OCCUPATIONAL HAZARDS

A volume in the series
Cornell Studies in Security Affairs
edited by Robert J. Art, Robert Jervis, and Stephen M. Walt

A list of titles in this series is available at
www.cornellpress.cornell.edu.

OCCUPATIONAL HAZARDS

Success and Failure in
Military Occupation

David M. Edelstein

CORNELL UNIVERSITY PRESS   ITHACA AND LONDON

First published 2008 by Cornell University Press
Printed in the United States of America

Library of Congress Cataloging-in-Publication Data

Edelstein, David M.
  Occupational hazards : success and failure in military
occupation / David M. Edelstein.
      p. cm. — (Cornell studies in security affairs)
  Includes bibliographical references and index.
  ISBN 978–0–8014–4615–3 (cloth : alk. paper)
  1. Military occupation.   2. United States—Armed Forces—
Foreign countries.   I. Title.   II. Series.

  D25.5.E34   2008
  355.4'90973—dc22

                                    2007033718

Cornell University Press strives to use environmentally responsible suppliers and materials to the fullest extent possible in the publishing of its books. Such materials include vegetable-based, low-VOC inks and acid-free papers that are recycled, totally chlorine-free, or partly composed of nonwood fibers. For further information, visit our website at www.cornellpress.cornell.edu.

Cloth printing   10 9 8 7 6 5 4 3 2 1

Contents

Acknowledgments

This book asks a simple central question: why do some military occupations succeed whereas others fail? The research on this project began in the fall of 2002 as the United States was preparing for its eventual invasion and occupation of Iraq. I was driven to write this book by an unease with the analogy so often drawn then between the potential occupation of Iraq and the post–World War II occupations of western Germany and Japan. In retrospect, the occupation of Iraq looked nothing like those occupations, and the United States paid a heavy price in its attempts to stabilize and rebuild Iraq. One goal of this book is to help explain why the United States encountered such difficulty. I identify lessons that one should learn not only from Iraq but also from the larger history of military occupation. My hope is that future political leaders might heed these lessons before again occupying a foreign country.

Though my name alone is on the cover of this book, it truly would not be before you without the help, support, and advice of numerous people. John Mearsheimer gave the shove I needed to begin work on this project, and he has been a faithful supporter throughout. Despite his substantial administrative responsibilities while I was writing this book, Stephen Walt was always quick to respond to an e-mail with words that were simultaneously critical, helpful, and encouraging.

Three friends and colleagues warrant special acknowledgment. During those inevitable frustrating moments that attend writing a book, Daniel Byman was always willing to read drafts and comment on them with remarkable alacrity. Ronald Krebs is simply the toughest critic that I have, and for this I am enormously grateful. Ron disagrees with parts of the argument presented in this book, but that has never interfered with his willingness to help me make it better. Jasen Castillo has been a friend and confidant since our days studying together at the University of Chicago. A few weeks before I submitted the manuscript for review, Jasen and I spent three invaluable hours in a conference room with nothing but coffee and a whiteboard, attempting to clarify the argument. These three—Byman, Krebs, and Castillo—deserve much of the credit for what succeeds in this book, but none of the blame for what does not.

I am grateful to numerous other colleagues who have provided comments and advice on parts of this book: Robert Art, Andrew Bennett, Nora Bensahel, Michael Brown, Charles Glaser, Donald Daniel, Alexander Downes, Tanisha Fazal, Matthew Kocher, Adria Lawrence, Keir Lieber, Robert Lieber, Charles Lipson, Robert Pape, Barry Posen, Elizabeth Stanley, and Leslie Vinjamuri. The book has also benefited from presentations in seminars at Columbia University, Georgetown University, Harvard University, the Massachusetts Institute of Technology, the University of Chicago, and the University of Virginia. An earlier version of the argument was published as "Occupational Hazards: Why Military Occupations Succeed or Fail," *International Security* 39, no. 1 (summer 2004): 59–91. At Cornell University Press, I thank Roger Haydon for his guidance, Karen Hwa, and Jack Rummel for copyediting the manuscript. David Prout ably and expeditiously prepared the index.

I am fortunate to have researched and written this book while on the faculty of the Edmund A. Walsh School of Foreign Service and the Department of Government at Georgetown University. Within Georgetown, my home has been the Center for Peace and Security Studies. As directors of the center, Michael Brown and then Daniel Byman have shown consistent devotion to the faculty. The center's staff, led by Bernard Finel, Natalie Goldring, and now Ellen McHugh, ensured that faculty can focus on their research and teaching. The center has also supported four outstanding research assistants, whom I thank for their help and their more than occasional willingness to chase wild geese for me: Christopher Machnacki, Christine Shoemaker, Philipp Bleek, and Dov Gardin. James Reardon-Anderson and Charles King, as chairs of the faculty of the School of Foreign Service, and Joshua Mitchell and George Shambaugh, as chairs of the Department of Government, have protected junior faculty so that we could focus on our research.

Georgetown has also been a wonderful environment because of the colleagues around me. Leslie Vinjamuri and I have endured the challenges and rewards of being junior faculty together. Dan Byman, Kate McNamara, Liz Stanley, Dan Nexon, Andy Bennett, Victor Cha, Bob Lieber, George Shambaugh, Tony Arend, Chris Joyner, Marc Busch, Bob Gallucci, Jennifer Sims, Don Daniel, and Sunil Dasgupta have made Georgetown an invigorating place in which to write this book and to study international relations more generally.

Both my family and my wife's family have been wonderfully supportive throughout this project. In particular, I thank my parents for their constant encouragement and for their emphasis on education above all else. My wife's family has welcomed me and supported me as one of their own. I am enormously thankful for it.

Finally, my wife, Robin, has offered endless support. Even when I doubted myself, she never did. She endured the highs and lows of this process with an astounding amount of patience and understanding. Our son, Levi, was born only two weeks after this book went off for review. He has brought perspective and an unimaginable level of joy into my life. As wonderful a wife as Robin is, she has unsurprisingly proved to be an equally amazing mother. For all of this and so much more than words can easily express, this book is dedicated to her with love and gratitude.

OCCUPATIONAL HAZARDS

THE CHALLENGE OF MILITARY OCCUPATION

"History points out the unmistakable lesson that military occupations serve their purpose at best for only a limited time, after which a deterioration rapidly sets in." General MacArthur wrote these words to the U.S. Congress less than two years after the occupation of Japan had begun.[1] In the rest of his letter, the Supreme Commander of the Allied Powers in Japan implored Congress to continue its support of the occupation while also noting that the occupation could not go on indefinitely without testing the patience of the Japanese population. More than fifty years later, in the midst of a fledgling insurgency in postwar Iraq, the U.S. administration harkened back to the post–World War II occupations of Japan and Germany as evidence that events in Iraq were not unprecedented. "There is an understandable tendency to look back on America's experience in postwar Germany and see only the successes," National Security Adviser Condoleezza Rice remarked to the Veterans of Foreign Wars on August 25, 2003. "But as some of you here today surely remember, the road we traveled was very difficult." Secretary of Defense Donald Rumsfeld invoked the German opposition group known as the "werewolves" and asked, "Does this sound familiar?"[2]

In the end, history confirms MacArthur's intuition. Ironically, the occupation of Japan is one of the few in history to succeed, and it took nearly seven years to do so. The more general conclusion reached from a survey of the history of military occupation is that most military occupations have ambitious goals that take a long time and substantial resources to be accomplished, but both occupied populations and occupying powers grow weary of extended occupations, undermining their success.

1

This book explains why most military occupations fail whereas few succeed. By doing so, it will reveal why the simple analogy invoked by Rice and Rumsfeld failed to appreciate the critical differences between post–World War II Germany and postinvasion Iraq. Ultimately, I conclude, military occupation is among the most challenging tasks of statecraft and, as a consequence, failure is much more common than success. When occupying powers do succeed, propitious conditions for occupation, most importantly the presence of an external threat to the occupied territory other than the occupying power itself, are the keys to success.

Central Question

Since 1815, there have been twenty-six completed military occupations, on my count, but only seven have succeeded. Why have occupations failed more often than they have succeeded? Answering this question is vitally important. Military occupations often have been critical turning points in international politics, with significant consequences for both the occupying power and the occupied population. In some cases, occupation lays the foundation for stable and productive long-term relations between the occupier and the occupied. In other cases, occupation breeds instability and animosity that lingers long after the occupation concludes.

Consider the beneficial effects of the American occupation of Japan on the development of postwar Japan or the ways in which the allied occupation of western Germany after World War II established the basic structure of the cold war. Less successful occupations, such as the American occupations of Haiti and the Dominican Republic in the early twentieth century, have had detrimental consequences. Most recently, the American-led occupation of Iraq potentially has implications for not only the future of Iraq but also more general Middle Eastern peace and the role of the United States in the world.

The issue of military occupations also promises to remain prominent in the years to come. In the wake of the terrorist attacks of September 11, 2001, the problem of failing and failed states has risen in prominence among both scholars and practitioners of international security.[3] Terrorist groups such as al-Qaeda may be able to find safe haven in weak or failed states that either cannot or will not prevent these groups from setting up camp in their territory. Great powers, such as the United States, cannot invade these failing states without anticipating the postconflict reconstruction that inevitably follows.

Military occupation is also often necessary in cases of "regime change." Most obviously, the defeat of Iraq and removal of Saddam Hussein from power in

2003 left a void in Iraq that was filled with an American-led occupation. Any future attempts at regime change, whether in Syria, Iran, or North Korea, may also require postconflict occupation. The leaders of great powers would be wise to recognize the challenges of occupation and the factors that are most conducive to occupation success before undertaking such an enterprise.

Aside from its clear policy relevance, understanding why military occupations succeed or fail also has theoretical implications. Scholars of strategic studies have long argued about the utility of military force as a tool for accomplishing goals such as democracy promotion.[4] In addition, military occupation starkly poses the question whether great powers can win over the population of occupied territories. Put in the vernacular of international relations theory, can occupying powers convince occupied populations to bandwagon with them rather than balance against them?[5]

Defining Military Occupation

Military occupation is the temporary control of a territory by a state (or group of allied states) that makes no claim to permanent sovereignty over that territory.[6] Military occupations require a military intervention force and usually include some form of administration, either civilian or military, to govern the occupied territory. Critically, the intended duration of a military occupation must be temporary and finite. That is, an occupying power must intend at the onset of the occupation to vacate the occupied territory and return control of the territory to an indigenous government.[7] A precise date for evacuation need not be specified, but it must be the intention of the occupying power to withdraw as soon as the goals of occupation have been accomplished.

Military occupation is distinct from other related concepts such as annexation, colonialism, intervention, and nation building. Annexation denotes the permanent acquisition of territory and incorporation of that territory into the annexing state's homeland. When the United States expanded across North America in the nineteenth century, its ambitions were annexation, not temporary occupation. A defining feature of occupation is precisely that the occupying power rejects annexation as the ultimate goal.

The critical distinction between occupation and colonialism lies in how states define their goals in the occupied territory. The intended duration of colonial ventures is much more ambiguous than the clear temporary intention of military occupation.[8] For example, I consider the British presence in Egypt from 1882 until 1954 to be an occupation, but I categorize the British presence in India as colonialism. As I discuss in chapter 3, the British leadership initially had little desire for an extended stay in Egypt, yet circumstances forced Britain to abandon its goal of a short-lived occupation. In India, on the other hand, London demonstrated little anxiety to evacuate until the forces of Indian nationalism and the costs of maintaining the empire drove it to withdraw in the aftermath of World War II. One of the distinguishing and most challenging features of occupation is that both parties—the occupying power and the occupied population—want the occupation to end. In colonialism, the population is likely to be far more desirous of an end to colonialism than the colonial power. The intention and willingness of an imperial power to sustain a lengthy colonial mission introduces different dynamics than those faced in a military occupation intended to be temporary.

As for intervention, all occupations require interventions, but not all interventions become occupations. A state may intervene in another state without occupying it. To be an occupation, the intervening power must take control of the occupied territory and exercise sovereignty over that territory for a significant length of time.[9] United States operations in Haiti and the Dominican Republic in the early twentieth century qualify as occupations, but U.S. operations in Grenada in 1983 and Panama in 1989 were interventions that stopped short of becoming occupations.

Finally, many military occupations have nation building among their goals, but the tools of nation building go beyond military occupation. This book, therefore, mostly refrains from commenting on the general merits of nation building except in cases when military occupation has been employed as a means to this end.

Using this basic definition of what is and is not occupation, I identify a universe of cases of twenty-six occupations about which judgments of success or failure can be reached and four ongoing contemporary occupations for which it is too soon to tell. The thirty total cases are listed in table I.1.

Appendix 1 includes a full discussion of the method by which I assembled this list. Perhaps the most difficult cases on which to decide involved the Soviet Empire in post–World War II Europe. Ultimately, I have decided to exclude these cases—East Germany, Czechoslovakia, Hungary, Romania, Poland, and Bulgaria—for two reasons. First, Soviet intentions were not for finite and temporary occupations but rather to build and establish a faithful empire. Second, although Moscow may have returned de jure sovereignty to indigenous governments in these countries at different points after the war and, thus, legally ended any occupation, the Soviet Union also made it clear that it would not tolerate any behavior that was inconsistent with Soviet objectives. In Hungary in 1956 and Czechoslovakia in 1968, the Soviet Union intervened militarily to crush movements that were perceived as contrary to Soviet wishes.[10]

Table I.1 Success and failure in military occupations, 1815–2007

TERRITORY (PRIMARY OCCUPIER) AND DATE	SUMMARY JUDGMENT
France (United Kingdom, Russia, Prussia, Austria), 1815–18	Success
Mexico (France), 1861–67	Failure
Ili (Russia), 1871–82	Mixed
Egypt (United Kingdom), 1882–1954	Failure
Cuba (United States), 1898–1902	Failure
Philippines (United States), 1898–1945	Mixed
Cuba (United States), 1906–9	Failure
Haiti (United States), 1915–34	Failure
Dominican Republic (United States), 1916–24	Failure
Istanbul (France, United Kingdom, Italy), 1918–23	Failure
Rhineland (France, United Kingdom, United States), 1918–30	Failure
Iraq (United Kingdom), 1918–32	Failure
Palestine (United Kingdom), 1919–48	Mixed
Saar (France), 1920–35	Mixed
Italy (United Kingdom, United States), 1943–48	Success
Eastern Austria (Soviet Union), 1945–55	Failure
Western Austria (United Kingdom, United States, France), 1945–55	Success
Western Germany (France, United Kingdom, United States), 1945–52	Success
Japan (United States), 1945–52	Success
Ryukyus (United States), 1945–72	Success
Northern Korea (Soviet Union), 1945–48	Success
Southern Korea (United States), 1945–48	Mixed
West Bank/Gaza (Israel), 1967–	Failure
Cambodia (Vietnam), 1979–89	Failure
Southern Lebanon (Israel), 1982–2000	Failure
Lebanon (Syria), 1976–2005	Failure
Bosnia (NATO/EU), 1995–	?
Kosovo (NATO), 1999–[a]	?
Afghanistan (NATO), 2001–	?
Iraq (United States, United Kingdom, Poland), 2003–	?

[a] The occupation of Kosovo has included a UN component—UNMIK—as well as a NATO component—KFOR. In this table, I refer to the KFOR component as UN cases are excluded from this set of cases.

Even if one disagrees with this decision to exclude these cases, my findings remain robust when the cases are included. The arguments I will make in subsequent chapters about the threat environment and strategies of occupation work well to explain the Soviet experience during the cold war. In fact, in the discussion of occupation strategies in chapter 2, I will briefly examine the Soviet use of coercion in Eastern Europe during the cold war to maintain its empire.

Goals and Means of Military Occupation

Explaining success and failure in military occupation must begin with an understanding of the goals of occupation and the means states utilize to achieve those goals. The fundamental and overriding goal of all military occupations is to ensure that the occupied territory does not pose a threat to the occupying power or its interests both in the short and the long term. Accomplishing this goal involves either the creation or restoration of political, economic, and social institutions that will be sustainable once the occupation concludes. This central security goal most often trumps other ideological goals. Whereas great powers may claim that they seek to install governments of a certain ideology such as democracy, they seek, first and foremost, to install regimes that do not threaten their interests regardless of their ideology. Similarly, with regard to reconstructing war-torn economies, the oft-cited post–World War II cases of Japan and Germany demonstrate how reconstructed industrial economies are sought by occupying powers not as an end in themselves but largely because they are geopolitically valuable and enhance the occupying power's security.[11]

Although the end goal of occupations tends to be similar, the means for achieving this goal differ. In some cases, occupying powers attempt to impose new political, economic, and social institutions on the occupied territory as a means of achieving their goal. In other cases, occupying powers believe that their objective can be achieved at less cost by employing more limited means that simply aim to restore existing institutions. As an occupation proceeds, occupying powers may recalibrate the means that they are using in order to lower costs, improve the chances of achieving security, or both. Understanding the varying means for seeking occupation success is important because these strategies have widely varying costs. Implementing a successful military occupation requires choosing means that are likely to effect security at the most reasonable cost.

To take one example of more limited occupation means, the allied occupation of the Rhineland in the aftermath of World War I sought to prevent the reemergence of a powerful and potentially threatening Germany.[12] Although France initially advocated Rheinish independence, none of the occupying powers ultimately hoped to install a particular government in the Rhineland; instead, their goal was simply to limit the ability of Germany to again pose a threat to their security. On the other hand, the U.S. occupation of Japan and the three-power occupation of western Germany after World War II are the best-known examples of occupation where comprehensive reconstruction was seen as the means to occupation success. The creation of new, democratic political institutions in those cases was valued precisely because it helped achieve the primary security objectives of the occupation.

Success and Failure in Military Occupation

Judgments of success or failure in military occupations are based on whether the occupying power accomplished its goals and at what cost.[13] A successful occupation creates conditions under which an occupying power can withdraw without concern for the security of its interests. As I will discuss in chapter 3, occupations can only successfully end when they leave behind a stable, indigenous government, and the postoccupation state is guaranteed of its security and nonthreatening to others. Ideally, the occupied territory is actually transformed from a wartime adversary into a reliable ally. Thus, the post–World War II U.S. occupations of Germany and Japan are viewed as successes, in large part, because of the remarkable transformation of these countries from bitter adversaries to reliable allies.[14]

Not only must these goals be accomplished in the short term, but they must be sustainable over the long term. Occupying powers that expend significant national resources on an occupation only to find themselves reintervening a few years later cannot be satisfied with the outcome of the occupation. Tracking the long-term ramifications of an occupation is essential for judging success or failure, but it can also be difficult to hold an occupying power responsible for developments years or decades after the occupation has ended.

The accomplishments of an occupation must also always be considered relative to the costs—both direct and indirect—of the occupation. The direct costs include the financial costs of the troops that must be deployed for a lengthy time to keep the peace in the occupied territory and the occupation administration that may be established. Additionally, any lives that are lost as a result of resistance to the occupation are a direct cost. The indirect costs of an occupation are more difficult to measure. They include the opportunity cost of the occupation. An ongoing occupation may preclude an occupying power from pursuing other national interests. Indirect costs also include any rivalry that might be generated with a third party as a result of the occupation. Finally, a state may incur an indirect reputation cost if an occupation does not go as well as hoped.

Measuring the costs of an occupation is usually quite difficult. Much of the financial cost of occupation is often included within military budgets in which it can be difficult to isolate the costs of the occupation alone. Even if one could find precise financial figures, it is still not clear that these would be a valuable indicator since cost is always relative. Paying an enormous sum of money to achieve a

valuable end may not be perceived as costly by a population or a country's decision makers. Indirect costs are even more difficult to measure concretely. Thus, in
the case studies below, I investigate the nature of the domestic debate over each
occupation as a proxy measure of cost. If leaders or the general public openly
questioned the cost of the occupation, then this provides some indication that
the occupation was perceived as expensive, even if precise financial figures or
measures of indirect costs are unavailable.

Success or failure, then, is judged by looking at the short- and long-term
accomplishments of an occupation relative to the expense of the occupation.
The historical record indicates that military occupations almost always cost a
considerable amount, last several years, and require thousands of troops. The
critical question then is how often occupations accomplish enough to justify
their costs. An occupation may cost a lot, but if it accomplishes equally as much,
then it can be considered a success. Even though the occupations of Germany
and Japan after World War II were time consuming and costly, few would argue
that the stakes did not warrant these costs. An occupation that costs a lot but does
not accomplish its goals is most disappointing. The American occupation of the
Philippines in the early twentieth century and the British occupation of Egypt
were lengthy and costly occupations where the reward may not have justified the
cost. If an occupation costs little and accomplishes little, then it may be a failure,
but it is not a costly failure. Finally, the ideal, but rare, occupation costs little but
accomplishes a great deal.

Coding occupations as successes or failures can be challenging. Consider the
example of the U.S. occupation of the Philippines. The occupation provided the
United States with a base of operations in the Pacific Ocean, but it also contributed to the emerging rivalry with Japan.[15] Eventually, the Philippines became a
democracy, but only decades after the occupation began and after the United
States waged a costly counterinsurgency campaign at the turn of the twentieth
century. Weighing these benefits and costs, I conclude that this occupation is best
thought of as a mixed success. Occupations coded as mixed successes offer some
positive benefit counterbalanced by a failure to accomplish all of the occupier's
goals or by significant costs, either direct or indirect.

Judging success or failure is further complicated by two additional considerations. First, occupying powers may change their means over the course of an
occupation, or they may, in fact, alter the very purpose of their operation. An
occupying power may initially be committed to the complete reconstruction of
an occupied territory's institutions as a means to achieving security. At some
point, the occupying power may opt for something more achievable but also
more tenuous for the long term. "Moving targets" like this make it difficult to
judge success or failure. In these cases, the basic judgment of success or failure

must still be relative to the goal of creating stability and security that is sustainable after the occupation ends. Alternatively, an occupying power may decide to alter the purpose of its operation from occupation to colonialism or annexation. As I will argue in chapter 3 in the context of the occupation of Egypt, when military occupations transform into colonialism or annexation, it is often because the occupying power encounters difficulties so severe that their leaders believe withdrawal is impossible.

The second difficulty with judging the success or failure of an occupation is that that judgment must be made relative to a counterfactual. Even if an occupation falls short of meeting the initial goals set forth by the occupying power, the result of the occupation may still be better than the alternative. A failed occupation may be preferable to having done nothing at all. Still, even if occupation is chosen only because it appears preferable to some hypothetical alternative, great powers still should (1) anticipate the possibility of occupation before engaging in war and (2) if war is necessary, then try to create conditions that are conducive to occupation success.

Table I.1 summarizes the historical record of military occupations. The summary judgments provided in the table are presented so that general patterns in the larger universe of cases can be evaluated, but one should be careful not to read too much into these summary judgments. As I just delineated, judging occupation success and failure involves a complicated calculation of costs, benefits, and alternatives. For this reason, appendix 2 provides a more detailed narrative summary of each case, along with the rationale for coding it as either a success, failure, or mixed success. At the most general level, however, the summary judgments are suggestive of the historical pattern of success and failure in military occupations.

An examination of the data yields two particularly notable findings. First, of the twenty-six occupations where summary judgments are possible, only seven were fully successful (27%), fourteen failed (54%), and five are classified as mixed successes (19%).[16] Second, of the seven successes, six are from the immediate post–World War II period, with the lone exception being the first occupation in the data set, the allied occupation of France after the Napoleonic Wars. These two findings raise critical questions. What explains the prevailing rate of failure among occupations? Why are the occupation successes clustered around the end of World War II? The remainder of this book is largely aimed at answering these questions.

One might argue that these results are unsurprising because military occupations are subject to certain selection effects. That is, states choose whether or not to occupy other countries, and they only choose to do so when they have few other options. Not all wars result in occupation, so perhaps only the most difficult of postwar environments necessitate occupation. Occupation, in other words, is a strategy of last resort. Thus, the universe of cases of occupations is a universe of hard cases, and we should expect to see failures. If occupation were attempted in a wider set of circumstances, the rate of success would be higher. Even if this is true, the evidence suggests that occupation can succeed, and it is, therefore, important to understand the reasons for success.

Why Military Occupation is Difficult

Military occupation is a difficult challenge because both sides—the occupied population and the occupying power—want the occupation to end as quickly as possible, but successful occupation often takes a long time and consumes considerable resources. Occupation often occurs in the wake of violent, destructive conflict that leaves chaos and disorganization behind. Even in a case where an occupying power seeks to establish security through the relatively modest means of reinforcing existing institutions, an occupation needs to last long enough for the occupying power to rebuild and ensure that its interests have been secured. More ambitious occupations that aim to create new political, economic, and social institutions in the occupied country will take even longer and cost even more. Importantly, occupation success is not simply a product of a significant resource investment and lengthy time commitment. Lengthy occupations that failed, such as the U.S. occupation of Haiti from 1915 until 1934, make this point clear. Time and resources, however, allow for the building of the political, economic, and social institutions that are necessary for long-term success.

Ironically, all sides want to see an occupation end quickly, yet achieving that desired goal in a mutually acceptable way can often be quite difficult. Unlike conquering or colonial powers, occupying powers often would rather devote their resources elsewhere. And unlike irredentist populations who seek attachment to another state, occupied populations long to govern themselves. To succeed, an occupying power must, therefore, achieve two difficult tasks: (1) it must convince the occupied population to accept a lengthy occupation, and (2) it must maintain its own commitment until occupation reforms have been successfully implemented.

The Occupied Population's Nationalism

The greatest impediment to successful military occupation is the nationalism of the occupied population. Nationalism refers to the desire of a population to govern itself or, put differently, to join an identifiable nation together with the governing institutions of the modern state. In the now-standard definition offered by Ernest Gellner, "Nationalism is primarily a political principle, which holds that the political and the national unit should be congruent."[17] Occupation is likely to invigorate nationalism inasmuch as it deprives a national group of self-determination. Two points about nationalism are worth emphasizing.

First, more than one nationalism may be present within the boundaries of an existing state. That is, there may be several identifiable national groups within a state that long for their own self-determination. In fact, the existence of multiple nationalisms within an occupied territory is likely to make the task of occupation more difficult. In these cases, the occupying power must locate a strategy for satisfying the nationalist desires of several groups, not just one. Different national groups may compete with each other for control of the same territory, for as Gellner observes, "It follows that a territorial political unit can only become ethnically homogenous, in such cases, if it either kills, or expels, or assimilates all non-nationals."[18] To say that nationalism undermines occupation may, therefore, refer to one unified nationalism or multiple nationalisms within an occupied territory.

Second, arguments that emphasize the causal role of nationalism can be criticized unless a way of measuring nationalism is identified. That is, if nationalism is a variable, then how do we measure the intensity of that nationalism independent of any outcome, such as insurgency, that we are studying? Rather than stipulating a specific metric for nationalism, I argue, instead, that military occupation is a particular affront to any occupied population's nationalism. If any event is likely to generate a strong nationalist response, then it is likely to be the usurpation of political authority by a foreign occupying power that has just defeated the occupied population in war.

Some critics dismiss nationalism-based "grievance" explanations by arguing that nationalism is present in much of the world, yet conflict is far more infrequent. Instead, these critics point to "greed" explanations and argue that conflict is a product of greedy motives and the capability to carry out insurgent campaigns.[19] The assumption underlying this argument is that nationalism is essentially a constant, and change cannot be explained with a constant. In reality, however, nationalism is not a constant, and military occupation represents a potent catalyst to the nationalist instinct for self-determination.

Occupation is so difficult largely because it invites both greed and grievance as motives for violence. In the aftermath of conflict, different groups may seek to gain control of the state and its resources out of greed. Postwar chaos creates conditions conducive to insurgency. Thus, groups may have both the motive and the capability to seize power. At the same time, the usurpation of sovereignty by a foreign power creates an acute grievance for nationalist groups. This combination of greed and grievance is a dangerous one for occupying powers and explains, in part, why military occupation has proven so difficult.

If nationalism is invigorated by occupation, then the question becomes how can occupying powers best manage that nationalism. How can they both reduce the grievances raised by invasion and occupation and limit the capabilities of their opponents to undertake insurgency? As Michael Hechter has argued, "Nationalism based on individual interests should wax and wane with personal circumstances. Therefore, it ought to be susceptible to shifts in state policy that accommodate nationalist demands or redress grievances. It also ought to be vulnerable to cooptation."[20]

To succeed, military occupiers must convince an occupied population to forestall its demands for sovereignty and tolerate—not necessarily welcome, but tolerate—the occupation.[21] Achieving this success is likely to be difficult, as the occupying power is often a military conqueror that the occupied population is predisposed to reject. Even if an occupying power is welcomed initially, that welcome is likely to obsolesce as the occupation continues and self-determination is continuously postponed.

If, however, an occupying power can convince the occupied population that it is better off tolerating an occupation, then the occupier will gain the time and support it needs to implement its desired reforms. With these reforms successfully implemented, the occupying power can withdraw confident that its long-term interests are secure. If, on the other hand, the occupied population concludes that it would rather be governing itself, then it will resist the occupation and make the accomplishment of occupation goals more difficult.[22] Long-term success will become elusive as the occupied population is likely to harbor resentment for having suffered through foreign occupation.

Nationalist desires for self-governance in opposition to occupation may manifest themselves in violent resistance, such as insurgency, or other forms of protest, such as labor strikes. Importantly, widespread, violent resistance against an occupation does not itself indicate that an occupation necessarily has failed, but violent resistance makes it more difficult for an occupying power to achieve its goals. Resistance impedes an occupying power's efforts to reconstruct the occupied territory in the manner that it desires and makes it less likely that the occupying power will be able to secure its interests for the long term. For the unsuccessful occupying power, a destructive feedback loop ensues. The tasks of occupation are made difficult by resistance, but the less the occupying power accomplishes, the more likely further resistance becomes. Once ensconced in this vicious cycle, occupying powers find it difficult to emerge successfully.[23]

The Occupying Power's Impatience

The challenge of occupation is not only to assuage the nationalist desires of the occupied population, but also for the occupier to sustain its commitment to the occupation. If occupation requires significant time and resources to succeed, then the occupying power must be determined to see the occupation succeed and be willing to devote sufficient resources to make that happen. Like any country, however, an occupying power has limited national resources and numerous demands on those resources. Especially in democracies, political leaders need to justify the expenditure of national resources on the occupation of a foreign country. If an occupying power faces violent resistance in the early stages of occupation, then it will become even more difficult for the government of the occupying power to garner the resources to sustain the occupation. As a further complication, occupation is often undertaken not because a victorious power necessarily wants to occupy another country, but rather because it feels compelled to occupy that country to ensure that the resources expended on defeating the country are not wasted. The occupying power is, thus, likely to feel pressures to reduce the resources available for an occupation, which only reduces the probability of success.

The Dilemma of Withdrawal

The final reason occupation is difficult is the challenge of deciding when to end an occupation. Occupations that end too soon may leave instability in their wake, but occupations that go on too long invite resistance against the occupying power. To succeed, occupying powers must establish the conditions that allow them to withdraw with sufficient confidence that their interests will not be threatened after withdrawal. This requires returning sovereignty to a stable, reliable indigenous government and ensuring that the occupied territory will be secure and nonthreatening after the occupation concludes. The challenge is to create these conditions before the resentment of the occupied population interferes with the achievement of the goals of the occupation.

Why Occupations Succeed or Fail

Not all occupations fail. Some occupations, such as the United States in Germany and Japan after World War II, succeed, and the primary goal of this book is to understand this variation. An effective theory of military occupation would explain three aspects of occupation: (1) variation in the nationalist level of resistance to occupation, (2) variation in the commitment of occupying powers to the occupation, and (3) the reasons some occupying powers are successfully able to end an occupation, but others are not. Chapters 1 and 2 confront the first two aspects. Chapter 3 addresses the third.

In the next chapter, I contend that one critical condition, the threat environment of the occupied territory, does more to shape the likelihood of occupation success or failure than any other factor. When a third-party external threat to the occupied territory is present and is perceived as such by the occupied population and the occupying power, then an occupation is more likely to succeed. An occupied population is more likely to accept an occupation when the occupying power can offer it protection that the population believes it needs, and an occupying power is more likely to commit to a geopolitically valuable territory that is threatened by some other state. The absence of such an external threat or the presence of an internal threat to the coherence of the occupied territory (an unfavorable threat environment), on the other hand, is likely to increase resistance to the occupation and, thus, increase the likelihood that the occupation will fail.

In chapter 2, I examine the strategies that occupying powers employ to conduct an occupation and explain the interaction between the threat environment of an occupation and strategies of occupation. Occupying powers have three types of strategies available to them: accommodation, inducement, and coercion. Accommodation is a strategy of engaging and co-opting political elites within the occupied society who can control the nationalist instincts of the population. A strategy of inducement attempts to gain the acquiescence of the occupied population by offering material benefits to the population. Finally, coercion employs military and police force in order to defeat any nationalist opposition to the occupation.

The initial threat environment of an occupation affects the strategic choices that occupying powers make and, through a process of feedback, subsequently affects the occupied population's perceptions of the threat environment. An initially unfavorable threat environment increases resistance and forces occupying powers to rely on coercion, which, in turn, only exacerbates the unfavorable threat environment. An initially favorable threat environment allows states mostly to refrain from coercion and, instead, accommodate and induce the occupied population, which, in turn, reinforces a favorable threat environment and allows for progress toward the conditions that allow an occupation to end successfully. All three of these strategies can succeed, but coercion is often more challenging as it may only convince an occupied population that the occupying power is, in fact, the greatest threat to its nationalist goals.

Finally, in chapter 3, I address the challenge of when to end an occupation and introduce the "occupation dilemma." Successful occupying powers must meet

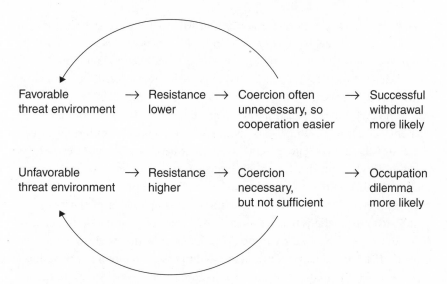

FIGURE 1.   The logic of military occupation

two conditions before they withdraw. First, they must return sovereignty to an independent, indigenous, and reliable government. Simultaneously, they must ensure that the occupied territory is secure from threats both internal and external, but also nonthreatening to its neighbors. This second condition can be met either through an alliance relationship or through support for the development and maintenance of an indigenous military. Occupying powers that have enjoyed a favorable threat environment are more likely to meet these conditions as such an environment facilitates the creation of stable, reliable, and secure institutions and reflects the common security interests between the occupied territory and the occupying power. Unsuccessful occupying powers are likely to confront the "occupation dilemma." The occupation dilemma occurs when unsuccessful occupying powers face a choice between either ending an occupation too soon or prolonging a costly and unsuccessful occupation. Occupying powers that face an unfavorable threat environment and that have been forced to rely on coercion are less likely to meet the conditions for successful withdrawal and, thus, more likely to confront the occupation dilemma (see fig. 1).

Existing Literature and Alternative Arguments

Given the historical importance of military occupations, it is surprising that there is so little scholarly literature on the subject. Put simply, there is no existing attempt to offer a theoretical explanation of why military occupations succeed or fail and to evaluate that theory with empirical evidence.[24] There are, however, several literatures that are relevant and that inform the analysis in this book.

To begin with, a sizeable literature has emerged in the last decade on the subject of nation building through military intervention and occupation.[25] Prompted by real world events in the Balkans, Haiti, Afghanistan, and Iraq, most of this literature emanates from the think-tank community in an effort to confront the challenges that the United States and other countries have faced since the end of the cold war. This literature has two major shortcomings that this study seeks to correct.

First, in their efforts to appeal to today's policymakers, the authors of these studies have eschewed deductive, theoretical thinking in favor of short-sighted policy recommendations that are often derived from and specific to the particular case about which they are writing. As a consequence, the conclusions of these reports offer little guidance for thinking about possible future military occupations. Further, the findings in these studies are usually based on an inductive study of past military occupation with more attention to correlation than causation. For example, a much-publicized 2003 RAND study of nation building points to the importance of troop and resource commitments for occupation success, but it fails to establish any compelling causal relationship between certain types of resources and occupation success or failure. The occupation of Iraq, it is suggested in that report, might succeed as the occupations of Germany and Japan did with sufficient time and resource commitments. This book does not deny the importance of resource commitments to occupation success; rather, it seeks to identify not only why great resources are sometimes necessary for occupation success, but also the deeper challenges that occupying powers must address in order to succeed.[26] It explains why those time and resource commitments are likely to be more forthcoming in some situations than in others, and it aims to demonstrate why the key to occupation success is not as simple as more resources, more troops, and more time.

Second, because the existing literature on nation building is primarily intended for policymakers dealing with a contemporary issue, the authors tend to focus on the question of how nation building can be done better rather than the question of whether attempting to nation build through force is a good idea at all. Although it is certainly valuable to generate lessons for the better conduct of nation building, it is perhaps even more important to look at the broader question of whether and when nation building through military occupation makes good grand strategic sense.

The voluminous historical studies of specific cases of military occupation is another important literature employed in this study. Military occupations are often critical events that serve to reshape defeated countries, so it is unsurprising that these cases would receive extensive attention from historians. In particular, the post–World War II occupations of Germany and Japan have been the subject of enormous historical analysis. Although this literature is vital to the empirical analysis contained in this book, it understandably makes little effort to offer more general conclusions about the conditions under which military occupations succeed or fail.[27]

Finally, there are two other literatures that are related, but not central, to this project. First, there is a significant international law literature on military occupation.[28] International legal scholars, however, tend to have a normative focus on the obligations of occupying powers, which differentiates their work from the empirical focus of this project. Second, there is a large literature on counterinsurgency.[29] Troubled occupations often encounter insurgencies, so the literature addressing counterinsurgency is pertinent and complementary to the arguments I make. This literature does not, however, deal with the broader question of why some occupations result in costly antioccupation insurgencies while others evolve peacefully.

Based on this existing literature as well as other discussions of the use of force in international politics, I derive three different alternative arguments to my own about the causes of occupation success or failure that I consider throughout the course of this book. First, as noted above, some have argued that the key to occupation success is the investment of time and resources. With a sufficient investment, military occupiers can overcome the challenges of occupation and accomplish their goals.[30] This argument is unsatisfying on both logical and empirical grounds. Logically, the argument has largely been presented as correlation, not causation. The United States did invest considerable resources in the successful occupation of Japan, for example, but I will argue that it was the threat environment surrounding Japan after World War II that best explains why the United States made this investment. Empirically, advocates of this argument have been forced to argue that certain nation-building exercises, most notably Kosovo, have been successful when the evidence for these claims is dubious. Measured per capita, the NATO and UN investment in Kosovo has been extraordinary, yet the future of Kosovo as a stable, independent political entity remains uncertain.

A second alternative argument attributes the success or failure of military occupation to the level of economic development in the occupied territory prior to the occupation. The occupation of highly developed countries is more likely to succeed because it is easier to rebuild a functioning economy and ensure that citizens are employed. In underdeveloped and nonindustrialized occupied states, occupation is more difficult because political challenges are compounded when a population is impoverished and unemployed. Like the argument about resource investment, this argument is largely derived from the successful occupations of post–World War II western Germany and Japan, both highly industrialized and developed economies before and during World War II.

My response to this argument is twofold. First, in chapter 2, I argue that occupying powers often adopt an inducement strategy that attempts to win over the occupied population by offering them material rewards. The ability of an occupying power to successfully implement an inducement strategy may, in part, be a product of how developed the occupied state's economy is. Conversely, when an occupied state has an underdeveloped economy, the occupying power will find it more difficult to induce the population into cooperation. Second, the initial instinct of the occupying powers in both postwar western Germany and Japan was to destroy the industrial economies that had powered those countries during World War II. Only when the threat from the Soviet Union emerged did the United States and its allies move quickly to the revitalization of these industrial economies. Thus, whether or not an occupying power takes advantage of the level of development in an occupied territory is itself a product of the threat environment.

The final alternative argument suggests that contemporary military occupations are more likely to succeed if they are multilateral. Multilateralism lends legitimacy to an occupation, which makes it both more likely that an occupied population will accept an occupation and that other countries will participate in an occupation.[31] In chapter 4, I argue that the multilateralism hypothesis is unconvincing. Drawing on the recent UN de facto occupations of East Timor and Kosovo, I demonstrate that multilateralism did little to appease the nationalist instincts of either the East Timorese or the Kosovars. To the extent that success has been enjoyed in East Timor it was a product of a favorable threat environment. Multilateralism does offer certain advantages: costs can be defrayed in a multilateral occupation, and pledges to end an occupation appear more credible when issued by the United Nations. But the legitimacy benefits of multilateral occupation have been overstated. The key to occupation, whether unilateral or multilateral, remains satisfying the nationalist desires of the occupied population and maintaining the commitment of the occupying power.

Research Design

Most of the evidence offered in this book takes the form of qualitative case studies. These case studies allow for careful examination of the causal logics that I suggest, but this careful examination can come at some price in terms of the ability to generalize about the findings. I supplement the case studies with broader assessments of the universe of cases of military occupation since 1815, but even this analysis is somewhat problematic given the absence of easily quantifiable indicators of the variables of interest.

I have chosen the cases in each chapter for a variety of reasons: variation in key independent and dependent variables, historical interest, and relevance to contemporary policy challenges. Table I.2 summarizes the logic of case selection. To assess the argument about the fundamental importance of the threat environment, I examine two cases in the next chapter that represent two common types within the larger universe of cases.[32] The first case, the occupation of western Germany after World War II, featured a prominent external threat (the Soviet Union). The case is, in many ways, typical of the other cases of U.S. occupation success after World War II. The second case, the U.S. occupation of Haiti from 1915 to 1934, featured no other external threat to the island aside from the occupying power itself. This case resembles other cases of U.S. occupation in the early twentieth century that usually followed smaller-scale interventions. As the

Table I.2   The logic of case selection

CASE	LOGIC	OUTCOME
CHAPTER 1: WHEN TO OCCUPY?		
Allied occupation of western Germany, 1945–52	Favorable threat environment	Success
U.S. occupation of Haiti, 1915–34	Unfavorable threat environment	Failure
CHAPTER 2: HOW TO OCCUPY?		
U.S. occupation of southern Korea, 1945–48	Unfavorable threat environment / Poor strategy	Mixed
Soviet occupation of northern Korea, 1945–48	Unfavorable threat environment / Effective strategy	Success
CHAPTER 3: WHEN TO LEAVE?		
U.S. occupation of Cuba, 1898–1902	Unfavorable threat environment / Premature withdrawal	Failure
British occupation of Egypt, 1882–1954	Unfavorable threat environment / Prolonged stay	Failure
U.S. occupation of Japan, 1945–52	Favorable threat environment / Successful withdrawal conditions met	Success
CHAPTER 4: WHO OCCUPIES?		
UN occupation of East Timor, 1999–2002	Multilateral occupation	Preliminary success
UN occupation of Kosovo, 1999–	Multilateral occupation	?

threat-environment argument expects, the occupation of western Germany was far more successful than the occupation of Haiti.

To evaluate how threat environment, strategies of occupation, and occupation outcomes interact, I investigate two cases with similar initial threat environments—the simultaneous occupations of southern Korea by the United States and northern Korea by the Soviet Union after World War II. The two occupations faced similarly unfavorable initial threat environments, yet they had significantly different outcomes, with the United States having less success in the south than the Soviet Union did in the north. Both of these cases also turn out to be outliers: the U.S. occupation of southern Korea was the only post–World War II U.S. occupation that did not have a great deal of success, and the Soviet occupation of northern Korea is the unusual case of an occupation that succeeded under an unfavorable threat environment. I will argue that it was the ability of the Soviet Union to implement an effective occupation strategy that led to success in the north while a poor occupation strategy led to a mixed outcome for the United States in the south.

Chapter 3 includes three cases that cover the variation in the decision to end an occupation. First, the United States withdrew too soon after its occupation of Cuba from 1898 to 1902. Second, Great Britain stayed too long in its occupation of Egypt from 1882 to 1954. Third, the United States established successful conditions for withdrawal before it ended its occupation of Japan in 1952, after almost seven years of occupation. Through these cases, I demonstrate the difficulty of identifying the proper time to end an occupation, the conditions that are necessary for successful withdrawal, and the occupation dilemma that arises in unsuccessful occupations.

Chapter 4 evaluates an alternative argument about the consequences of multilateralism in contemporary military occupation. I consider two cases of de facto military occupation—East Timor and Kosovo—undertaken under the auspices of the United Nations. These two cases represent the closest that the United Nations has come to undertaking occupations as I have defined an occupation. The cases allow for considering whether the imprimatur of a multilateral body makes a significant difference in the conduct of an occupation. In addition, the East Timor and Kosovo cases test whether the logic of the argument for explaining the success or failure of an occupation undertaken by a single country could also be extended to UN operations.

Finally, in the conclusion, I present preliminary evidence from two ongoing cases of occupation, Iraq and Afghanistan. These are not formal case studies but rather potential contemporary applications of the argument. Afghanistan is particularly useful, for there a conquering power chose not to pursue the complete occupation of a defeated country.

Two concerns might be raised about the cases selected. First, do too many of the cases have the United States as the primary occupying power? Whereas it is true that the United States is featured prominently among the cases, this is not unwarranted. Not only has the United States historically been the most frequent occupier, there is also good reason to think that the United States will continue to be a leading occupier. Occupations are most often undertaken by great military powers, and there is no greater military power in the foreseeable future than the United States. Further, the cases of the Soviet occupation of northern Korea, the British occupation of Egypt, and the multilateral nature of the occupation of western Germany do add some variation into the identity of the occupying power.

Second, are too many of the cases from the immediate post–World War II era? In fact, four of seven cases (excluding Kosovo and East Timor) are from the period, but the selections are justified for two reasons. First, western Germany and Japan are so often pointed to as exemplars of the possibility of successful military occupation that it is worth examining the reasons for their success and investigating whether they provide lessons that are applicable in other cases. Second, northern and southern Korea not only provide an interesting quasi-experiment, but southern Korea is also the only U.S. occupation in the immediate post–World War II period that did not have a great deal of success.[33]

Ultimately, this book concludes that military occupation is among the most difficult tasks of statecraft. Often, as in Germany and Japan after World War II, occupation is both inevitable and necessary. In other cases, however, states embark on military interventions that are neither inevitable nor clearly necessary but that will require postintervention occupation. Not only do we need to ask how occupations can be conducted better, but more fundamentally, we need to ask whether the project of social, political, and economic reconstruction that is often incumbent on military occupiers is a task that should be welcomed. I begin this exploration in the next chapter with an argument about the importance of threat environment to occupation outcomes.

WHEN TO OCCUPY
The Threat Environment

The most successful occupations in history were in many ways the most ambitious and radically transformational. They were also among the most surprising. The United States and its allies fought lengthy and vicious wars against both Germany and Japan, yet were then able to occupy both countries and transform them from fascist, militaristic, and highly nationalistic enemies into democratic and peaceful allies. There is a simple explanation for why these occupations, despite their apparent difficulty, were able to succeed while others have failed: the threat environment of the occupied territory. By "threat environment," I mean both external threats and internal threats that may challenge the security, survival, and integrity of an occupied territory. In postwar Germany and Japan, the presence of an external threat, the Soviet Union, perceived as a threat by both the occupied population and the occupying power, created conditions conducive to occupation success. In other cases, where occupied territories have either faced an internal threat to their integrity or where no threat has been perceived, occupations have been less successful.

The Threat Environment

Recalling that a successful occupying power must placate the occupied population and maintain its own commitment to an occupation, the influence of the threat environment on occupation success is best understood by examining the perspective of both the occupied population and the occupying power.

The Occupied Population

When an occupied population perceives that another country poses a threat to its future security, it will welcome an occupying power that is both willing and able to protect it from that threat. As a consequence, the occupied population will offer little resistance to the occupying power, allowing the occupier time to rebuild political and economic institutions within the occupied country and create conditions conducive to a successful withdrawal. Nationalist populations are willing to suppress their desire for self-determination if doing so allows for protection from an external threat.[1]

Occupied populations determine their external threat environment by assessing the relative threat posed by the occupying power as opposed to other third-party states. In some cases, the occupying power itself will appear to pose the greatest threat to the nationalist desires of the occupied territory. In these cases, the occupied population will reject the occupation. In other cases, the occupied population may perceive another third party as the greatest threat to their long-term self-determination. Assessments of threat are based on the capabilities and intentions of the states involved. To measure relative threats, occupied populations are likely to examine the ideology and track record of the potential threats: Does a power typically restore sovereignty to other societies that it may have occupied? Is the future promised by the occupying power more attractive than the alternatives?

Occupied populations are less willing to suppress their nationalist instincts when the occupying power does not offer it protection from an external threat. The population will see less need for the occupation and will be more likely to resist the occupation. Such resistance may persuade an occupying power either to react violently and further antagonize the occupied population or to evacuate the occupied territory prematurely. In either case, the lack of an external threat contributes to the ultimate failure of the occupation by making it more difficult for the occupying power to accomplish desired reforms during the occupation.

An occupied population's views about the protection offered by an occupying power are likely to be affected by three different factors. First, the composition of the occupied population may determine whether or not an external threat is perceived. In a state with many different national groups that have a history of conflict between them, it is unlikely that all of the groups will agree on whether the greatest threat to their self-determination is posed by the occupying power or by some other third-party threat. In particular, groups within a state are unlikely to agree on the most compelling threat if at least one of the groups has an affinity with a neighboring and potentially threatening state, seeks to dismantle the occupied territory into more than one state, or aims to gain disproportionate control over the territory. Even a minority population can undo an occupation if it allies itself with an external threat or if it perceives the occupying power, not another foreign country, as the greatest threat to the security of the occupied country. Whereas, then, the population and the occupier's interests may coalesce around a commonly perceived external threat, an internal threat to the coherence of the occupied territory is more likely to lead to occupation failure.[2]

Second, the level of external threat is determined not only by the presence of a nearby aggressive power, but also by the vulnerability of the occupied territory. Threat is a relative variable that is determined not only by the nature of external powers, but also by the status of the occupied territory itself. The threat posed by the capabilities of an external power is exacerbated when the occupied territory itself is particularly weak. Occupied territories left prostrate and defeated by the conflict preceding the occupation are likely to be more vulnerable to potential predators that are looking to capitalize on the weakness of the state. Destructive conflict may also leave the occupied population less capable of mounting a violent, determined opposition to a postconflict occupation. Other occupied populations that feel liberated and less in need of protection, rather than defeated and vulnerable, are likely to feel less threatened and, therefore, resist occupation.

Third, threat is not simply a structural variable determined by the presence of external powers. The initial absence or presence of a powerful external threat is significant, but perceptions of threat can be either reinforced or transformed by the strategies that occupying powers pursue once an occupation is underway. Thus, it is useful to distinguish between initial perceptions of threat at the outset of an occupation and subsequent perceptions of threat once an occupation is underway. In the next chapter, I examine how the occupied population's initial perception of threat affects the strategic choices of occupying powers and how those strategies, in turn, affect the occupied population's subsequent perception of threat.

The Occupying Power

An external threat also persuades an occupying power to maintain its commitment to an occupation. Occupying powers are continuously tempted to evacuate the occupied territory. By doing so, they may conserve resources and end their involvement in a foreign country. Unless an occupying power is seeking empire, it should want to terminate an occupation, not prolong it. The pressures to end an occupation can be intense. On the domestic front, groups opposed to the occupation may argue that the occupation is both unwise strategically and an unnecessary expenditure of vital national resources. If the occupied population violently resists occupation, then the pressure to end the occupation is likely only to increase as the death count among occupying soldiers continues to rise.

An external threat provides a justification to an occupying power's domestic audience for prolonging an occupation. Occupying powers have an interest in defending an occupied territory from an external threat. Otherwise, the cost of intervening in and occupying the territory in the first place will have been wasted. When an external threat is present, the leaders of an occupying power can better persuade their domestic audience that a longer occupation is necessary. In particular, when the occupied territory is perceived as vulnerable to predators as a result of the preoccupation conflict, the occupying power may feel compelled to protect that territory. Less vulnerable territories will likely appear less threatened and, therefore, less worthy of the costs of occupation.

When either an external threat is absent or the occupied territory is beset with internal threats, it is more likely that the occupying power will face pressures to end its occupation. Internal threats raise the prospect that an occupying power will become entangled in a costly and unproductive civil war. Domestic audiences will not see the value in prolonging a dangerous and costly occupation when it requires becoming a participant in another country's civil war. These pressures may tempt an occupying power to end an occupation prematurely without having established the conditions for long-term stability.

In sum, the most important predictor of occupation success is a favorable threat environment: the presence of an external threat to the occupied territory from which the occupying power is willing and able to protect it. Most often, the threat perceived by the occupied population and the occupying power will be the same, common threat. In theory, a successful occupation could result from a threat environment in which the population perceives one threat and the occupying power perceives another. In this unlikely case, the occupying power's presence may still provide protection to the occupied population even if two different threats are motivating the population and the power.

When the threat environment is unfavorable—an external threat is absent or the primary threat is an internal threat—occupation is less likely to be successful. This analysis reveals two important auxiliary hypotheses. First, occupation is more likely to succeed in territories that have been left prostrate and vulnerable by the preoccupation conflict. Weak postconflict states are more prone to predatory behavior by other neighboring states. Vulnerability amplifies the threat posed by any external power. Second, the occupation of geopolitically significant territory is more likely to succeed. Such territories are both more likely to be threatened and more likely to generate a commitment from an occupying power to offer protection than territories on the periphery of the international system that are less likely to be threatened and that are perceived to be of lesser value.

Evidence on the Threat Environment

To evaluate the effect of the threat environment on occupation success or failure, I present two forms of evidence. First, in Table 1.1, I code each of the thirty
cases of military occupation since 1815 for the threat environment and examine
whether these factors correlate with success or failure. Second, to more closely
evaluate the central hypothesis on external threat, I examine two cases that
represent ideal types: the occupation of western Germany after World War II and
the U.S. occupation of Haiti from 1915 to 1934.

Table 1.2 summarizes the data set with regard to the threat environment
argument. Appendix 2 provides a slightly more detailed discussion of the threat
environment in each case. In all five of the cases in which an external threat was
present, the occupation succeeded. In five of the seven cases of occupation success, the occupied territory faced an external threat. The only occupations that
succeeded without such a threat present were the allied occupation of France
after the Napoleonic wars and the Soviet occupation of northern Korea after
World War II. The allied occupation of post-Napoleonic France was a multilateral occupation that quickly restored the prewar monarchy and aimed to do little
more. Although the French population merely tolerated rather than welcomed
the occupation, the allied powers were able to accomplish their goal relatively
quickly before both they and the population lost patience with the mission.[3] Few
cases of occupation since have attempted to restore either a monarchy or a prewar regime. In the next chapter, I discuss the other outlier, the Soviet occupation
of northern Korea, which succeeded primarily because of an effective strategy of
coercion that overcame the initial unfavorable threat environment.

Of the fifteen cases in which there was no external threat to the occupied
territory, ten (67 percent) failed and only two fully succeeded. Further, in four
of the six cases of occupation in which there was a major internal threat to the
occupied territory, the occupation failed and the other two achieved only mixed
success. In theory, one could also find cases with both an internal and an external threat, but unsurprisingly, there are no cases in the data set that featured
both an internal threat and an external threat that was perceived by a strong
majority of the occupied population. If the population is divided internally,
then it would be surprising to find that population agreeing on the threat posed
by an external power. All of these findings are consistent with the hypotheses
presented above.

To further evaluate the importance of the threat environment, I present two
detailed case studies. These cases represent prominent types of cases in the data
set—one in which the threat environment was propitious for occupation success
(the allied occupation of western Germany after World War II) and one where

Table 1.1 Threat environment and occupation results

TERRITORY (PRIMARY OCCUPIER) AND DATE	INITIAL THREAT ENVIRONMENT	SUMMARY
France (United Kingdom, Russia, Prussia, Austria), 1815–18	None	Success
Mexico (France), 1861–67	None	Failure
Ili (Russia), 1871–81	None	Mixed
Egypt (United Kingdom), 1882–1954	None	Failure
Cuba (United States), 1898–1902	None	Failure
Philippines (United States), 1898–1945	Internal	Mixed
Cuba (United States), 1906–9	Internal	Failure
Haiti (United States), 1915–34	None	Failure
Dominican Republic (United States), 1916–24	None	Failure
Istanbul (France, United Kingdom, Italy), 1918–23	None	Failure
Rhineland (France, United Kingdom, United States), 1918–30	None	Failure
Iraq (United Kingdom), 1918–32	None	Failure
Palestine (United Kingdom), 1919–48	Internal	Mixed
Saar (France), 1920–35	None	Mixed
Italy (United Kingdom, United States), 1943–48	External (Germany, then Soviet Union)	Success
Eastern Austria (Soviet Union), 1945–55	None	Failure
Western Austria (United Kingdom, United States, France), 1945–55	External (Soviet Union)	Success
Western Germany (France, United Kingdom, United States), 1945–52	External (Soviet Union)	Success
Japan (United States), 1945–52	External (Soviet Union)	Success
Ryukyus (United States), 1945–72	External (Soviet Union)	Success
Northern Korea (Soviet Union), 1945–48	None	Success
Southern Korea (United States), 1945–48	None	Mixed
West Bank/Gaza (Israel), 1967–	None	Failure
Cambodia (Vietnam), 1979–89	Internal	Failure
Southern Lebanon (Israel), 1982–2000	Internal	Failure
Lebanon (Syria), 1976–2005	Internal	Failure
Bosnia (NATO/EU), 1995–	Internal	?
Kosovo (NATO), 1999–	Internal	?
Afghanistan (NATO), 2001–	Internal	?
Iraq (United States, United Kingdom, Poland), 2003–	Internal	?

Table 1.2. Summary of threat environment and occupation results

| | | OCCUPATION RESULT | | |
		SUCCESS	MIXED	FAILURE
	External	5	0	0
Threat	None	2	3	10
	Internal	0	2	4

the threat environment augured occupation failure (the U.S. occupation of Haiti from 1915 to 1934). The German case is selected because of both its historical importance and its representative nature. The case is in many ways typical of the occupations that the United States undertook in the immediate aftermath of World War II. Although this was a case of multilateral occupation, I focus primarily on the United States since it quickly assumed a leadership role within the occupation. The case of Haiti is more obscure, but likewise, it is representative of a broader class of American occupations undertaken in the first half of the twentieth century. Later in the book, I address two cases—Kosovo and Iraq—where an internal threat has undermined occupation.

The Allied Occupation of Western Germany, 1945–1952

World War II in Europe ended in May 1945, and by 1955 the West German economy had been rebuilt, West Germany was a member of the North Atlantic Treaty Organization (NATO), and the country was emerging as a model of Western liberal democracy.

To be clear, success in the occupation of western Germany did not come easily. In the early months of the occupation, the Western allies faced popular resistance brought on by a shortage of food, a devastated infrastructure, and a dysfunctional economy.[4] Germans, like others who have been occupied, wanted to rule themselves and were suspicious of the intentions of their occupiers, in particular the French.[5] In this case study, I will argue that the threat posed by the Soviet Union, amplified by the vulnerability of Germany in the wake of World War II, enabled the occupation of western Germany to succeed.

The looming Soviet threat lessened the likelihood of nationalist resistance from the occupied population and increased the willingness of the occupying powers to see the occupation through to a successful conclusion. Germans recognized that they were going to be occupied by somebody after World War II, and if the choice was between being occupied by the United States, the United Kingdom, and even France or, alternatively, the Soviet Union, then most west Germans preferred occupation by the Western powers.[6] At the same time, although many in the United States wished that the their government could retrench in the wake of World War II, the threat posed by the Soviet Union bound the United States to the European continent and to the occupation of Germany.

GOALS AND MEANS

The success of any occupation must be judged relative to the goals of the occupation and how the occupying powers hoped to accomplish those goals. Winston Churchill, Franklin Roosevelt, and Josef Stalin devised the basic goals and means of the occupation of Germany at the Yalta conference in February 1945.[7] While envisioning a future unified Germany, the three leaders agreed to divide Germany into four temporary occupation zones—American, British, Soviet, and French. Germany was to continue to be treated as a single country and was to be governed during the occupation period by an integrated Allied Control Council (ACC) with representatives from each of the four occupying powers.[8] Germany would be forced to surrender unconditionally to the Allies and accept the punishment meted out to it.[9]

The Allies did not agree on everything at Yalta. Perhaps most importantly, they disagreed on the size and form of reparations that Germany would pay. Stalin called for the extraordinary sum of $20 billion in reparations, half of which would go to the Soviet Union, but Churchill objected that such extreme reparations would condemn Germany to poverty and prevent her peaceful reintegration into Europe. Unable to agree on a reparations agreement, the Big Three decided instead that they would create a reparations commission that would assess the appropriate amount and form of reparations that Germany would pay.[10]

Inspired by the treasury secretary Henry Morgenthau, the allies originally intended to impose a harsh and punitive peace on the Germans. Regarding the critical industrial heartland of the Ruhr Valley, Morgenthau suggested that "this area should not only be stripped of all presently existing industries but so weakened and controlled that it can not in the foreseeable future become an industrial area."[11] To accomplish this, all industrial equipment would be removed from the Ruhr and the region would be governed by an international body appointed by the United Nations. Notably, it was not just the United States that adopted the punitive spirit of the Morgenthau Plan. The British Foreign Office declared, "The primary purpose of the Occupation is destructive and preventive and our measures of destruction and prevention are only limited by consideration for (1) the security and well-being of the forces of Occupation, (2) prevention of unrest among the German people, (3) broad considerations of humanity."[12]

Morgenthau's punitive agenda was reflected in the U.S. Joint Chiefs of Staff planning directive for postwar Germany, JCS 1067.[13] JCS 1067 laid out four means by which the general goal of creating a stable and peaceful Germany would be accomplished. First, Germany would be demilitarized. The enormous military machine of the Third Reich had to be completely dismantled to ensure that Germany would never again pose a threat to European security. Second, Germany would be denazified. Supporters of Nazism would have to be, at a minimum, removed from positions of power and, in some cases, punished for their actions. Third, Germany would be decentralized. The highly centralized government of the Nazi period had to be replaced by a more diffuse federal system that would prevent the concentration of power in any single person or group. Finally, Germany would ideally be democratized. The Allies aimed to convince the German people that totalitarianism had led to the destruction of their country. Instead, the German people should embrace liberal democracy.

At Potsdam in July 1945, the differences among the Big Three on questions of reparations and occupation administration became more pronounced. Stalin insisted that the Soviet Union be paid extensive reparations to be drawn proportionally from the four zones of occupation. After the Americans and the British rejected this idea, the Allies agreed instead on a plan whereby the Soviets were to receive 15 percent of "usable and complete industrial capital equipment" in the western zones in return for food and other commodities from the Soviet zone.[14] On top of that, the Soviets would receive an additional 10 percent of industrial capital that was deemed unnecessary for the peacetime German economy. The parties also agreed at Potsdam to allow the Soviets to expel ethnic Germans from Eastern Europe "in an orderly and humane manner."[15] As a consequence, western Germany was inundated with 11 million refugees and deportees in the wake of World War II.[16]

THE EMERGING THREAT ENVIRONMENT

As predicted, the course of the occupation of western Germany shadowed the increasing threat perceived from the Soviet Union. Following Potsdam, relations between the Western allies and the Soviet Union continued to deteriorate. Most importantly, the Soviet occupation authorities quickly violated the reparations provisions that had been agreed to at Potsdam by extracting more resources from their occupation zone than they were permitted. A fundamental disagreement emerged among the allies over how much economic capacity western Germany needed to function. Because the Soviets were entitled to 10 percent of unnecessary German industrial capacity, they had every incentive to diminish the economic needs of western Germany. The Western allies, increasingly concerned about the poor conditions in their occupation zones, sought to raise the standard. In April 1946, the U.S. commander in Germany, General Lucius Clay, angered the Soviets by announcing that he was suspending reparations deliveries from the American zone until a satisfactory agreement could be reached on an import-export policy for Germany.[17]

Then, in May 1946, Secretary of State James Byrnes called for the demilitarization of Germany.[18] When Moscow rejected Byrnes's plan in July, the threat perceived from the Soviets was amplified, and the Western powers moved even further to solidify the Western occupation zones in opposition to the Soviet zone. Byrnes invited any of the other occupying powers economically to unite their zones with the American zone. Facing severe problems paying for reconstruction in their own zone, the British quickly accepted. The British zone had industrial resources, but London lacked the financial resources to fully support the occupation.[19] Meanwhile, the U.S. occupation zone was largely agricultural and stood to benefit from the industrial resources of other zones. Even though it could have benefited from zonal unification, France remained opposed to any movement toward centralized authority within Germany, so it opted not to unify with the other Western zones at this point.[20]

As the outlines of the cold war began to emerge, the more punitive aspects of the original strategies intended to create security—denazification and demilitarization—were supplanted by tactics meant to ensure that Germany did not become a part of the Soviet sphere of influence. Following the suspension of reparations in the spring of 1946, Secretary of State Byrnes's speech in Stuttgart on September 6, 1946, marked yet more movement away from the punitive policies of the Morgenthau Plan and JCS 1067, and the arrival of policies focused on ensuring the place of western Germany in the Western European system of institutions and alliances.[21] Since social instability was seen as a condition abetting the spread of communism, Germany could no longer be allowed to founder. In the speech, Byrnes first called for a revision of the level of industry plan that guided the deindustrialization policy. If Germany was to become a peaceful member of the European system, then it must be allowed to have a functioning economy and Germany's people must be provided with adequate food in order to survive. Second, Byrnes appealed to German nationalism by acknowledging that Germans must soon again be allowed to govern themselves. Although Byrnes explicitly committed the United States to continuing participation in the occupation, he also appreciated that the goal of democratization would never be accomplished without beginning the process at the state and local level. The draconian measures of the Morgenthau Plan had been completely rejected. Future geopolitical goals took precedence over punishment for the past.[22]

UNIFICATION OF THE WESTERN ZONES

On January 1, 1947, the American and British occupation zones were united into what came to be called "Bizonia." The unification was strictly economic, but nonetheless, it symbolized the widening gulf between the Western allies and the Soviet Union. Once again, the foreign ministers convened in Moscow in March and April 1947, but the divisions were now irreparable. Moscow continued to seek a resumption of reparations while London and Washington were already moving forward toward the creation of an independent western Germany. By the summer of 1947, the United States had pledged in the Marshall Plan to lend substantial financial support to the countries of Europe in order to prevent the spread of communism in these countries. In July, JCS 1779 superseded JCS 1067 as guidance for the U.S. military government in Germany and reflected the movement started by Byrnes in Stuttgart away from a vengeful occupation to an occupation aimed at ensuring the western Germany would be allied with Western Europe.[23] Consistent with this move, the level of industry plan for western Germany was significantly revised by the Bizonal Commission. Total allowable industrial production was raised from 70–75 percent of 1936 levels to 90–95 percent.[24] Raising German industrial production would presumably raise the German standard of living and convince Germans to reject Soviet-sponsored communism.

In February 1948, the United States pushed further during the Council of Foreign Ministers meeting in London, proposing the creation of a common currency among the four zones of occupation. In early June, France finally agreed to join with the United States and Great Britain in a western German state with a common currency. From the Soviet perspective, the adoption of a common currency in the three Western zones without Soviet participation fundamentally violated the pledge that the allies had made to treat Germany as a single economic unit. From the Western Allied perspective, however, Soviet violations of the reparations agreements reached had long ago abrogated the Potsdam agreement. The Soviets responded with a blockade of Berlin. The common currency, combined with other policy reforms allowing for increased German exports, was a boon to the German economy. Before the currency reform, industrial output was at 47 percent of 1936 levels. After the currency and export reforms, industrial production rose to 89 percent of 1936 levels by March 1949.[25]

In addition to revitalizing the economy, the occupying powers appealed to German nationalism as a way of signaling that the Western occupation posed less of a threat than the Soviet Union. The three Western allies along with Belgium, the Netherlands, and Luxembourg agreed to move Germany further in the direction of self-government. The agreements reached in London in 1948 called for the creation of a representative constituent assembly that would meet and draft a constitution for an independent, federal West Germany.[26] The confluence of economic and political developments in the summer of 1948 pushed further toward the consolidation of a western Germany that would be well-entrenched in Western Europe and protected from the threat posed by the Soviet Union.

In sum, by the time of the Berlin blockade in 1948, leaders in both Germany and their Western occupiers understood that the goal of creating a peaceful, unified Germany was now infeasible. Instead, the Western allies worked to prevent communism from gaining a foothold in western Germany. As the Soviet threat emerged, the occupation of western Germany was decreasingly about denazification and deindustrialization and increasingly about how best to guarantee the security and friendship of western Germany.

END GAME

The Western allies continued to attempt to demonstrate to Germans that the West promised self-determination while the Soviets promised only continuing oppression. The German assembly, the Parliamentary Council, began meeting in September 1948 with sixty-five members elected by the parliaments of each German state. Over the following several months, the Parliamentary Council discussed the form of the German government, and in particular, the level of centralized authority in the new German state. On February 10, 1949, the Parliamentary Council submitted its final draft of the German Basic Law to the military governors. After intense negotiation between the Germans and the Allies, a revised Basic Law was accepted by the Parliamentary Council, and the Basic Law was then ratified by the German state legislatures between May 16 and May 22. Bundesrat elections were held in Germany three months later, and Konrad Adenauer of the Christian Democratic Union was elected the first chancellor of the Federal Republic of Germany, West Germany, in September. One month later, the German Democratic Republic, East Germany, was created.

Even as West Germany was becoming a semisovereign state in 1949, the occupying powers reserved important areas of policymaking for themselves. Through an Occupation Statute that was agreed to at the same time as the Basic Law, the occupying powers essentially remained in control of German foreign and trade policy and retained the power to intervene in German affairs in an emergency.[27] In addition, an International Ruhr Authority was created to supervise production and exports from the industrial Ruhr Valley. German sovereignty was, therefore, highly circumscribed even after 1949. The Germans were, however, able to use the Soviet threat as leverage to convince the occupying powers to end the unpopular program of denazification. Although denazification remained important to the occupying powers, retaining geostrategically significant Germany in the Western bloc was far more important.[28]

The priorities of both the Germans and Allies continued to shift after 1949. For the Germans, priorities included ending the limiting Occupation Statute, regaining full sovereignty, and becoming a member of the Western alliance to ensure protection from the Soviet threat. The Allies, on the other hand, were still concerned about the threat that an independent Germany might pose, so they sought to integrate Germany into the West as a means of weakening any potential German threat while simultaneously protecting Germany from the looming Soviet threat.[29]

The solution to granting West Germany full sovereignty while simultaneously guaranteeing that it would not threaten the security of Europe was to embed West Germany in a series of European institutions. The first of these institutions, the European Coal and Steel Community, replaced the International Ruhr Authority in April 1951. The treaty, which included West Germany, France, Italy, and the Benelux countries, placed European coal and steel industries under supranational control. Germany would again benefit from the industrial potential of the Ruhr Valley without being able to exploit those resources to threaten its neighbors.

Second, the Allies and Germany hoped to solve the problem of German rearmament by creating a European Defense Community (EDC).[30] With the outbreak of the Korean War, the perceived Soviet threat once again asserted itself, and it was increasingly evident that a rearmed Germany could be a great benefit in the cold war struggle against the Soviet Union. At the same time, other Western Europeans hesitated to endorse the rearmament of their erstwhile enemy, and Germans themselves embraced a pacifism that precluded consideration of rearmament. Under the EDC proposal, Germany would be permitted to rearm, but all of its forces would be committed to the EDC, precluding any German aggression. Meanwhile, Adenauer made the EDC proposal palatable to the German public by demanding that, in exchange, the Occupation Statute be repealed and that Germany be granted full sovereignty.[31]

On May 26, 1952, the General Treaty, abrogating the Occupation Statute, was signed in Bonn between the Western occupying powers and the Federal Republic of Germany. A day later, the EDC treaty was signed in Paris. Although the EDC eventually collapsed when the French Chamber refused to ratify it in August 1954, the rearmament of Germany signified a turning point in Germany's integration into the West. This integration culminated in 1955 when Germany became a full member of the North Atlantic Treaty Organization.

EVALUATING THE OCCUPATION

The occupation of western Germany must be considered a success. Not only did Germany become a liberal democracy with a thriving industrial economy, but it also became an important member of the North Atlantic Treaty Organization. These accomplishments were sustained throughout the lengthy cold war. All of this occurred without any substantial resistance, violent or otherwise, to the lengthy occupation. The costs to the United States, Great Britain, and France of occupying Germany were not insignificant. Though Germany was forced to pay for direct occupation costs, western Germany became eligible for Marshall Plan aid in December 1947.[32] Between money from the Marshall Plan and funds authorized in 1946 under the Government and Relief in Occupied Areas (GARIOA) budget, western Germany received more than $3 billion in aid from the United States alone in the occupation period. Rising occupation costs were a concern for all three of the occupying powers, prompting the economic unification of the American, British, and French zones in 1947 and 1948. Even though the costs of occupying Germany were significant in both dollars and time commitment, the occupation was essential to the emerging cold war struggle with the Soviet Union.[33] It is difficult to imagine an alternative strategy other than occupation that could have achieved Western goals in Germany.

WHY THE OCCUPATION OF WESTERN GERMANY SUCCEEDED

The post–World War II occupation of Germany demonstrates the effect that the threat environment can have on occupation outcomes. No population enjoys being occupied, but if the occupying power offers valuable protection against another threat, then the population will tolerate the occupation. In this case, the threat from the Soviet Union led the West German population to accept the occupation by the United States, United Kingdom, and even its perennial rival, France. Arriving with reports about the abusive behavior by communist authorities in the Soviet Union and other Central and Eastern Europe countries, the millions of refugees from these areas confirmed the threat posed by Soviet-style communism.[34] As historian John Lewis Gaddis writes of Soviet behavior, in particular the mass rapes, in eastern Germany, "These semi-sanctioned mass rapes took place precisely as Stalin was trying to win the support of the German people, not just in the east but throughout the country. He even allowed elections to be held inside the Soviet zone in the fall of 1946, only to have the Germans—women in particular—vote overwhelmingly against the Soviet-supported candidates."[35] Norman Naimark, a leading historian of Soviet behavior in eastern Germany, observes, "Many [eastern Germans] succumbed, acquiesced, and even joined the system, although many escaped to the west. Simultaneously, many in the West grew increasingly determined to avoid the fate of their brethren in the East, and some were willing to resort to open resistance in order to do so."[36] As news of Soviet behavior in the east arrived in western Germany, Germans came to view the prospect of Soviet-control as far more threatening than Western occupation.[37]

To understand how western Germans perceived the relative threat posed by the Soviet Union as opposed to the occupying powers, it is useful to look at both public opinion and the opinion of important leaders. Fortunately extensive public opinion polling was conducted in the American zone of occupation. In October 1945, an Opinions Survey Section was established in the Intelligence Branch of the Office of the Director of Information Control, Office of Military Government. Over the following four years, this agency conducted seventy-two major surveys of German public opinion, about one every three weeks. The Opinion Survey Section initially limited its surveys to the southern section of the American zone of occupation, including Bavaria, Hesse, and Wuerttemberg-Baden. Gradually, however, surveys were also conducted in the American zone of West Berlin as well as the American-controlled port city of Bremen.[38]

The public opinion polls conducted in Germany during the occupation reveal the threat that the Germans perceived from the Soviet Union. For example, in a poll taken in October 1947, 70 percent of Germans polled believed that that United States would have the greatest influence on world events in the following ten years. The Soviet Union polled second with only 13 percent. These results by themselves are not particularly revealing, but what is more interesting is that of those who had selected the United States, 78 percent believed that that influence would be in the interest of peace. Conversely, 88 percent of those who chose the Soviet Union believed that dominant Soviet influence would result in war.[39]

When asked that same month which occupying power they trusted most, 63 percent selected the United States, 45 percent said Great Britain, 4 percent identified France, and none selected the Soviet Union. In the same survey, 84 percent of Germans in the American zone of occupation said that they would choose the Americans again as their occupying power if they could turn back history.[40] Germans in the American zone also had negative impressions of life within the Soviet Union. Less than 5 percent of those surveyed in April 1948 believed that

that Soviet policy was determined by the will of the people and that people got along well within the Soviet Union.[41]

During the Berlin blockade, Germans welcomed the relief offered by the Western powers. Ninety-eight percent of West Berliners believed that the Western powers were correct in staying in Berlin rather than retreating. Eighty-two percent of Germans interviewed believed that the image of Western powers had improved among Germans while a roughly equal number believed that Soviet popularity had declined as a result of the crisis in Berlin. The German desire to see the Western powers remain is particularly telling given the overwhelming fear of war among Germans at the time. By July 1948, 82 percent of the Germans interviewed believed that war was likely within a decade, up from 42 percent in August 1947. Seventy-three percent expressed that the Berlin crisis itself might be a sufficient catalyst for war.[42] Foreseeing war, Germans embraced, rather than rejected, the protection that the Western allies offered against the Soviet Union.

In addition to public opinion, the opinions of prominent elites are significant. The occupying powers successfully identified and promoted German leaders who shared their belief in the threat posed by the Soviet Union. Konrad Adenauer recognized the seriousness of the threat posed by the Soviet Union and the need to join the West in order to resist this threat. As Adenauer writes in his memoirs, "Soviet Russia was making it quite clear that for the time being she was not willing to release the German territory she had been allowed to take over, and that moreover she had every intention of gradually drawing the other part of Germany towards her as well. There was only one way for us to save our political liberty, our personal freedom, [and] our security . . . : we must form our firm links with the peoples and countries that shared our views concerning the state, the individual, liberty, and property."[43] Adenauer's greatest fear, in fact, was that the Western allies did not appreciate the seriousness of the threat posed by the Soviet Union. As a consequence, Adenauer attempted to convince both the Americans and the British to strengthen their commitments to the security of western Germany.[44]

Kurt Schumacher, leader of the Social Democratic Union, represented the primary opposition to Adenauer, and Schumacher too agreed on the threat posed by the Soviet Union. Occupation officials did, in fact, have significant concerns about Schumacher, but those concerns were about the strength of Schumacher's nationalism, not his sympathy to communism. The Western allies feared that Schumacher would reject any occupation as a precursor to the permanent division of Germany.[45] But neither Adenauer nor Schumacher believed that Soviet-inspired communism posed less of a threat to German nationalism than Western liberal policies.

Finally, consider the memories of John McCloy, high commissioner of Germany from 1949 until 1952: "Another element was the spur which we always had at this stage—the fear of the Soviet Union, the fear of the Russians. There they were, across the way in Berlin, pressing. . . . We could do no wrong [in Berlin] because the importance of showing ourselves in Berlin was so apparent to the Berlin population that it was almost a delight to go up to Berlin . . . while down in the zone we were apt to be criticized."[46] In other words, the U.S. occupation was most readily accepted by the German population that was in closest proximity to the Soviet threat. Further away from that threat, the population was more likely to resist the continuing occupation.

The threat posed to western Germany was amplified by the prostrate nature of Germany in the wake of the war. Germans had not been liberated; they had been defeated. Little opposition to occupation was evident, as Germans were desperate for the assistance that the Western allies were willing and able to offer.[47] The so-called "werewolves"—German military officers trained to disrupt any occupation activities—revealed themselves to have little capability or will to interfere with the occupation.[48]

The Western occupation promised Germany help in reconstructing a once-proud nation and protection from the looming threat of the Soviet Union. In the immediate aftermath of the war, a U.S. Army observer reported, "More than 20 million Germans are homeless or without adequate shelter. The average basic ration is less than 1,000 calories. The ability to wage war in this generation has been destroyed."[49] Major cities were almost entirely destroyed—93 percent of the houses in Düsselfdorf, 75 percent in Frankfurt, and 66 percent in Cologne.[50]

United States leaders were concerned that this level of destruction left Germany vulnerable to the threat of Soviet-sponsored communism. General Clay worried about the German choice "between becoming a Communist on 1500 calories and a believer in democracy on 1000 calories. It is my sincere belief that our proposed ration allowance in Germany will not only defeat our objectives in middle Europe but will pave the road to a Communist Germany."[51] The vulnerability of Germany compelled the allied occupied powers to commit resources to the occupation. Increasing food rations and allowing Germany industry to reconstitute itself was seen as vital to helping Germany rebuild from the devastation of World War II.[52] Once the United States and its allies began to help in the reconstruction of Germany, it only reinforced the sense that the Soviet Union posed the most significant threat to German security. At the same time, the existing industrial infrastructure in Germany lessened the costs to the occupying powers, making the occupation more affordable.

The threat posed by the Soviet Union also helped to sustain the allied commitment, in particular the U.S. commitment, to the occupation. In the wake of World War II, there was considerable doubt about the willingness of the United States to maintain a forward military presence in Europe. The minutes of the meeting among the Big Three at Yalta on February 5, 1945, record, "[President Roosevelt] replied that he did not believe that American troops would stay in Europe much more than two years. He went on to say that he felt that he could obtain support in Congress and throughout the country for any reasonable measures designed to safeguard the future peace, but he did not believe that this would extend to the maintenance of an appreciable American force in Europe."[53] Roosevelt, of course, uttered these words at a time that he still maintained some hope for great power cooperation in the aftermath of the war. Within two years, however, the looming Soviet threat was employed to motivate the American people and the U.S. Congress to continue supporting the occupation of Germany.[54]

In sum, the threat environment in postwar western Germany satisfied both conditions necessary for a successful occupation: it made a lengthy and costly occupation more acceptable to the German population and more palatable to the United States, United Kingdom, and France.

The U.S. Occupation of Haiti, 1915–1934

The U.S. occupation of Haiti from 1915 until 1934 is instructive because, unlike the German case, there was no external threat that led the Haitians to embrace the American occupation or the United States to see the continuing occupation as in its interests. In the absence of this threat, the Haitian population became impatient with a foreign occupation, and the United States began to question why it was devoting national resources to the occupation of Haiti.

GOALS AND MEANS

The immediate, precipitating cause of U.S. intervention in Haiti was the overthrow and subsequent execution and dismemberment of Haitian President Vilbrun Guillaume Sam in July 1915. Sam was the seventh Haitian president since 1910, and the overthrow of his regime gave the United States a pretext on which to intervene in order to prevent the emergence of anarchy in Haiti. On July 28, an initial U.S. force of 330 soldiers and marines landed in Port-au-Prince and were shortly reinforced by several hundred more.[55] The United States had begun an occupation of Haiti that would ultimately last almost two decades.

The U.S. government intervened in Haiti with three goals. First, it wanted to prevent the complete political disintegration of Haiti. For President Wilson, the imperative was quite clear: "There is nothing to do but to take the bull by the horns and restore order . . . and put an end to revolution. . . . In other words, we consider it our duty to insist on constitutional government there and will, if necessary, if they force us to it as the only way, take charge of elections and see that a real government is created which we can support."[56] This motive alone is, however, unsatisfying, for it cannot explain the timing of the United States intervention in Haiti. Political unrest was endemic to Haiti, yet the United States found 1915 to be the appropriate year to intervene.

Second, the United States intervened in Haiti in order to protect the investments of private American citizens and banks in Haiti. This argument is consistent with American behavior elsewhere in the Western Hemisphere, but it is somewhat undercut in the case of Haiti by the relatively miniscule American investment in Haiti prior to the occupation. In 1913, the United States had approximately $4 million invested in Haiti, a paltry 0.32 percent of total U.S. investments in Latin America.[57] The United States intervention may have been motivated, in part, by a desire to secure future areas of investment for the United States, but it is implausible to argue that the United States acted to secure current investments in Haiti.

Third, the United States wanted to prevent what it perceived as German ambitions to establish a base of operations in the Western Hemisphere.[58] The newly built Panama Canal was of vital strategic importance, and German control over Hispaniola would have granted the Germans unacceptable control over access to the canal. As Secretary of State Robert Lansing explained in 1922 to Senator Medill McCormick, chairman of the Senate Select Committee on Haiti and Santo Domingo, the United States was motivated by "a desire to forestall any attempt by a foreign power to obtain a foothold on the territory of an American nation which, if a seizure of customs control by such a power had occurred, or if a grant of a coaling station or naval base had been obtained, would have most certainly been a menace to the peace of the Western Hemisphere, and in flagrant defiance of the Monroe Doctrine."[59] Consistent with the Roosevelt Corollary to the Monroe Doctrine, leaders in Washington feared that Haiti might become unstable and fall into German hands, which would have had negative strategic and economic repercussions.[60] Thus, strategic considerations explain both the motive and the timing of the U.S. intervention in Haiti.

THE THREAT ENVIRONMENT

The Haitian population was immediately hostile to the U.S. marines who undertook the occupation of its country and denied Haiti its sovereignty.[61] The greatest threat perceived by the Haitians was the U.S. military rather than any other third party. Although U.S. marines found control relatively easy to gain in the coastal regions, the woody interior regions were dominated by local militias, known as *cacos*, who vehemently opposed the American occupation and remained loyal to the exiled political leader and presidential candidate Rosalvo Bobo.[62] Eventually, the *caco* rebels were overpowered by the U.S. marines, and by the fall of 1915 most of the *caco* resistance had temporarily subsided.

The U.S. occupation authorities did little to prevent the recurrence of hostility when they handpicked Philippe Sudre Dartiguenave to be the Haitian president and had him elected in a sham election in August 1915. Subsequently, the United States pursued negotiations with the Haitian government to legalize the American occupation, and in February 1916 the Haitian Senate unanimously approved a treaty granting the United States wide-ranging control over Haiti.

The treaty was to remain in force for ten years from the date on which ratifications were exchanged, May 3, 1916. It granted the United States control over the Haitian economy and finances and provided for five treaty services: a Customs Receivership, an Office of the Financial Adviser, a Constabulary, a Public Works Service, and a Public Health Service. The United States would also organize, train, and provide officers for a Haitian gendarmerie that would be responsible for public safety.[63] Despite the ostensible existence of a Haitian government under Dartiguenave, the American occupiers dictated the treaty to the Haitian people. Almost a year later, in March 1917, the treaty was extended until 1936.

Consistent with the security goal of the occupation, the United States acted to eliminate the German presence in Haiti once the occupation began. In 1917, the United States proposed alterations to the Haitian constitution that would limit German influence with Haiti. More specifically, the new constitution opened up Haiti to American economic penetration by eliminating a five-year residency requirement for land ownership. Such a policy favored newly arriving American interests while reducing the economic influence of Germans who had previously moved to and invested in Haiti.[64] When the Haitian National Assembly refused to ratify the constitution, the U.S. occupation administration disbanded the legislature, with the approval of President Dartiguenave. Subsequently, the new constitution was approved in a plebiscite of the Haitian people under the watchful eyes of American marines.[65]

After the Haitian government finally declared war on Germany in 1918, leading Germans in Haiti were interned, and any Germans owning land in Haiti had that land stripped from them. Colonel John Russell remarked that World War I had "afforded an opportunity for the elimination of [Germans] from commerce and politics, and it is hoped that by this time this has been effected."[66]

Meanwhile, by continuing to usurp Haitian sovereignty and offend the Haitian people, the American occupation authority did little to endear itself to the Haitian population. In particular, marine colonel Smedley Butler, who was in command of the Haitian gendarmerie, discovered an 1863 Haitian law that provided for the creation of a corvée. Under the law, "public highways and communications will be maintained and repaired by the inhabitants, in rotation, in each section through which roads pass, and each time repairs are needed."[67] Local peasants were compelled to contribute labor to the building of infrastructure if they could not afford to pay a tax instead (which very few Haitian peasants could). Although the corvée system proved productive—supporting the construction of a widespread road network—it also generated considerable discontent among the Haitian population.[68] The conduct of the United States only exacerbated the unfavorable threat environment that existed at the onset of the occupation.

Despite the official abolishment of the corvée system by the end of 1918, the system continued unofficially in the more remote regions of Haiti where American commanders had wide leeway to direct their provinces. In particular, in the Hinche region, a *caco* revolt began in the face of continued abuses by the Haitian gendarmerie under the command of U.S. marines. Between July and September 1918, U.S. marines and the Haitian gendarmerie engaged in 80 armed skirmishes with *caco* rebels, and between July and September 1919, another approximately 131 skirmishes took place. Eighteen hundred and sixty-one of the 2,250 Haitians killed in the first five years of the occupation were killed during the 1919 clashes.[69] Despite having inferior equipment and forces, the *cacos* presented a significant challenge by taking advantage of their local knowledge and employing unconventional guerrilla warfare tactics.

Meanwhile, domestic pressure in the United States to end the occupation of Haiti began to grow. Before long, details of atrocities committed by U.S. marines in Haiti became public knowledge.[70] The behavior of the United States in Haiti and the simultaneous occupation of the Dominican Republic became issues in the 1920 U.S. presidential election with special congressional hearings convened in 1920 and 1921 to consider the U.S. role in Hispaniola.[71]

Eventually, the revelations of American atrocities and the defeat of Germany in World War I prompted the United States to reconsider the occupation altogether. With the end of the war and the defeat of Germany, the security motivation for the occupation of Haiti had disappeared. As Hans Schmidt relates, "With the end of the European war, the military occupation was no longer necessary to safeguard American strategic interests; moreover, Wilson was faced with the embarrassing contradiction implicit in championing the rights of small nations at the 1919 Versailles Peace Conference while simultaneously maintaining military control over Haiti."[72] Instead, the U.S. rationale for remaining in Haiti shifted. Between 1922 and 1925, the United States extended almost $23 million in loans to Haiti that refinanced the Haitian debt away from French lenders and into the hands of American bankers. The United States opted to remain in control of Haiti in order to protect American economic interests in the island that had grown during the occupation and prevent a return to the anarchy that preceded the occupation.[73]

HAITIAN NATIONALISM RESURGENT

For most of the remainder of the decade, Haiti remained relatively quiet.[74] Had the United States been able to withdraw in the mid 1920s and leave a stable and secure government, then the occupation of Haiti might be viewed as more of a success. But, at the same time that Haiti was quiet, it was not making much progress toward legitimate self-determination. The Unites States was primarily interested in protecting its own interests, not in improving Haitian society or stabilizing an indigenous Haitian government.[75] Both the peasants, who faced continuing repression, and the elites, who were dispossessed of their privileged position in society, continued to oppose the occupation.

Haitian nationalism finally reasserted itself in 1929. On October 29, students at Service Technique agricultural college in Damien walked out in protest over scholarship reductions.[76] The student strike spread by early November to include a general strike led by customs workers in Port-au-Prince. High Commissioner John Russell responded by imposing martial law and a curfew, suspending press operations, and revoking the independent status of the Haitian Garde.

The uprisings of late 1929 were the result of a confluence of two factors. First, in October 1929, Haitian President Louis Borno, at the urging of the occupation authority, canceled elections that were scheduled to be held in 1930. The U.S. feared the antioccupation results that were likely in a free and fair election. Second, the Haitian economy was showing few signs of improving. The combination of a weak coffee crop and declining coffee prices caused Haiti's rural peasants to suffer.

The situation only further deteriorated as a result of an incident in Cayes on December 6. After being surrounded by an angry mob of fifteen hundred Haitian peasants, twenty marines opened fire. High Commissioner Russell reported that twelve Haitians were killed with twenty-three wounded whereas the Haitian press reported that twenty-four had been killed and fifty-one wounded.[77] Just days before this incident, President Herbert Hoover had stated his desire to find some long-term solution to the Haiti situation, but the Cayes Massacre would make it that much more difficult for the United States to remain in Haiti in order to create the stability necessary for a successful end to the occupation.[78]

Ultimately, the protests in Haiti quieted after Borno declared his intention not to seek a third term as president. Nonetheless, the riots of 1929 had again drawn attention to the occupation in the United States. Debates in Congress focused on the hypocrisy of a democratic United States not allowing genuine democracy in Haiti. Foreign audiences as well vocally criticized the continuing occupation of Haiti in the wake of the Cayes Massacre.[79] As a consequence, by 1930, the priority of the United States was to bring the occupation to a conclusion as quickly as possible.[80] Neither the Haitian population nor the United States perceived any foreign threat that could motivate a continuation of the occupation.

END GAME

In February 1930, President Hoover charged the Forbes Commission, chaired by W. Cameron Forbes, a former governor of the Philippines, to travel to Haiti in search of a way to satisfy both the United States and Haitian nationalists without further bloodshed. The Forbes Commission eventually lauded the accomplishments of the occupation under John Russell but also criticized the administration for not making more progress toward Haitian self-rule.[81] The United States would only be able to withdraw from Haiti, the commission reported, if it were able to prepare the Haitians to govern themselves and provide for their own security.

Following the election of an ardent Haitian nationalist, Stenio Vincent, as president in November 1930, the United States replaced the much-disliked John Russell with Dana Munro. Munro was explicitly instructed to avoid interfering in Haitian domestic politics as a means for facilitating U.S. withdrawal from Haiti. Even though Munro attempted to work toward "Haitianization" of everything from public works to the gendarmerie, the critical issue remained creating protections for U.S. financial interests so that the United States could safely and confidently withdraw.[82]

After lengthy negotiations, the two sides finally agreed on the Executive Accord of August 7, 1933. The accord provided for an American fiscal representative who would supervise the Haitian economy, including customs, taxation, and the budget. The Haitian government was not permitted to increase its indebtedness, and the American supervision would continue until all outstanding bonds were liquidated (which was not scheduled until 1952). In return, Washington agreed to withdraw the occupation troops by October 1934, about a year and a half before the 1936 date that was stipulated in the treaty authorizing the occupation.

The Executive Accord was unpopular in both Haiti and the United States. Haitians wondered why the United States was being allowed such extensive control over their economy. In the United States, many questioned why national resources were being expended to protect private American bondholders.

In the end, though, the accord was the only agreement that could satisfy the needs of both sides. In July 1934, President Roosevelt visited Cap Haitien and announced that U.S. troops would leave Haiti about two months earlier than previously expected. On August 15, 1934, the final U.S. marines departed Haiti.

EVALUATING THE OCCUPATION

The United States went into Haiti with three primary goals: preventing German control over the island, ensuring opportunities for American investments in Haiti, and preventing Haitian society from decaying into anarchy. Although the occupation prevented Germany from gaining control over Haiti, it is unclear that Germany ever had any ambition to attempt to control the sea lines to the Panama Canal.[83] In other words, preventing a German takeover of Hispaniola can count neither for nor against the occupation. Although Haiti has never posed a significant threat to U.S. national security, it has remained a hemispheric thorn in the side of the United States. In terms of political developments and creating an environment stable for U.S. investment, when the occupation ended, the Haitian political system unsurprisingly returned to the corrupt ways that had preceded (and endured during) the U.S. occupation.[84]

It is difficult to assess the total cost of the occupation of Haiti. On the one hand, at its peak, the U.S. only had about three thousand troops committed to Haiti and there were relatively few American lives lost during the occupation.[85] On the other hand, the occupation did last for nineteen years and became a source of controversy and contention in U.S. domestic politics. At a time of international upheaval, Haiti was never the top story in U.S. foreign policy, but its place in the 1920 presidential election suggests that the costs and conduct of the occupation of Haiti were not insignificant matters. Haiti returned to American domestic political debate after the Cayes Massacre in December 1929 and again became a controversial topic within the United States. Even though the costs were only moderate, the accomplishments of the occupation of Haiti failed to justify the expense.

From the perspective of Haiti, the occupation also cannot be considered a success. The U.S. occupiers worked hard to build infrastructure and create public institutions, but these quickly deteriorated once the occupation ended. In the long-term, the Haitian political system returned to the system of cronyism that had dominated before the U.S. intervention. For Haitians, the occupation protected them against a threat they did not perceive and did little in the long-term to improve their country.

WHY THE U.S. OCCUPATION OF HAITI FAILED

The initial U.S. intervention and occupation was premised, in part, on the threat that imperial Germany supposedly posed to control of Haiti and, therefore, to control over the sea-lanes to the Panama Canal. In March 1915, Secretary of State William Jennings Bryan warned President Wilson, "There seems to be some sympathetic cooperation between the French and German interests in Haiti." Wilson responded, "This whole matter has a most sinister appearance."[86] The intervention in Haiti was largely motivated by traditional Monroe Doctrine concerns, but the threat that Germany supposedly posed was not sufficient to allow for occupation success. As predicted, the absence of a sustained external threat, perceived by both the occupying power and the occupied population, impaired the ability of the United States to accomplish its goals.

First, the Haitian people never shared the U.S. fear of German imperialism. Occupation by any foreign country was not welcome by a Haitian population that had only achieved its independence from France in 1804. Further, of all the foreign powers involved in Haiti, the United States was seen as the greatest threat to Haitian independence. The Haitian elite consistently had better relations with the French and Germans than they did with the Americans. The French, by their colonial legacy, had social ties with much of the Haitian elite, and the Germans, through marriage and other social mechanisms, intermingled with members of Haitian society. By contrast, the United States role in Haiti was mostly from a distance with few Americans actually living in Haiti. L. Ton Evans, a pioneering missionary of the Baptists of the United States who spent twenty-eight years in Haiti prior to testifying before Congress in 1920 on the state of the occupation, commented that once the occupation began the Haitians grew to miss the Europeans: "While European and German politicians and profiteers exploited the Haitian Government and customs, they were wiser than to meddle with the senate and chambers of the people or attempt such a stupid and mad things as the rape of Haiti's constitution."[87] Once the United States took control over Haitian customs, the only significant source of income for the Haitian government, the Haitian population became even more embittered.[88]

Second, once World War I ended in 1918, the security motivation for the U.S. occupying Haiti disappeared with the defeat of Germany. As a consequence, U.S. interest in Haiti waned. Even when the threat from Germany was obviated, however, the United States found itself incapable of completely extricating itself from Hispaniola. In the process of extending the occupation treaty until 1936, the United States had also engrained itself deeper into the Haitian economy. In particular, the United States sought to further limit European influence in Haiti by floating a loan to the Haitians to pay off any debt owed to France. If the United States had withdrawn, Haiti likely would have defaulted on its loans, and the U.S. administration would have been held responsible for the economic loss. After Germany's defeat, however, the United States had little enthusiasm for continuing the occupation.

Why, then, did the U.S. occupation of Haiti ultimately last nineteen years? If the Haitians wanted the United States to leave and the United States had lost interest in the occupation, then should not withdrawal have been attractive to both sides? After 1918, the United States did, in fact, begin to seek a way out of the turmoil in Haiti, but economic interests precluded a quick and clean withdrawal. The U.S. occupation essentially stagnated in the 1920s. The actual costs were not excessive, but the potential costs of withdrawal appeared to prohibit evacuating the island. As a consequence, the United States remained in Haiti until the early 1930s when the cost of staying clearly exceeded the probable costs of leaving.

In the end, the tragic flaw of the occupation of Haiti is captured in a conversation between a departing U.S. marine officer and Georges Léger, a prominent Haitian attorney and public figure. The marine told Léger, "You'll be glad to see us go and the occupation end." To which Léger responded, "Yes. I will be absolutely honest. We know how you have helped us in many ways and we appreciate that. But after all, this is our country and we would rather run it ourselves."[89] Haitian nationalism resented any foreign military occupation, especially when Haiti was unthreatened from abroad. Without a favorable threat environment, the United States found it difficult to succeed over nearly two decades of occupying Haiti.

Conclusion

Before ending this chapter, it is worth considering one alternative argument that could potentially explain both the Germany and Haiti cases. According to this argument, it was the relative economic development of Germany compared to Haiti that allowed the United States and its allies to succeed in western Germany but not in Haiti. More generally, the history of military occupation reveals that most occupied countries have lacked industrial development and that the occupation of these poor countries has most often been unsuccessful.

It is undoubtedly true that the industrial base of Germany contributed to occupation success. Put simply, this industrial base allowed Germany to more quickly rebuild a successful economy, but the initial instinct of the occupying powers, reflected most prominently in the Morgenthau Plan, was to remove all of Germany's industrial power and leave it a barren, prostrate power in the center of Europe. Only when the threat from the Soviet Union became clearer, and the importance of incorporating the West German economy into the anti-Soviet bloc became apparent, did the occupying powers abandon the Morgenthau Plan and turn to the rapid reconstruction of the German economy. The initial impulse simply to neuter Germany was abandoned as the geostrategic significance of German recovery became evident. As early as June 1946, Secretary of War Robert Patterson wrote James Byrnes that the reconstruction of Germany's economy was a matter of national security.[90]

In Haiti, on the other hand, the U.S. occupation would surely have been aided by greater industrial development in Haiti that would have lowered the costs of occupation for the United States. At the same time, however, Haiti had only gained its independence a century before the American intervention, and the denial of sovereignty that attended the occupation was rejected by the Haitians. In fact, more economic development in Haiti may only have intensified the Haitian desire to govern themselves in the absence of any postwar destruction. Haitians were only likely to tolerate a foreign occupation if it promised protection against some other external threat, and no such external threat existed.

The threats perceived by occupied populations are not entirely structural and exogenous. As both cases in this chapter suggest, the strategies that occupying powers adopt are significant as well. In Germany, the Western decision to address food shortages and then to allow the reconstruction of the German economy reinforced an initially advantageous threat environment. In contrast, the coercive strategies employed by the United States in Haiti only further undermined the U.S. presence there, exacerbating the Haitian sense that the greatest threat to its independence was from the United States, not any other country. The way in which occupations are conducted, therefore, is not only a response to the threat environment of an occupied territory, but also reshapes and reformulates the occupied population's perception of threat. In the next chapter, I examine the question of occupation strategy.

HOW TO OCCUPY
Strategies of Occupation

The threat environment of an occupied territory is not a static, exogenous factor. Whereas certain elements of threat, such as the capabilities of a neighboring state, may be particularly important for shaping the initial threat environment of an occupied territory, an occupied population's perceptions of threat are also shaped by the strategies pursued by an occupying power once the occupation is underway.

Strategies of Occupation

Occupying powers have three general types of strategies available to them: accommodation, inducement, and coercion.

Accommodation

A strategy of accommodation attempts to satisfy the nationalist demands of an occupied population by incorporating elements of that population into the governance of the occupied territory. Successful strategies of accommodation co-opt local elites into the occupation project. Those elites come to see the occupation as a means for ensuring their own position of power within the occupied territory both during and after the occupation. Ideally for an occupying power, these elites, in turn, convince the occupied population to suppress its nationalism and accept the period of occupation. By making the end result of the occupation look more attractive, accommodation gains the quiescence of the occupied population and can reinforce an initially favorable threat environment. When successfully implemented, a policy of accommodation minimizes resistance to the occupation, which lowers the cost of the occupation to the occupying power. Poor strategies of accommodation, on the other hand, only reinforce the occupied population's doubts about the intentions of the occupying power.[1]

There are two key elements to a successful strategy of accommodation. First, the occupying power must ally with local elites who share the occupying power's goals and interests. Within any society, there may be an array of elites from which to choose, and occupying powers must locate elites who are willing and able to help the occupying power succeed. Because of the potential power that comes with being the "accommodated elites," local elites may compete for the favor of the occupying power. In divided societies with multiple national groups, in particular, defeat and occupation may unleash previously suppressed national forces that vie for control over the rebuilding society. At the same time, elites must be careful, for co-opted elites may lose credibility among the occupied population.

Second, accommodation can benefit both the occupying power and the chosen elites, but those elites must be able to control the local population. If the occupying power chooses elites who do not have the support of the population or who cannot generate that support, then not only will the population's nationalism not be suppressed, but it may actually be aggravated by the choice of unpopular elites. As the case study of the U.S. occupation of southern Korea presented below demonstrates, occupying powers encounter great difficulty when they choose elites who do not have the support of the population. A poorly executed accommodation strategy is unlikely to succeed.

Aside from the direct advantages that a successful strategy of accommodation can provide, such a strategy may have the added benefit of amplifying the sense of external threat that an occupied population perceives. Elites who have been co-opted into the occupation project, and credibly promised that they will have control over the country after sovereignty is restored, are more likely to see the occupying power as a lesser threat to the occupied territory's security and self-determination. Practiced well, then, a strategy of accommodation not only has its own independent positive effects, but it also reinforces the threat environment of the occupation. In post–World War II Japan, the United States wisely chose not to exclude the emperor from the postwar political system. Even though the emperor's role was relegated to symbolism, retaining the emperor and co-opting him into the occupation project sent an important message to the Japanese people that the United States had respect for Japanese culture, traditions, and national identity.[2]

From the perspective of an occupying power, accommodation is a relatively low-cost strategy with a potential high reward. If occupying powers can employ local elites to assist in the occupation, then their own investment in the occupation can be reduced. Perhaps most important, a successful strategy of accommodation reinforces a favorable threat environment, enables progress toward ending an occupation, and lays the foundation for a stable relationship between the occupied territory and the occupying power after the occupation concludes.

Accommodation, however, can also be a challenging strategy to implement in the chaotic conditions that often characterize postwar, occupied societies. Groups are likely to compete for the favor of the occupying power, or alternatively, they may aim to be seen as the leading opposition to the occupation. In this context, identifying reliable elites, whose goals are stability and not simply furthering their own interests, to co-opt can be difficult for an occupying power.

Inducement

A strategy of inducement provides resources to the occupied population in an effort to buy its acquiescence. The logic behind this strategy holds that if an occupied population sees its welfare improving under occupation, then it will tolerate the occupation. Nationalist demands for self-determination are, according to the logic of this argument, a lower priority than economic well-being.

To the extent that an occupied territory has been destroyed in war and requires help in rebuilding the material of society, inducement is a requirement of any occupation strategy. The destruction wrought by war often provides a "honeymoon period" for occupying powers during which an occupied population will suspend its demands for self-determination if the occupying power is offering assistance that improves the material welfare of the population. Inducement, in these cases, is both a product of a favorable threat environment in which an occupied territory is particularly vulnerable and can reinforce a favorable threat environment by demonstrating the benevolent intentions of the occupying power.

Inducement is often a necessary strategy for occupation success, but it is generally not sufficient. Inducement alone cannot solve the political problem of nationalism that is at the heart of the difficulty of occupying another society. Occupied populations may accept the material benefits of occupation, but they will also simultaneously grow weary of being denied self-determination. When patience runs out and when the honeymoon period ends, the denial of sovereignty trumps the provision of resources.

From the perspective of the occupying power, inducement is potentially a very expensive strategy. It promises to consume great resources in a small amount of time without necessarily producing great returns. Inducement is, however, made easier when the occupied territory has indigenous resources and industry that can provide the foundation for reconstruction. In these cases, such as in Germany and Japan after World War II, inducement can complement already existing resources. Building from scratch demands an even higher level of resource commitment from the occupying power. In this way, this argument captures an alternative explanation for occupation success that focuses on economic development and industrialization as an explanation for occupation outcomes. Economic development does assist occupying powers by making it easier for them to revive an economy that may have been destroyed by war. Thus, inducement is easier when there is an economic base to utilize as part of the inducement strategy.

The causal logic behind the strategy of inducement, however, begs a question: why are some occupying powers willing to devote the necessary resources to occupation success while others are not? The answer to this question returns us to the consideration of the threat environment. Occupying powers are more likely to expend valuable resources when there is a significant external threat posed to the occupied territory. Conversely, when there is no external threat or an internal threat to the occupied territory, occupying powers are hesitant to expend great resources on an inducement strategy. To the extent that inducement is applied as a strategy, then, it is likely to be the product of the geopolitical significance of and perceived threats to the occupied territory. Consider the example of post–World War II western Germany. The initial U.S. instinct in western Germany was, as expressed in the Morgenthau Plan, to eliminate the industrial capacity of the country. As the cold war emerged, however, the United States recognized that German industry would be vital to defeating communism. The U.S. commitment to the economic reconstruction of Germany was a result of the threat posed by the Soviet Union.[3] Extensive inducement is practiced then when the threat environment encourages it.

Prescribing a strategy of inducement also poses a difficult methodological problem. To date, there is no reliable guide for how many resources are sufficient for occupation success. The only efforts to do this are largely inductive and lack explanations for why a certain amount or types of resources are necessary for success. Further, the most prominent effort to correlate resource expenditures with occupation success and failure produces some odd findings. For example, in terms of per capita assistance in the first two postconflict years, Bosnia and Kosovo rank as much as ten times higher than Japan and western Germany, yet few would argue that those resources have led to resounding nation-building successes in either Bosnia or Kosovo.[4] This places the analyst in an untenable position: failure is attributed to "insufficient" resources while success is chalked up to "sufficient" resources. Without any reliable *ex ante* guide to how many resources are necessary for success, the argument that inducement leads to occupation success is nonfalsifiable.[5]

All that said, the provision of resources is often a necessary component of a successful occupation strategy, even if it is rarely sufficient.

Coercion

Coercion is the use or threatened use of military force to defeat any elements of the population that resist or threaten to resist an occupation. By doing so, the occupying power may lessen the nationalist resistance and make it easier to accomplish the goals of occupation.

Coercion in occupations can take the form of either explicit, actual violence, or latent violence that deters violent opposition to occupation. Military occupiers may employ violence in order to destroy any opposition. Occupiers may also use the threat of violence to quell any resistance before it erupts. "A well-behaved occupied country is not one in which violence plays no part," Thomas Schelling observes. "It may be one in which latent violence is used so skillfully that it need not be spent in punishment."[6]

Violent opposition to occupation can inhibit successful accommodation and inducement strategies, so coercion becomes a necessary prerequisite to these more cooperative strategies when significant opposition is present. When coercion succeeds as an occupation strategy, it eliminates this opposition to the occupation and enables the occupying power to then pursue more cooperative strategies that can ultimately lead to occupation success.

Both forms of coercion—actual violence and latent violence—pose challenges to an occupying power. Unless actual violence completely eliminates those who would resist the occupation, coercion may have the adverse effect of generating more recruits to the opposition. In particular, if coercion turns into a full-fledged counterinsurgency campaign, then the animosity between the occupied population and occupying power may increase rather than diminish. This fighting between the occupied population and the occupying power is likely to exacerbate an already poor threat environment. Actual violence is also a difficult strategy to implement from the perspective of the occupying power.[7] It is likely to be a costly strategy, both in terms of human and financial costs. Particularly in an unfavorable threat environment, such costs may lead to calls for a premature end to the occupation. In short, violence may introduce all of the problems of counterinsurgency that great powers have encountered throughout history.[8]

A strategy of latent violence such as deterrence may avoid many of the costs involved in a strategy of actual violence, but it also poses other difficulties. Most fundamentally, a deterrent signal from an occupying power must be credible enough to persuade an occupied population to refrain from engaging in antioccupation violence. An occupying power employing latent violence must locate ways to communicate the severity of retaliatory violence that will meet any resistance, and it must convince the population that it is willing to pay the costs that may inhere in the use of actual violence to control an occupied population.

Coercion can succeed, however, if the occupying power adopts a well-designed coercive strategy and is willing to pay the high costs of an extended military effort. Coercion succeeds by essentially "clearing the decks" of any opposition to the occupation, making room for the occupying power and any supporters it has to implement occupation reforms. In Northern Korea, for example, the coercive occupation strategy after World War II used the latent threat of violence and imprisonment to encourage any unhappy citizens to immigrate to southern Korea. Once those citizens were incarcerated, killed, or chased away, the threat environment had improved. Those left behind shared a much more common perception of threat posed by southern Korea and the United States.

One can see the challenges posed by relying on coercive strategies in the policies of the Soviet Union in Central and Eastern Europe during the cold war.[9] As I discussed in the introduction, Soviet behavior in Central and Eastern Europe straddles the line between occupation and empire. Whichever conclusion one reaches, Soviet behavior is still instructive as an illustration of the advantages and disadvantages of relying on coercion. As Vladislav Zubok and Constantine Pleshakov describe, "Millions of forced refugees, arrests of opposition members, and brutal persecution of intellectuals in Eastern Europe, amounted to a hidden but quite powerful dimension of Soviet foreign policy. It was a traditional policy of the empire, but a more barbaric one. This occupational policy deeply affected millions of people and did irreparable damage to the image of Stalin's Soviet Union in Central Europe."[10]

The use of both explicit and latent coercive violence allowed the Soviet Union to create a buffer zone on its western borders. Further, throughout the cold war, the Soviet Union maintained sizeable troop presences throughout Central and Eastern Europe that likely acted to deter those populations from actively resisting Soviet occupation. When populations did rise up against communist rule, they were forcefully rebuffed as in Hungary in 1956 and Czechoslovakia in 1968. The heavy reliance on coercion enabled the Soviets to maintain an unfriendly empire for more than forty years. At the same time, however, the Soviets never enjoyed the willful acquiescence of those populations to Soviet control, and the Soviets were forced to expend resources to maintain control over these states. Soviet coercion only continuously reinforced an unfavorable threat environment, making subsequent violence even more necessary. In short, Soviet policy in Central and Eastern Europe demonstrates not only the potential for coercion as a strategy for maintaining control of an occupied territory but also the difficulties of employing such strategies over the long-term.[11]

In the end, most occupying powers employ some degree of both actual and latent violence in their occupations of foreign countries. After all, it should not be overlooked that military occupation often involves the deployment of large numbers of troops in order to provide security and deter the outbreak of anti-occupation violence. What is less clear, however, is whether coercion on its own can succeed as a strategy of occupation. More likely, the more that an occupying power needs to depend on coercion to control an occupied population, the more difficult an occupation is likely to be. Conversely, when an occupying power can minimize the use of coercion—either actual or latent violence—then the power is likely to find occupation easier.

Strategies and the Threat Environment

The strategies the occupying powers pursue are both a product of the initial threat environment and subsequently shape the threat environment. Depending on the threat environment, certain strategies may be necessary and others may be sufficient for occupation success.

Favorable Threat Environment

In an initially favorable threat environment, occupying powers usually face less resistance. As a consequence, occupying powers can focus on more cooperative strategies of accommodation and inducement. Cooperative strategies allow the occupying power to begin the process of constructing stable and secure political institutions in the occupied state. In turn, these cooperative strategies reinforce the favorable threat environment. As the occupied population benefits from the cooperative strategies, it perceives the occupying power as less of a threat to its interest in national self-determination. This process of positive feedback moves an occupation in a successful direction and ultimately allows the occupying power to move toward the creation of a stable, secure, and reliable indigenous government.

Unfavorable Threat Environment

An initially unfavorable threat environment increases resistance to the occupying power. In the face of resistance, defeating the resistance through coercion becomes a necessary strategy for occupation success. Occupying powers operating in an unfavorable threat environment fail when they either opt not to pursue a coercive strategy or they pursue a poorly designed coercive strategy. Importantly, while coercion is necessary in this situation, it is not sufficient for occupation success. Coercive strategies are a prerequisite for more cooperative strategies that ultimately allow for the building of stable institutions. Such cooperative strategies cannot be implemented, however, until resistance has been controlled.

Just as cooperative strategies reinforce favorable threat environments, coercive strategies are likely to exacerbate unfavorable threat environments as the occupying power develops an adversarial relationship with at least a segment of the occupied population. Such antagonism only invites more resistance, making coercion even more necessary. A dangerous feedback loop ensues.

This does not imply that all occupations in unfavorable threat environments are doomed to failure, but simply that occupation will be more difficult under such circumstances. To succeed, an occupying power must successfully coerce resistance and transition into cooperative strategies that build institutions that ultimately allow the occupation to end. The Soviet occupation of North Korea discussed below is an example of such a case in which coercive and cooperative strategies were successfully combined, but this case is, as expected, an outlier in the larger universe of cases.

In sum, most occupying powers combine carrots and sticks in the conduct of their occupation, but the key point is whether the predominant strategy is cooperative or coercive. In an initially favorable threat environment, a predominately cooperative strategy is often largely sufficient for success. In an initially unfavorable threat environment, a coercive strategy is necessary, but not sufficient, for occupation success. In such an environment, the successful occupying power must first achieve coercive success and then implement cooperative strategies. Not surprisingly, the implementation of such a strategy is difficult and has most often eluded occupying powers in an unfavorable threat environment. Occupations are also prone to positive feedback effects.[12] That is, occupation strategies are not only a product of the initial threat environment, they also tend subsequently to reinforce that threat environment. Cooperative strategies pursued in a favorable threat environment are likely to reinforce that threat environment. Coercive strategies pursued in an unfavorable threat environment are likely to exacerbate that threat environment. To be clear, a poorly executed accommodation or inducement strategy can fail just as a poorly executed coercion strategy, but accommodation or inducement is more likely to succeed than coercion. Table 2.1 summarizes the relationship between threat environment and strategies.

Table 2.1   The relationship between initial threat environment and strategies of occupation

		OCCUPATION STRATEGIES	
		COOPERATIVE	COERCIVE
Initial threat environment	Favorable	Easiest scenario: cooperation reinforces favorable threat environment	Latent violence may be necessary, but actual violence is less necessary in a favorable threat environment
	Unfavorable	Successful coercion is a prerequisite for cooperative strategies in an unfavorable threat environment	Most difficult scenario: coercion exacerbates unfavorable threat environment

Evidence: The Occupations of Korea

Presenting a simple table of the occupation strategies employed in all twenty-six completed occupations since 1815 is impractical. As noted, most occupying powers pursue a combination of cooperative and coercive strategies with the critical difference being in emphasis. Instead of such a table, I present detailed case studies of two simultaneous cases: the U.S. occupation of southern Korea and the Soviet occupation of northern Korea, both beginning immediately after World War II and lasting until 1948. These two cases represent an unusual quasi-experiment in the social sciences. Toward the end of World War II, the United States and the Soviet Union arbitrarily divided the Korean Peninsula into two occupation zones, yet the two occupations had varying levels of success. The initial threat environment hypothesis would predict that the two occupations would have similar unfavorable outcomes, yet the Soviets had far more success in northern Korea than the United States had in southern Korea.

The two occupying powers pursued different strategies of occupation that I contend account for the differing outcomes in these two cases. Although the Soviet Union successfully employed coercion in the north, the United States had less success at coercion in southern Korea, only further antagonizing a population that was resistant to occupation from the outset. Successful coercion eliminated opposition to the occupation and eventually allowed the Soviet-sponsored regime to adopt other more cooperative policies in northern Korea whereas unsuccessful coercion in the south was only made worse by poorly executed strategies of accommodation. These two cases are valuable not only because of the natural comparison, but also because they both constitute outlier cases. The U.S. occupation of southern Korea is the only one of the immediate postwar U.S. occupations that did not succeed. The Soviet occupation of northern Korea, on the other hand, is the rare case in which an occupying power was able to overcome an initially unfavorable threat environment through the successful implementation of a strategy of coercion.

In mid August 1945, the United States and the Soviet Union agreed to divide Korea at the Thirty-eighth Parallel with the Americans granted responsibility for the postwar management of southern Korea and the Soviets given the same for northern Korea. Although there certainly were differences between northern and southern Korea—the north was more industrial to name one—the Koreans thought of themselves as one nation prior to their division in 1945. As Anna Louise Strong, who visited northern Korea during the occupation years, points out, "No Korean recognized the Parallel as a proper division. It cut across a national life whose food was in the South and whose industries were in the North. . . . Koreans felt themselves a single nation."[13] For most Koreans, the end of World War II and the defeat and expulsion of Japan after decades of Japanese colonialism signaled a long-awaited opportunity for self-determination.[14] Both the Soviets and the Americans faced the difficult challenge of occupation: managing the nationalism of a population longing for self-determination.

I will argue that the successful Soviet occupation of northern Korea is an exceptional case that demonstrates the possibility of occupation success even in an initially unfavorable threat environment. In the north, the threat of imprisonment and violence against opponents of the occupation and the Kim regime successfully coerced opposition to leave for southern Korea. Successful coercion allowed the Soviet Union to adopt a political strategy of supporting Kim Il-Sung that accommodated Korean nationalism and, thus, aided the Soviets in overcoming an unfavorable threat environment. Finally, on the heels of successful coercion, the Soviets were able to offer economic and social reforms to the North Korean people that led them to acquiesce to the occupation.

In the south, the United States made two critical strategic misjudgments in the face of an unfavorable threat environment. First, efforts to coerce opposition only generated more antagonism and reinforced the unfavorable threat environment. Second, the United States made an ill-advised choice to throw its support behind Syngman Rhee, a conservative who did not enjoy the support of most of the Korean population. Absent successful coercion, the accommodation of an unpopular elite resulted in an unsuccessful occupation strategy. Finally, especially after the lack of immediate success in southern Korea, the United States was reluctant to devote substantial resources to southern Korea because of other geopolitical priorities. In both cases, an initially unfavorable threat environment made success unlikely, but the Soviets proved more adept at crafting a successful strategy with a foundation in coercion.

The U.S. Occupation of Southern Korea, 1945–48

When World War II ended in 1945, Korea was liberated from more than three decades of Japanese colonial rule. To govern its colony, Japan supplanted the existing Korean political institutions with Japanese-run institutions, replaced Korean with Japanese as the official language, and gave authority only to those Koreans who were willing to collaborate with the Japanese. During this period, repressive Japanese rule only served to foment Korean nationalism, most notably in a series of uprisings in 1919.[15]

In the 1940s, as World War II progressed toward an eventual Japanese defeat, President Franklin Delano Roosevelt began to envision a system of trusteeship that would manage the dissolution of the Japanese empire. Such a trusteeship system would guide former colonial subjects toward independence, maintain U.S. presence and influence, and it was hoped, avert postwar tension between the great powers. For Korea, in particular, trusteeship was necessary because it did not have the indigenous economic or political resources to manage its own independence.[16] In a document titled "Korea: Political Problems: Provisional Government" of May 4, 1944, the U.S. Inter-Divisional Area Committee on the Far East observed, "The exclusion of Koreans from important political posts for the past thirty-five years has emasculated them politically and has deprived them of all experience in managing a state."[17]

GOALS AND MEANS

In November 1943, the leaders of the United States, Great Britain, and China convened in Cairo to consider a series of wartime and postwar issues, including the postwar fate of Japan's colonial holdings. At the end of the conference, the leaders issued a critical, yet ambiguous, endorsement of eventual Korean independence, "The aforementioned three great powers, mindful of the enslavement of the people of Korea, are determined that *in due course* Korea shall become free and independent."[18] For the United States and its allies, the phrase "in due course" reflected FDR's trusteeship vision.[19] Koreans, however, worried that the declaration signaled yet a further denial of sovereignty.[20] Liberated from Japanese colonialism, Koreans desired independence, not further occupation.

Whereas trusteeship was the favored outcome, U.S. policymakers in Washington considered alternatives if trusteeship were to fail. Soviet control over the entire East Asian mainland was not an acceptable alternative to multilateral trusteeship. In the fall of 1943, a State Department paper worried,

Korea may appear to offer a tempting opportunity [for Soviet premier Josef Stalin] . . . to strengthen enormously the economic resources of the Soviet Far East, to acquire ice-free ports, and to occupy a dominating strategic position in relation both to China and to Japan. . . . A Soviet occupation of Korea would create an entirely new strategic situation in the Far East, and its repercussions within China and Japan might be far reaching.[21]

The result was a parallel track of planning within the U.S. State Department for a postwar occupation of Korea.[22] As late as July 1945, many U.S. military planners were content to allow the Soviets to take the entire Korean Peninsula because of the high toll that they expected conquering all of Korea would take.[23] The successful test and then use of two atomic weapons altered American thinking. Rather than allowing the Soviets to enter the war and establish a strong presence in East Asia, the goal of the United States became to limit Soviet influence in East Asia and conclude the war before the Soviets could conquer all of Korea.[24] With the fate of trusteeship still unclear and the war about to end, the U.S. State-War-Navy Coordinating Commission suggested that the United States propose the division of Korea into two occupation zones at the Thirty-eighth Parallel, which Stalin then accepted.[25] By early September, the United States had hurriedly moved the XXIV Corps into southern Korea. For the next three years, as many as forty-five thousand U.S. troops would occupy the southern half of the Korean Peninsula. The United States hoped to placate Soviet ambitions by offering it control of the north.[26]

The Basic Initial Directive for the occupation, SWNCC 176/8, of October 17, 1945, stated that the goal of the occupation was to "foster conditions which will bring about the establishment of a free and independent nation capable of taking her place as a responsible and peaceful member of the family of nations."[27] The United States had both short- and long-term security goals for its occupation of southern Korea. First, in the short term, U.S. leaders wanted to ensure that the entire Korean Peninsula did not fall into Soviet hands—"free and independent."[28] Second, looking toward the long term, American leaders believed that Korea was not yet ready for self-rule. Therefore, a period of occupation was necessary to manage the Korean transition to independence and create the conditions for an effective government that was friendly to the United States.[29]

STRATEGIES OF OCCUPATION IN SOUTHERN KOREA

The United States occupation authority was not, however, well-prepared for these tasks. General John Reed Hodge, the occupation commander, did not receive detailed instructions for the occupation for the first nine months that he was in Korea.[30] Grant Meade, who participated in the American Military Government in Korea, later identified five specific flaws in the planning for Korea: (1) a lack of instruction in political matters for the administrators of the occupation, (2) little foresight in the training of the occupying army, (3) no tailoring to the specific challenges of Korea, (4) an emphasis on combat operations rather than governance, and (5) a general failure to prepare for the tasks of military government.[31] James Matray reports that one member of the American military government nicknamed the occupation, "operation trial and error."[32]

The United States did not enjoy a favorable threat environment when it embarked on the occupation of southern Korea. With the era of Japanese colonialism coming to an end, Korean nationalism began to reassert itself. Much of the southern Korean population did not perceive any external threat greater than the United States, and as a consequence, resistance to the occupation emerged. As a consequence of the lack of preparedness and poor knowledge of local Korean conditions, the initial U.S. strategy for conducting the occupation of Korea was to rely on the institutions and individuals that had administered the Japanese colonial state in Korea.[33] This strategy only exacerbated the difficulties in the early period of the occupation. Further, Korea had not been a major battlefield of World War II, so Koreans were not prepared to suppress their nationalism in deference to help in reconstruction.

As soon as it was apparent that Korea was destined to be occupied, both left and right in Korean society mobilized in opposition. The Committee for the Preparation of Korean Independence (CPKI) was founded in August under the leadership of Yo Un-Hyong, but this body soon foundered on the political divisions that existed within Korean society. These divisions produced the leftist Korean People's Republic (KPR) and the right-wing Korean Democratic Party (KDP). Among the KPR leadership were both socialists and communists who were firmly committed to Korean independence and undoing the Japanese colonial legacy.[34] The KDP was a merger of various conservative parties in Korean society, including advocates of the Korean Provisional Government (KPG), a conservative, nationalist exile government that had fled Korea to Chongqing after the 1919 uprisings against Japanese rule.[35]

THE FAILURE OF COERCION AND ACCOMMODATION IN SOUTHERN KOREA

Faced with this emerging divide in Korean politics, General Hodge chose to back the Korean right, in general, and more specifically, Syngman Rhee, one of the conservative Koreans exiled during the colonial period. This would prove to be an ill-thought-out and premature strategy of accommodation. Rhee and his right-wing allies were not particularly popular among the general Korean population.

Without first defeating the opposition to the occupation through coercion, such a strategy of accommodation was unlikely to succeed. Hodge, however, made this choice for two reasons. First, Hodge was an inveterate anticommunist. In a November 25 report to General Douglas MacArthur in Japan, Hodge advised that the United States must issue a "declaration of war" on communism. Hodge warned, "If activities of Korean People's Republic continue as in the past, they will greatly delay time when Korea can be said to be ready for independence."[36] The occupation commander easily dismissed the KPR as communist, even if elements of it were far from ardent communists.

Second, Hodge's primary goal was to accelerate U.S. withdrawal from Korea. In Hodge's view, the United States was in a vulnerable position having occupied only the southern part of the Korean Peninsula, but the United States could not consider withdrawal until he was certain that a communist government would not take over in southern Korea. The Korean right, in Hodge's view, was more likely to form a strong government that would resist communism. "Hodge was laying a foundation for conservative political dominance," notes James Matray, "But his main motive was hastening U.S. military withdrawal."[37]

Hodge was not the only one who believed that the occupation should be concluded as quickly as possible. In a cable to Secretary of State James Byrnes on September 15, 1945, H. Merrell Benninghoff, the political adviser in Korea, warned that "South Korea can best be described as a powder keg ready to explode at the application of a spark." As Benninghoff interpreted the situation, "Koreans did not understand why they were not given complete independence soon after the arrival of American troops."[38] Then, in October, the State-War-Navy Coordinating Subcommittee for the Far East issued SWNCC 101/4, which assessed the prospects for trusteeship and occupation in Korea. Among other conclusions, the report offered, "No time has been set as to when Korea should become independent but this should, of course, be accomplished as quickly as possible after liberation. . . . It would therefore seem advisable to terminate military occupation as early as practicable."[39]

In December 1945, the foreign ministers of Great Britain, the Soviet Union, and the United States once again convened, this time in Moscow, for the next round of negotiations over postwar arrangements. After years of halting negotiations, the foreign ministers finally agreed to a joint trusteeship of Korea that should be as short and limited in scope as possible. A Soviet-American Joint Commission would oversee the process of transition from international trusteeship to Korean independence.[40]

For the United States, the agreement on trusteeship fulfilled the promise of a cooperative, multilateral approach to Korea that would allow for a smooth transition to Korean independence and the eventual unification of the country. The

Soviet Union was more skeptical of trusteeship, but Moscow endorsed the Joint Commission concept when it recognized that trusteeship would give it an opportunity to consolidate communist control over northern Korea. Among Koreans, the initial reaction to the trusteeship was uniformly negative. Once again, the occupying powers were deferring Korean independence. Rhee made his own views of trusteeship quite clear: "If there is any government that tries to force us to trusteeship, we thirty million Koreans would rather prefer our death in fighting for our freedom than in going under trusteeship."[41]

By the end of 1945, the United States was facing all of the familiar challenges of occupation. No commonly perceived external threat motivated southern Koreans to accept the occupation, and the American attempt to placate Korean nationalism through the trusteeship proposal was met with skepticism. Further, the American decision to back Rhee was a poorly executed strategy of accommodation. At the same time, the likelihood of a short occupation in Korea appeared to diminish as U.S.–Soviet tension increased. Washington was reluctant to continue to pay the cost of occupation, but it was also heavily invested in Korea and concerned about a communist takeover of the entire peninsula if the occupation was abandoned.[42] General Hodge summarized his views that Korea was heading toward an "abyss" in a mid-December memo to General MacArthur that was then passed on to the Joint Chiefs of Staff. "Every day of drifting under this situation," reported Hodge, "makes our position in Korea more untenable and decreases our waning popularity and our effectiveness to be of service. . . . The Koreans want their independence more than any one thing and they want it now." Hodge went on to warn that the imposition of trusteeship in Korea would actually lead to physical revolt. He concluded, "I would go so far as to recommend that we give serious consideration to an agreement with Russia that both the US and Russia withdraw forces from Korea simultaneously and leave Korea to its own devices and an inevitable internal upheaval for its self purification."[43]

THE SEARCH FOR AN EXIT

The United States would not, however, simply follow Hodge's advice and withdraw. Hodge was specifically instructed not to recognize any particular government as the official government of southern Korea because doing so would cement the division of Korea and foreclose the peaceful unification of the country.[44] Further, many in the U.S. government did not trust Rhee to lead Korea and were reluctant to recognize Rhee's KDP as the representative government of Korea.[45] Finally, withdrawal from southern Korea might lead to a communist takeover of all of Korea, which would potentially pose a threat to other U.S. interests in Asia, including Japan.

In early January 1946, Korean leftist groups abruptly switched positions, endorsing the terms of the Moscow accords.[46] Suddenly, the Soviet Union and Korean communists became allies in their support of the Moscow trusteeship agreement. The apparent consolidation of Soviet control over northern Korea and the reversal of the southern Korean left on the subject of trusteeship contributed to Hodge's mounting concern about the growth of communism in Korea.[47] The United States found itself in the difficult position of simultaneously preparing for meetings of the trusteeship's Joint Commission while also maintaining its support for right-wing Koreans who vehemently opposed any trusteeship. Rhee and his supporters made this conflict even more difficult for the United States by couching their claims to independence in language that was meant to appeal to the liberal democratic foundation of the American political system.[48] No commonly perceived threat motivated the United States and southern Koreans to cooperate in continued occupation, and the attempt to accommodate southern Korean nationalism through either trusteeship or the support for Rhee was failing.

The Joint Commission opened its first official meetings in Seoul on March 20, 1946. By early May, the talks had dissolved over a disagreement about which groups deserved representation at the talks. The Soviet representatives argued that only groups that supported the Moscow accords should be allowed to participate in the negotiations. Such a restriction would have excluded the right-wing Korean groups that the United States was now backing in southern Korea. United States representatives, on the other hand, insisted that all groups, even those opposed to the Joint Commission, were entitled to participate.

When the Joint Commission adjourned on May 8, the United States began to consider alternative ways that it could bring the occupation to a quick, but successful, conclusion. On July 16, 1946, Truman wrote to the U.S. ambassador in Paris, Edwin Pauley, "I agree with you that Korea is, as you aptly phrase it, 'an ideological battleground upon which our entire success in Asia may depend.'"[49] From 1946 on, U.S. policy in Korea was dominated by one attempt after another to locate a strategy that could extricate the United States from Korea without turning the entire peninsula over to the Soviet Union.

Once again, the United States would attempt to introduce a political solution meant to accommodate Korean nationalism. This time, the attempt took the form of sponsorship of a left-right coalition government in southern Korea.[50] Even though Hodge remained committed to the Korean right, a coalition government, it was hoped, would allow the United States to withdraw, knowing that a strong, representative government was in place in southern Korea. By the end of June 1946, General Hodge had endorsed the coalition, and by the fall, elections were scheduled for a South Korean Interim Legislative Assembly (SKILA).[51] According

to the election provisions, the occupation administration would be able to supplement the election results with its own selections in order to balance political
representation in the SKILA. The SKILA elections were held in October with conservative parties winning the majority of the seats. This victory was largely facilitated by the boycott of leftist parties, political intimidation, and the high turnout
of Korean landed voters. In an effort to save the coalition effort, Hodge used his
selections to appoint moderate rightists and leftists to the assembly, but the SKILA
failed to achieve a quorum when it convened in December. The end result was a
coalition that was never viewed as legitimate by any of the major political interests
in Korea: the left dismissed the elections as fraudulent while the Korean right felt
wronged by Hodge's efforts to balance the assembly through his selections.[52]

Meanwhile, Korean dissatisfaction with the U.S. occupation authorities continued to rise. In the fall of 1946, the Autumn Harvest Uprisings began. On
September 23, 8000 railroad worker in Pusan went on strike, which was followed
by a more general strike of 251,000 workers and a series of protests and uprisings primarily directed against Korean police forces across the peninsula. In the
first two weeks of November more than fifty separate incidents were reported
in southern Korea. A combination of economic problems in southern Korea,
including widespread unemployment, seemingly unfair rice collection policies,
rampant inflation, as well as U.S. favoritism toward the right, produced these
uprisings in the Korean countryside.[53]

The Korean right, with the support of the U.S. occupation authority, responded
with a strategy of coercion. As predicted, when the threat environment is unfavorable, occupying powers must respond with coercion in order to control the occupied population. By the time the uprisings ended, most of the Korean Communist
Party and many other presumed instigators in southern Korea—as many as thirty
thousand people—were imprisoned.[54] More than two hundred policemen and a
thousand protesters were killed in the uprisings. On October 28, 1946, MacArthur
wrote to Chief of Staff Dwight D. Eisenhower with concern about the growing
influence of the Communist Party in Korea and the unfortunate consequences
of the coercive strategy employed by the United States and its Korean allies: "In
this connection the Russian propaganda program in North Korea is making tre-
mendous capital on recent and current Communist disorders in South Korea, and
building up the Americans as the most cruel and sadistic imperialists in the entire
world, who destroy innocent Koreans with tanks and airplanes."[55]

In reality, however, the uprisings of 1946 were not coordinated by any national leftist party in an effort to incite a national communist revolution; rather,
they were a series of local revolts in protest of specific policies being pursued
by the occupation administration. As Bruce Cumings persuasively concludes,
"The autumn uprisings, far from being pathological anomalies or the work of

scheming individuals, were the predictable and logical culmination of more than a year of unheeded Korean demands for meaningful reforms, labor unions, peasant unions, and self-governing organs of power."[56] The individual uprisings were easily squashed by the Korean national police, but the dissatisfaction with the occupation administration and its right-leaning policies that were at the root of the uprisings remained even after they were defeated. Coercion had the effect of alienating much of the Korean population instead of leading it to welcome the continuing U.S. presence. Rather than alleviating the unfavorable initial threat environment, coercion only exacerbated it.

In the wake of the unsuccessful SKILA elections and the autumn uprisings, the United States looked for yet another way out of Korea in early 1947.[57] One option was to recognize Syngman Rhee as the legitimate ruler of southern Korea and end the occupation. As Hodge lamented, "Rhee is nuisance [sic] in that he wants everything done his own impractical way and wants to head separate Govt of South Korea. However, we cannot and must not overlook his potential to do irreparable damage unless carefully handled."[58] Rhee embarked on a three-month trip to Washington in early 1947 to convince U.S. leaders to let him rule southern Korea without interference, but Washington remained reluctant to entrust Korea to Rhee.

THE DEBATE IN WASHINGTON

As the United States struggled to find a strategy that would enable it to extricate itself from Korea, a vigorous debate ensued in Washington over the value of Korea and whether or not the United States should continue to expend valuable resources on the occupation at all.[59] The United States was spending more than $1 million per day on the occupation at a time when it was attempting to scale back its military spending from the high levels of World War II.[60]

In early 1947, the argument over the strategic importance of Korea manifested itself in a debate about how much additional financial aid to grant to southern Korea. President Truman eventually submitted a request for a one-year $215 million aid program to South Korea, down from the three-year $600 million program that the State Department had originally suggested, but this proposal was tabled in the summer of 1947 by a reluctant Congress that was already being asked to foot the bill for the ambitious Marshall Plan in Europe.[61] The United States had not yet found a way to overcome the initially unfavorable threat environment and the resurgence of Korean nationalism. In the absence of a compelling enough threat to southern Korea, the United States was unwilling to devote substantial resources as part of an inducement strategy.

The debate over the geopolitical significance of Korea and the advisability of continuing the occupation was carried out primarily between the State

Department and the War Department. The State Department argued that the occupation of Korea was critical to U.S. credibility throughout East Asia and, in particular, to its continuing commitment to Japan. Korea, according to Dean Acheson, might be a "military liability," but "control of all Korea by Soviet or Soviet-dominated forces . . . would constitute a strategic threat to U.S. interests in the Far East."[62] The United States, according to the State Department, had to continue the occupation and the devotion of substantial financial resources to it.

The War Department, however, placed a low priority on Korea, arguing instead for a quick exit from the peninsula.[63] The occupation of Korea required forty-five thousand troops that, in the absence of the occupation of Korea, could be redeployed to more strategically important locations.[64] Further, the War Department argued that the U.S. military forces in Korea were unlikely to prevail if conflict did break out on the peninsula. Secretary of War Robert Patterson warned, "The current situation in Korea is potentially explosive." Patterson advised, "I am convinced that the United States should pursue forcefully a course of action whereby we get out of Korea at an early date and believe all our measures should have early withdrawal as their overriding objective."[65] By April 1947, the Joint Chiefs of Staff had concluded that Korea was not particularly important to the United States. JCS 1769/1 is worth quoting at length:

> From the security viewpoint the primary reasons for current assistance to Korea would be that, as a result of the 38th parallel agreement, this is the one country within which we alone have for almost two years carried on ideological warfare in direct contact with our opponents, so that to lose this battle would be gravely detrimental to United States prestige, and therefore security, throughout the world. . . . *However, this suspicion could quite possibly be dissipated and our prestige in these same western European countries enhanced if a survey of our resources indicated we could not afford to resist our ideological opponents on all fronts and we publicly announced abandonment of further aid to Korea in order to concentrate our aid in areas of greater strategic importance.*[66]

The JCS went on to identify Korea as the fifteenth most important country to U.S. national security out of the sixteen it considered, placing it ahead of only the Philippines. Secretary of Defense James Forrestal wrote to the secretary of state, "The Joint Chiefs of Staff consider that, from the standpoint of military security, the United States has little strategic interest in maintaining the present troops and bases in Korea."[67] George Kennan summarized the implication of the military's belief that Korea was not essential to U.S. security, "Our policy should be to cut our losses and get out of [Korea] as gracefully but as promptly as possible."[68] The military did not wish to see Korea lost to the Soviet Union, but they hoped to apply a generally passive containment strategy as opposed to the more active approach advocated by the State Department.

In short, to stay in Korea would require a dedication of resources that Congress was increasingly reluctant to grant, especially with growing opposition within the military to the occupation.[69] But the War Department's suggestion to withdraw from Korea posed two problems. First, as the State Department pointed out, southern Korea remained vulnerable to communist infiltration. Beginning on August 26, General Albert Wedemeyer visited Korea as part of a fact-finding mission in East Asia. Wedemeyer concluded that without continued funding of the occupation, Korea was likely to suffer an economic and political breakdown, making it susceptible to communist infiltration. To withdraw from Korea would "cost the United States an immense loss in moral prestige among the peoples of Asia; it would probably have serious repercussions in Japan and would more easily permit the infiltration of Communist agents into that country; and it would gain from the Soviet Union prestige in Asia which would be particularly important in the peripheral areas bordering the Soviet Union, thus creating opportunities for further Soviet expansion among nations in close proximity to the Soviet Union."[70]

Second, Syngman Rhee was becoming more vocally opposed to the continuation of the occupation, but American leaders feared that an independent Rhee would be belligerent and unpredictable. In July, MacArthur relayed General Hodge's dire assessment of the situation in Korea to the secretary of state: "In my opinion the Korean situation is more precarious today that at any time since the occupation began."[71] Joseph Jacobs, the political adviser in Korea, sent his own pessimistic appraisal of the situation to the secretary of state on September 8, "All groups except the leftists want American money, aid and assistance and armed protection (some are so impudent as to assume we owe it to them) but they want no control or supervision."[72] Rhee could not be trusted with American resources, and the concern remained that Rhee would attempt to unify the Korean Peninsula by military force if left unsupervised by the United States.

AN APPEAL TO THE UNITED NATIONS

After a failed attempt to reconvene the Joint Commission in the spring and summer of 1947, the United States asked the United Nations to supervise elections in Korea. A successful turn to the United Nations would allow the United States to achieve its goals of lessening the costs of occupation while simultaneously creating an independent Korea under legitimate indigenous leadership. Korean nationalism would be accommodated, and the U.S. expenditure of resources would be lessened. The move to the United Nations had the added benefit of appealing to Korean conservatives, who saw UN involvement as leading toward the end of the occupation and long-sought Korean independence.

The Soviet Union, however, opposed the involvement of the United Nations because of its concern that national elections would not turn out in its favor (northern Korea had a smaller population than southern Korea).[73] Leftists in southern Korea followed the Soviet lead and also opposed the American proposal for UN-supervised elections. In an effort to trump the U.S. initiative, the Soviets proposed instead a mutual withdrawal of all troops from Korea.[74] The proposal gained the Soviets a useful public relations victory, but it was essentially a nonstarter. The United States still was not prepared to withdraw from Korea and leave open the possibility of communist conquest of the entire peninsula.[75] General Hodge supported the UN initiative, but also argued the United States should hold the elections even if the United Nations was not involved. Elections—either under U.S. or UN supervision—would finally allow the United States to withdraw.[76]

On November 13, 1947, the UN Temporary Commission on Korea (UNTCOK) was established to supervise national elections in Korea by the spring of 1948. On May 8, 1948, UNTCOK-supervised elections were held in southern Korea. Despite communist-inspired protests in the south against the elections, the exclusion of the northern part of the peninsula, and evidence of voter intimidation, the UNTCOK endorsed the results of the election and a conservative victory in southern Korea.

END GAME

Once it was clear that the UN-supervised elections were likely to take place, Washington's attention again turned to how it could extricate itself from Korea. NSC 8, issued on April 2, 1948, established U.S. policy as seeking as early an exit from Korea as was feasible: "It should be the effort of the U.S. Government through all proper means to effect a settlement of the Korean problem which would enable the United States to withdraw from Korea as soon as possible with the minimum of bad effects." The United States, however, needed to be cautious: "Unless the US, upon withdrawal, left sufficient indigenous military strength to enable south Korea to defend itself against any but an overt act of aggression, U.S. withdrawal could be interpreted as a betrayal by the US of its friends and allies in the Far East and might well lead to a fundamental realignment of forces in favor of the Soviet Union throughout that part of the world."[77] With the formal selection of Syngman Rhee as the Korean president in July 1948 and the founding of the Republic of Korea on August 15, the door appeared to be open for the United States to contemplate its withdrawal from the peninsula. Secretary of State George Marshall warned, however, that the United States must remain flexible in its plans for withdrawal, "While every effort should be made to bring about the withdrawal of our occupation forces from Korea by the end of the current year as presently contemplated, sufficient flexibility should be maintained in the preparation and execution of withdrawal plans to make possible changes in the implementation of such plans which UN action or other developments may make advisable."[78]

Withdrawing immediately from Korea after the promulgation of South Korea was not as easy as it might seem. Faced with the prospect of having to defend his country, Rhee now asked that the United States *not* leave immediately. Although Rhee wanted political independence, he realized that he would be unable to repulse an invasion from the north. Washington, therefore, had two options: it could either arm Rhee and allow him to defend South Korea or the United States could maintain a military presence in South Korea as a deterrent to the north. Both of these options were unattractive. Rhee had already demonstrated a bellicose character, but maintaining a U.S. presence would continue to consume valuable American resources.

The United States settled on a middle ground. The United States would not completely withdraw from Korea at the end of 1948 as some had hoped, but neither would it commit indefinitely to protect South Korea. By the end of 1948, only about eight thousand U.S. troops—down from a high of forty-five thousand—remained in Korea. In March 1949, NSC 8/2 committed the United States to a full withdrawal from Korea by June 30 of that year.[79] In order to placate Rhee, a Korean Military Advisory Group was formed to assist the Korean president in forming a military that could defend South Korea. The final fifteen hundred U.S. troops withdrew on June 29, 1949.

The U.S. occupation hardly produced long-term stability in southern Korea. As early as the spring of 1948—even before the elections were held—rebellions broke out both on Cheju Island and in Yosu Province.[80] In Cheju alone, as many as thirty thousand people were killed over nearly a year of insurgent fighting against the powerful Korean right and its police.[81] A year later, by the fall of 1949, the guerrilla insurgency in South Korea had grown to include approximately eighty thousand guerrillas.[82] Once U.S. troops had withdrawn and Rhee no longer was hamstrung by the dominant U.S. military presence, the South Korean president embarked on a concerted strategy to crush all leftist opposition to his rule. By the spring of 1950, the combination of a harsh winter and Rhee's aggressive tactics had significantly damaged the insurgency, but Rhee's popularity in South Korea had further plummeted. After initially postponing scheduled elections in the spring of 1950, Rhee allowed elections to take place on May 30 under pressure from the United States. The results of the elections, in which many of

Rhee's opponents were elected, demonstrated that the support for Rhee's rightist rule, relatively weak to begin with, was further dissipating.[83]

EVALUATING THE OCCUPATION

Recall that the United States had short- and long-term security objectives in Korea. First, it wanted to protect southern Korea from communist aggression. Second, it wanted to shepherd southern Korea toward independence under a government friendly to the United States. In terms of protection from the threat posed by North Korea, the presence of the United States guaranteed security until its withdrawal in 1949. But the success of occupations must be judged on the stability they leave behind after the occupying powers withdraw. Otherwise, the occupation may have been all for naught. Even before the occupation had ended, domestic unrest erupted in southern Korea. Then, the Korean War broke out a year after the United States left, forcing the United States to intervene to defend South Korea.[84] If occupations are to be judged in terms of the stability that they leave behind after they leave, then the U.S. occupation of southern Korea must be deemed a failure.

As for the second goal, the United States encountered mixed success in its efforts to guide Korea toward independence with a government friendly to the United States. Washington found itself in the uncomfortable position of supporting Syngman Rhee's repressive regime, if only because it was viewed as the only credible opposition to Soviet-inspired communism. By the end of the occupation, the United States did not even have much control over Rhee. According to James Matray, "By 15 August 1948, when the U.S. occupation formally ended with the inauguration of the Republic of Korea, [Military Governor] James Hodge's actions had so alienated Syngman Rhee that the new president of South Korea was no longer responsive to U.S. influence and advice."[85]

The U.S. occupation not only struggled to achieve its stated goals. It also cost the United States far more than many within the U.S. government thought that the occupation was worth. Costs cannot easily be measured simply in dollar figures or troops committed; rather, cost is a product of the value of the goal being sought. General Hodge and others initially hoped that the occupation of southern Korea would be short. Withdrawal, however, proved to be elusive. Even though Korea itself was never viewed as inherently all that valuable to the United States, the costs to U.S. credibility of withdrawing were viewed by many as perhaps higher than the costs of staying.

Were there better options than occupation available to the United States in the fall of 1945? Did the United States have to occupy Korea as it basically had to occupy Japan and western Germany after the war? Unlike Germany and Japan, Korea was not a defeated power following the war. To the contrary, it was a liberated country, looking forward to its own independence. Although it is likely that the Soviet Union would have conquered southern Korea in the absence of the U.S. occupation, the critical question is whether preventing this was worth the cost of the occupation. This is a debatable counterfactual question with no easy answer.

In sum, the U.S. occupation of southern Korea was more failure than success. The occupation left South Korea insecure and in the control of a democratically elected, but illiberal and somewhat unpredictable, leader. That said, the occupation was not a complete failure. Though the occupation was more expensive than many in Washington had hoped, it also was relatively short-lived. The U.S. did successfully install a regime that mostly shared America's interests even if it was not totally reliable. Finally, the occupation laid some foundation for the extended U.S.–South Korean alliance that continues to this day, though the occupation itself did less to cement this relationship than did the U.S. intervention on the south's behalf in the Korean War.

WHY THE U.S. OCCUPATION OF SOUTHERN KOREA HAD MIXED SUCCESS

The Korean population desired independence, not occupation, from the outset. Although the Koreans were grateful for the help of the United States in liberating them from Japanese control, they wanted to rule themselves.[86] In terms of initial threat environment, the population itself was unconvinced that any other external threat was greater than the United States. Faced with an unfavorable threat environment, the United States faced a difficult challenge of implementing a successful occupation strategy. Unable to coerce the southern Korean population and then accommodate that population, the U.S. occupation ultimately failed to create a stable postoccupation South Korea.

First, consider the strategy of coercion employed in southern Korea primarily by the new southern Korean police and army, but with the backing of the United States. Given the unfavorable threat environment facing the United States, coercion was a necessary element of the occupation strategy, but coercion only served to intensify the difficult conditions of the occupation. Although a strategy of coercion successfully quashed opposition in 1946, opposition returned with greater strength in 1948 as the end of the occupation approached. Both immediately before and after the UN-supervised elections in 1948, the guerrilla insurgency against the Rhee government intensified in southern Korea.[87]

Second, in the absence of successful coercion, U.S. efforts at accommodating Korean nationalism also were unsuccessful. From their arrival, the United States did little to instill confidence in the Korean people that they would be able to choose independent, indigenous political leaders. The initial American decision to rely on Japanese and their Korean collaborators for staffing the military government made many Koreans immediately suspicious of the United States.[88]

Successful accommodation requires backing an elite who can manage the nationalist instincts of the population. The United States, however, chose to put all of its support behind the right-wing leadership of Syngman Rhee, despite the presence of alternative leaders who could have generated more support among the Korean people. As Bonnie Oh observes, "In their fear of communism, [U.S. occupation authorities] blindly supported noncommunists, who did not necessarily have either the interest or the support of the majority of the Korean people."[89] U.S. intelligence reported, "Whether their strength is spontaneous or forced is a matter of conjecture; but the fact remains that the leftist group, mainly through the organizational force of the People's Republic, represents the majority of the people of South Korea."[90] Without the occupation, it is likely that the left-wing KPR probably would have taken power in southern Korea within months of the end of the war.[91] Far from assuaging the southern Korean people's desire for self-determination, American support for Rhee only drove left-leaning southern Koreans to rise up against the occupation and against the emerging Rhee regime. Though the Korean right was pleased that elections would finally result in independence, the Korean left continued to protest and dismissed the elections as fraudulent.[92]

What about inducement? Would more U.S. resources have helped to resolve the difficulties in the U.S. occupation of southern Korea? Again, with an unfavorable threat environment, resources alone could not succeed until resistance had been coerced. Although it is true that the 1946 autumn uprisings were, in part, the result of rice shortages and more general economic difficulties in southern Korea, a simple resources argument cannot adequately explain the outcome in this case.[93] Even Hodge's political advisor Jacobs recognized that money and resources alone could not buy success. Poignantly, Jacobs observed in September 1947, "History cries loudly that the fruits of democracy come forth only after long evolutionary and revolutionary processes involving the expenditure of treasure, blood, and tears. Money cannot buy it; outside force and pressure cannot nurture it."[94] Opposition to the U.S. occupation was based on a popular desire for self-determination and opposition to the imposition of the conservative leadership of Rhee.

In short, the strategic choices that the United States made in southern Korea only exacerbated the unfavorable threat environment that was already working against U.S. success. For many Koreans, the greatest threat to their self-determination was the continued presence of the U.S. occupation. To be clear, southern Koreans did not prefer to be under the control of the Soviet Union either; their preferred outcome was for both emerging superpowers to leave the peninsula.[95] The absence of a commonly perceived external threat increased resistance and made coercion necessary. The strategy the United States pursued of unsuccessful coercion combined with support for Rhee only cemented the views of many southern Koreans that the United States was the greatest threat it faced.

United States impatience also contributed to the failures of the U.S. occupation in Korea. As early as the fall of 1945, General Hodge argued that the occupation should be as short as possible. In 1947, the State Department, the War Department, the president, and Congress debated the merits of continuing the expensive occupation. Whereas many within the State Department argued that the United States had to stay in Korea for reasons of credibility, few argued that Korea itself was intrinsically worthy of the costs of the occupation.

To the extent that a shortage of resources was a problem in southern Korea, it was a problem because important decision-making elements within the United States, namely Congress and the military, did not see the value in expending limited national resources on a country that was not that integral to U.S. national security and where the United States was unlikely ultimately to succeed militarily. Without more troops, the United States would have to "run if war comes," as an aide wrote Secretary of the Army William Draper, but there was little inclination in Washington to provide more troops to southern Korea when other strategic priorities were considered more important.[96] Questions about the value of a continuing occupation of southern Korea only grew as the occupation failed to show immediate returns in its first few years.

In an unfavorable threat environment, occupying powers must manage first to employ coercion and then transition to more cooperative strategies that can foster conditions conducive to successfully ending an occupation. The United States did little to shift the Koreans' calculation of threat through the failed strategies of coercion, accommodation, and inducement that it pursued. In fact, these failed strategies only exacerbated the unfavorable threat environment. The end result was an occupation that ended too early with Korea vulnerable and under the control of a leader who was largely unresponsive to American wishes. Not until the early 1950s, when North Korea emerged as a clearly recognized threat to South Korea, was the U.S. presence welcomed in South Korea.

The Soviet Occupation of Northern Korea, 1945–1948

When the Soviets arrived in northern Korea in August 1945, they were not much better prepared for the task than the Americans were in southern Korea. As

Andrei Lankov summarizes, "The commanders of the 25th army knew nothing about the country which they now unexpectedly had to govern."[97] Widespread raping and looting did little to endear the Soviets to the Koreans immediately on their arrival.[98] Yet, by the time the last Soviet occupation troops departed North Korea at the end of 1948, the Soviets had largely achieved their occupation goals. Opposition to the occupation was mostly muted and the Soviets were able to establish and support a government that was friendly to Soviet goals. Northern Koreans were initially as anxious as southern Koreans to regain their sovereignty in the wake of the defeat of Japan. Unlike the Americans in the south, however, the Soviets implemented a successful strategy of coercion that encouraged emigration of those who opposed the emerging northern Korean state. The success of the coercive strategy enabled the Soviets subsequently to adopt a more cooperative strategy with emerging northern Korean leaders.

GOALS AND MEANS

The first Soviet troops arrived in northern Korea on August 10, 1945.[99] Soviet occupation goals were dominated by geopolitical concerns. Stalin saw little need for a large and visible Soviet presence in northern Korea. He simply aimed to keep Korea out of the hands of either Japan or the United States, and he coveted the warm-weather ports available in northern Korea.[100] Soviet leaders recognized early on that Korea was a relatively low priority and that their ambitions in northern Korea would be relatively limited.[101]

Kathryn Weathersby has uncovered a planning document prepared by two officials of the Second Far Eastern Department in preparation for the Potsdam Conference in July 1945. The document summarizes Soviet thinking on the Korea question and reaches five main conclusions. First, the Russian struggle against Japan in the Russo-Japanese war was "an historically justified act," but Russia lacked sufficient strength at the time to defeat the Japanese and prevent the spread of Japanese influence onto the Korean Peninsula. Second, accordingly, now that it had been defeated, Japan must be forever excluded from the Korean Peninsula. Third, not only must Korea be denied to Japan, it must also be denied to any other great powers that would seek to exert their influence there. Thus, "the surest guarantee of the independence of Korea and the security of the USSR in the East would be the establishment of friendly and close relations between the USSR and Korea." Fourth, the report anticipates that the Korea question may be complicated by the interests of both the United States and China on the peninsula. Fifth and finally, the report asserts that if a trusteeship of Korea is established, then the Soviets must be a party to that trusteeship.[102] General Ivan Chistiakov, the commanding general of the Soviet Army of Occupation, the Twenty-fifth Army, declared that "the Red Army has no ideas for establishing the Soviet system in Korea or obtaining Korean territory. The private and public properties of the people in North Korea are *under the protection* of the Soviet Army authorities."[103]

STRATEGIES OF OCCUPATION IN NORTHERN KOREA

The Soviets did not establish an elaborate formal occupation administration in the north, maintaining instead a relatively light presence appropriate to their occupation goals. As Charles Armstrong observes, "The Soviet Union did not need, nor did it attempt, pervasive control of North Korean society."[104] The actual and latent use of coercive violence was critical to the Soviet occupation strategy in northern Korea.[105] The violent tactics that attended the initial Soviet invasion of Korea sent a signal about the possible repercussions of opposing the Soviet occupation. As a consequence, even though many large landowners were displeased by the Soviet and Kim's agenda, the opposition was relatively muted.[106]

On October 3, 1945, the Soviets established the Soviet Civil Administration, which was to shadow the Korean political institutions that were being created at the same time. Moscow also dispersed advisers, *komendaturas,* to each province to work with the local Korean officials and People's Committees.[107] The Soviets did ensure that communists had a majority role on the local People's Committees. At the national level, however, the occupying army demonstrated an initial willingness to work with multiple political interests within northern Korea. The Soviets engaged a variety of leaders, including Cho Man-Sik, a leading Korean conservative nationalist, in an attempt to craft a governing coalition of the most important political interests in the region.[108] In November, Cho was appointed as leader of the newly formed Five Province Administration Bureau.[109]

Ultimately, however, the ambitions of a conservative like Cho were incompatible with the interests of the Soviet Union, but finding friendly, communist leadership within northern Korean was not easy. To the extent there were native communists in Korea, they were based in Seoul under the leadership of Pak Hon-Yong, and the Soviets were reluctant to rely on a Communist Party that was based in southern Korea. Without a strong native Communist Party in place when they arrived, "the Soviet authorities had to create an artificial base for their policies by establishing a local Communist party from scratch while simultaneously making agreements with local nationalists whom they hoped to win to their side."[110]

THE RISE OF KIM IL-SUNG

With potential opposition largely subdued through both explicit and latent violence, the Soviets attempted to accommodate northern Korean nationalism by supporting Kim Il-Sung. Kim was born outside of Pyongyang, but migrated to Manchuria at an early age. In the 1930s, he commanded a unit of the Northeast Anti-Japanese United Army, where he rose to prominence as a result of his success in fighting the Japanese. Eventually, when a concerted Japanese effort squashed much of the guerrilla activity in Manchuria, Kim and his soldiers retreated across the border into the Soviet Union, where they were incorporated into two Soviet base camps. By the end of the war, Kim had risen to the level of captain in the Soviet Army.[111]

Kim returned to northern Korea in mid September 1945. On October 14, seventy thousand Koreans welcomed "General" Kim Il-Sung.[112] Kim was particularly attractive to both the Soviets and northern Koreans for at least four reasons. First, he had established his bona fides as an anti-Japanese Korean nationalist by fighting against Japan in Manchuria and resisting efforts to subsume the Korean nationalist movement under the Chinese Communist Party. Second, Kim had never been captured and interrogated by the Japanese, so his loyalty to the Korean nationalist movement had not been compromised. Third, he had a legion of soldiers under his command that he brought with him on his return to Korea from his training in the Soviet Union. Fourth, Kim had a youthful appearance and abundant appeal to the Korean people.[113] Unlike the Americans in the south, the Soviets had located a leader who would both be loyal to Moscow and enjoyed the support of the northern Korean people.

Opposition to the emerging Soviet occupation was not entirely absent. Most importantly, on November 23, 1945, a group of several hundred middle school students gathered at the former colonial courthouse in Sinuiju, where the headquarters of the North P'yong'an Provincial Korean Communist Party had been established. The students were protesting the removal of a school principal by the communist-dominated People's Committee. In response, Korean security forces and Soviet troops opened fire on the students, killing two dozen and wounding hundreds.[114] The Sinuiju incident pales in comparison to the violence seen over the course of the American occupation of southern Korea, but the incident does appear to have affected the approach that Kim took to consolidating his control over Korea. Charles Armstrong argues, "Sinuiju seems to have made a profound impact on Kim and convinced him of the dangers of a ruling party alienated from important segments of the population, particularly the youth."[115]

The effect of the Sinuiju incident on Kim is evident in his December 17 speech accepting the position of chairman of the northern Korea branch of the Korean Communist Party. In the speech, Kim highlighted both his loyalty to communist ideals, which satisfied the Soviets, and his desire to broaden the appeal of the party, satisfying his and his people's nationalist instincts. "The Communist Party will be able to perform its duty only if it is organized in the most centralized manner, if iron discipline bordering on military discipline prevails in it, and if its Party center is a powerful and authoritative organ," but at the same time, "If we do not continually strengthen our ties with the masses, teach them, and, in addition, learn from them, the Communist Party . . . will not be able to become a truly mass party, competent to lead the entire working people."[116]

On February 8, 1946, the assembled communist leaders of northern Korea agreed to form a North Korea Provisional People's Committee (NKPPC), which created at the national level a structure mimicking the People's Committees that already existed at the local level. The NKPPC was the embryo of what was later to become the North Korean state.[117] Over the course of the summer of 1946, the process of political consolidation continued with the formation of the Democratic National United Front (DNUF) in July and the North Korea Worker's Party in August. The disparate communist parties that had existed when the occupation began were, by the end of the summer of 1946, consolidated under the rule of Kim Il-Sung.[118] Finally, in September 1946, the DNUF supervised People's Committees elections in which a claimed 99.6 percent turned out to support the communist ticket.

By the end of 1946, a few important patterns emerged in the conduct of the Soviet occupation of northern Korea. First and most importantly, while Kim's regime did its best to adopt a populist message that appealed to the nationalist instincts of the northern Korean people, this strategy only came after a successful strategy of coercion. Critical media was shut down, opposition leaders were imprisoned, and disgruntled citizens were encouraged to emigrate to the south.[119] As expected, coercion was a necessary precursor to accommodation in an unfavorable threat environment. Those who were displeased with the reforms undertaken in northern Korea were free to leave for southern Korea, where a more conservative government was taking shape. More than 1 million people emigrated from northern to southern Korea over the course of the occupation.[120] Most of those who remained in northern Korea endorsed Kim's political agenda.[121] As an additional benefit, the massive refugee flow enabled the north to embed its own agents among the refugees.[122] The refugee flow did, however, also have significant costs for northern Korea. Among the refugees were some of the most qualified individuals within northern Korean society.[123] Unable to refill these technical and administrative positions, the North Koreans were forced to turn to the Soviets for assistance in running northern Korea. Numerous Koreans were sent to the Soviet Union to be trained, and by the end of 1947, two thousand Soviet-trained Koreans were operating North Korea's factories.[124]

Second, in 1946, Kim Il-Sung, with Soviet support, consolidated his rule. The first step in this direction came with the Soviet decision to support the trusteeship plan that came out of the Moscow conference in December 1945. As in the south, the Moscow agreement for trusteeship enraged northern Korean nationalists who longed for independence, not further occupation. In response, the Soviets employed coercion to control any opposition to the occupation. The most vocal of those who opposed trusteeship, including the erstwhile Soviet coalition member Cho Man-Sik, were imprisoned.[125]

With the conservative nationalists out of the way, the stage was set for Kim Il-Sung to create a northern Korean government under his control. Coercion makes accommodation easier by removing potential opposition. While communists in the south set their sites on the ambitious and perhaps unreasonable goal of Korean unification and the nationalists rejected the trusteeship agreement altogether, Kim emerged as a leader whose goals were both consonant with Soviet goals for northern Korea and who was responsive to the political desires of the remaining northern Korean population.

INDUCEMENT IN NORTHERN KOREA

Successful coercion paved the way not only for the accommodation of northern Korean nationalism through Kim but also for the inducement of the Korean population through economic and social policy. Kim, with Soviet support, began to implement a series of reforms in Korean society that garnered him the allegiance of the northern Korean people. By the end of 1946, the new quasi-government of northern Korea had undertaken land reform, labor reform, gender equality reform, and the nationalization of major industries. The first and perhaps the most significant of these reforms was the land reform undertaken in March 1946. According to a U.S. State Department report, in 1945, almost 75 percent of the total farm land in Korea was cultivated by tenants. One-half of the total farm households in Korea were landless, and an additional third rented the land that they farmed. As a result of the land reform of March 1946, around 2.3 million acres of farmland were redistributed to approximately 800,000 families.[126] The land reform was a key step in Kim's continuing effort to make the Communist Party appealing to the mass of the Korean people. As the U.S. State Department concluded, "By this one stroke, half the population of northern Korea was given a tangible stake in the regime and at the same time the northern Korean government gained an important propaganda weapon in its campaign against the south."[127] The U.S. military estimated that Kim's emerging regime enjoyed the ardent support of 70 percent of northern Korea's farmers after the land reform was enacted.[128]

As additional components of the inducement strategy, the fledgling northern Korean government, still under Soviet occupation, also introduced labor and gender equity reform. The labor reforms called for an eight-hour work day, fixed daily food norms, a standardized wage scale, two weeks' paid annual holiday, the right to collective bargaining, and the elimination of child labor in dangerous industries.[129] The gender equality law introduced on July 30 gave women equal rights to participate in politics, economic opportunity, the right to education, and freedom of choice in marriage and divorce.[130]

How responsible were the Soviets for all of these reforms during 1946? Most of these initiatives appear to have been Kim's, but northern Korea was still an occupied territory. The Soviets were not prepared to see Kim Il-Sung act in ways that were inconsistent with Soviet interests in northern Korea, but the Soviets were willing to countenance Kim's political program and sustain a relatively light presence as long as the Soviet geopolitical end goals could still be achieved. By April 1947, the number of advisers to the Korean central government had dropped from around two hundred to only thirty. As Cumings concludes, "This Soviet presence simply cannot be compared to fully-functioning satellites in Eastern Europe, which had thousands of Soviet staff people and advisers."[131]

The Soviets did play a more active role in helping the northern Koreans rebuild their economy. While the Soviet Army engaged in looting on its arrival in Korea, American Edward Pauley concluded in early 1946 that there was "little if any evidence" of industrial resources being stripped from North Korea. "No substantial removals of plant equipment have been made in the plants visited by the mission," wrote Pauley after visiting northern Korea.[132] To the contrary, the Soviets were offering extensive help in rebuilding North Korea's industrial infrastructure. By the eve of the Korean War, the North Korean economy had largely recovered thanks, in part, to extensive assistance from Moscow. "Thus, by the time the Korean War broke out, North Korean economic production had, in aggregate, fully recovered from the economic downturn caused by the end of colonial rule," argues Charles Armstrong.[133]

END GAME

In 1947, as the United States shifted its focus to the United Nations as a possible avenue for ending its occupation of southern Korea, the Soviet Union allowed northern Korea to further establish itself as an independent political entity. In February and March, elections were held for the hamlet, ward, and township levels of the People's Committees. Meanwhile, the Soviets responded to the U.S. plan for UN-supervised elections with a proposal for the immediate withdrawal of foreign troops from all of Korea and pledged their intention to withdraw from Korea in September regardless of what happened with the United Nations.

In 1948, the division of the Korean Peninsula into two separate countries became official. The northern Korean regime moved further along that path with the founding of the Korean People's Army in February. At the same time that preparation was underway for the UN-supervised elections in southern Korea, Pyongyang organized its own conference of Korean political parties in order to counter southern claims to legitimacy.[134] Three weeks after the Republic of Korea was founded in the south on August 15, the Democratic People's Republic of Korea was established in the north on September 9. Confident that North Korea was in the firm control of Kim's communist leadership and a developing military, Moscow could now consider ending the occupation of North Korea. By the end of 1948, the final remaining Soviet troops in North Korea were withdrawn.

EVALUATING THE OCCUPATION

The Soviet occupation of northern Korea was a success, especially relative to the U.S. occupation of southern Korea. Soviet goals in North Korea were primarily geopolitical—keeping the Korean Peninsula out of unfriendly hands. To achieve this, the Soviets sought the creation of a government "friendly to the Soviet Union."[135] Whereas Kim may have aimed at unifying the Korean Peninsula, Stalin's goals were simply to prevent anybody else from controlling the peninsula.[136]

By the time the Soviets left at the end of 1948, these goals had been successfully accomplished at a relatively low cost. The Soviet Union acquired an ally and trading partner in North Korea. Even though Kim emerged as one of the most independent leaders within the Soviet bloc, he generally did not act in ways contrary to Soviet interests, nor in ways that endangered Soviet interests in Northeast Asia.[137]

The cost of the occupation can be measured by looking at both the need for deploying occupation troops to northern Korea and the financial expense of supporting the fledgling North Korean state. In terms of troops, the initial Soviet presence in northern Korea was around 40,000 troops, similar to the size of the U.S. presence in the south. By mid 1946, according to the U.S. State Department, the Soviets were able to reduce this presence to 10,000.[138] Compared, for example, to the 240,000 troops the Soviets had in Romania in November 1946, the Soviet presence in northern Korea seems especially light.[139]

The Soviets arrived to find that the North Korean infrastructure had been largely destroyed by the Japanese in the last days of World War II. The economic problems of northern Korea were only compounded by the mass exodus of highly trained individuals to southern Korea during the occupation. As a consequence, the occupation of northern Korea required a significant Soviet investment. In 1946, the Soviets sent 740 million rubles in aid to northern Korea.[140] By one estimate, the value of Soviet exports to northern Korea during the occupation was approximately equal to total government spending by the northern Korean government.[141] Poor data and the nature of the Soviet communist economic system make it difficult to determine just how expensive this occupation was for the Soviets in real terms, but Charles Armstrong concludes that the Soviets "gave more than they got."[142] There is no evidence, however, that Moscow viewed the occupation of northern Korea as prohibitively expensive.

At an acceptable cost, then, the Soviets managed to ensure that the entire Korean Peninsula would not fall under American or Japanese control. In addition, a friendly government was securely in place by the time that the Soviets left at the end of 1948.

WHY THE SOVIET OCCUPATION OF NORTHERN
KOREA SUCCEEDED

Largely through a successful strategy of coercion followed by more cooperative policies, the Soviet occupiers were able to overcome the initially unfavorable threat environment. After a brief initial attempt at a coalition strategy that included noncommunist Korean nationalists, the Soviets in North Korea quickly adopted a strategy of coercing and repressing all opposition. All those who opposed the Moscow trusteeship agreement of December 1945 were imprisoned. Over the course of 1946 and 1947, all opposition, including in the media, to Kim's leadership was systematically repressed.

Unlike some other cases, the strategy of coercion was largely successful in northern Korea. The initial Soviet invasion, complete with raping and plundering, sent a signal to the northern Korean population of the likely costs of resisting the occupation. The Soviets largely avoided the negative consequences of coercion by encouraging, with the threat of violence and imprisonment in the background, a large number of those opposed to the reforms being implemented to leave for the south.

Coercion was not sufficient for success, but it was a prerequisite for the strategy of accommodation that followed. As the U.S. State Department noted, "In achieving its objectives in north Korea, the Soviet Union encouraged Korean nationalism and yet prevented this force from turning against the Soviet Union as it had against the Japanese."[143] The Soviets fostered the rise of Kim Il-Sung, a communist and a nationalist, who instituted a series of reforms that endeared himself to the North Korean people. Through Kim, the Soviets pursued a strategy that both accommodated Korean nationalism and induced the Koreans to cooperate by offering improved economic conditions. "The 'mass party' conception provided millions of poor peasants with status and position hardly dreamed of by their parents, thus forming a popular basis for Kim Il Sung's political power," observes Bruce

Cumings.[144] Philip Deane, a reporter for the London *Observer,* notes that northern Koreans were quite proud of their accomplishments under Kim's regime, including the spread of literacy.[145] By not insisting that the northern Korean leadership tow the entire Soviet line, the Soviets prevented the rise of any major antioccupation insurgency. As Charles Armstrong argues, "Unlike the Americans with their military government in the South, the Soviets in the North let Koreans run the show early on, while exerting a powerful influence behind the scenes."[146]

Nationalism was not absent in northern Korea, but the Soviets simply did a more effective job of suppressing and then accommodating this nationalism than the Americans did in southern Korea. To be clear, northern Koreans were no great fans of the Soviet Union. Like any occupied population they wanted the occupation to end, but those who remained after the coercion and emigration of the early occupation also supported many of the reforms implemented by Kim's regime.[147]

For the Soviets, meanwhile, protecting northern Korea from American or Japanese aggression warranted the necessary investment of money, troops, and time. Colonel General T. F. Shtikov represented Soviet interests at the opening of the Joint Commission meetings in March 1946: "The Soviet Union has a keen interest in Korea being a true democratic and independent country, friendly to the Soviet Union, *so that in the future it will not become a base for an attack on the Soviet Union.*"[148] The Soviets were willing to invest in the occupation as long as it promised certain geopolitical benefits to Moscow.

As Bruce Cumings argues, "The Soviets had pursued a highly cost-effective strategy in creating a regime that was responsive both to their minimum demand—a friendly border state—and to the desires of the mass of Koreans in the liberation era."[149] Over the course of the occupation, Moscow and Pyongyang developed a symbiotic relationship. Eventually, by clearing northern Korea of any opposition through a concerted strategy of coercion, the threat environment was transformed in northern Korea. What had initially been unwelcome by Korean nationalists was later viewed as essential protections from the threat posed by southern Korea and its American occupiers. Kim relied on the Soviet Union for protection, and the Soviet Union relied on Kim to provide stable communist leadership. "From Kim Il-Sung's perspective, dependency on the Soviets was strategically necessary," Bruce Cumings concludes. "The Chinese Nationalists occupied much of Manchuria at the start of this period. Were they to maintain control, Kim would have a tiger at the front door and a wolf at the back. Chiang and Rhee would unquestionably seek to squeeze north Korea like an irritating pimple."[150] The consolidated Democratic National United Front, formed in the summer of 1946, explicitly aimed at defeating U.S. imperialism.[151] The northern Korean communists also intensified their campaign in 1947 to introduce the communist revolution to southern Korea. In September, a special school was established in Kandong, outside of Pyongyang, with the purpose of training specialists to carry out illegal activities against the emerging southern Korean regime.[152] And, on the founding of the Korean People's Army in February 1948, Kim accused U.S. occupation forces of "working to divide and recolonize our nation."[153] Until Kim could build up the Korean People's Army to the point where it could independently defend North Korea, Kim was forced by the threats he faced to accept the Soviet occupation.

Comparing the Occupations of Southern and Northern Korea

The occupations of southern and northern Korea began with almost identical threat environments, yet they ended very differently. In the immediate aftermath of World War II, Koreans longed to be an independent, unified country, occupied by neither the United States nor the Soviet Union. Korea was not destroyed or defeated, but instead it was liberated from Japanese colonialism. To explain the varying occupation outcomes, one must turn to the strategies that each of the occupying powers pursued. Given the unpropitious threat environment confronting the United States and the Soviet Union in their occupations of southern and northern Korea, successful occupation required an effective strategy of coercion to control resistance to occupation followed by more cooperative strategies that could build sustainable institutions.

The Soviet occupation more successfully implemented a strategy of coercing and chasing away opposition than did the United States in southern Korea. Left behind in the north was a government and population that largely welcomed the protection that Moscow offered. Rhee, supported by the United States, also attempted coercion in the south, but with considerably less success. Rhee's repressive tactics only further antagonized leftist opposition. Unlike in the north, the resistance in the south chose to stay and fight rather than leave. Emigration to northern Korea was unattractive for the southern Koreans who did not welcome the prospect of living under the coercive Soviet occupation regime in the north anymore than they welcomed U.S. occupation in the south.

With coercion paving the way, the Soviets also adopted successful strategies of political accommodation and inducement in northern Korea. Together, the Soviets and their chosen Korean protégé found a way to harness that nationalism rather than developing an antagonistic relationship with nationalist northern Koreans.[154] Once in power, Kim adopted a series of land, labor, and gender equity reforms in 1946 that were popular with the northern Korean people.

The U.S. attempt at political accommodation in southern Korea was less successful. Failed coercion made accommodation more difficult, and failed accommodation only made coercion more necessary. Rhee was certainly a nationalist, but his conservative political views were not supported by the majority of the southern Korean people. Far from assuaging the nationalist instincts of the undaunted southern Korean people, the U.S. choice of local allies only antagonized large segments of the southern Korean people, leading in some cases to violent rebellion. Rather than overcoming an unfavorable threat environment, U.S. strategies exacerbated that threat environment. As the United States continued actively to support Rhee, it appeared less likely that it would allow the Koreans to choose their own political leadership. Erik Van Ree succinctly summarizes, "The major difference was that the Russians used the People's Committees; the Americans dismantled them."[155] Or as Wayne Peterson and Hilary Conroy write, "While the United States was a Johnny-come-lately to the cause of Korean nationalism, the Soviets and the Chinese opposed the Japanese and supported the Koreans and Korean nationalism to a greater extent than the United States had."[156]

Can the dissimilar outcomes in these two cases be explained simply by the choice of local leaders? Were the Soviets simply lucky to find Kim while the United States was unlucky in backing Rhee? The choice of a leader certainly mattered in this case, but there also was clearly more to the varying outcomes than simply the choice of leaders. Most important, the success of the Soviet occupation of northern Korea demonstrates that an effective strategy of coercion can lead to a successful occupation. Kim's success in the north was less about him and more about the campaign of coercion that preceded and attended his rise to power. In the south, meanwhile, the failure of coercion meant that any rightwing leader, Rhee or not, was going to encounter difficulty establishing control over southern Korea. Relying on coercion to bring about occupation success in an adverse threat environment is difficult. Unless coercion is sufficiently repressive and can truly eliminate resistance to the occupation, whether through forced immigration or the violent suppression of opposition, coercion may have the detrimental effect of worsening the threat environment by making the occupying power appear even more as the primary threat to the nationalist desires of the occupied population.

Conclusion

When the threat environment surrounding an occupation is unfavorable, as it was in Korea after World War II, then the occupying power must first implement a strategy of coercion. Coercion, however, introduces the danger of generating more resistance to the occupation and only a greater sense that the occupying power is the greatest threat that the population faces. The North Korean case is an exceptional case where an occupation succeeded despite an unfavorable initial threat environment. Soviet success was enabled by a highly effective and ruthless strategy of coercion followed by effective political accommodation. The South Korean case is more typical. The effort to coerce and control southern Korean opposition to the occupation failed, and as a consequence, efforts to accommodate southern Korean nationalism were unsuccessful. Under more favorable threat environments, occupying powers can refrain from coercion and rely instead primarily on cooperative strategies that are more likely to gain the support of the occupied population.

WHEN TO LEAVE
The Occupation Dilemma

In this chapter, I address a final challenge that all military occupiers face: when to end an occupation? The decision to end a military occupation is critical since occupations are, by definition, intended to be temporary. Even occupied populations that may welcome the protection offered by an occupying power desire an eventual withdrawal that leaves the population secure but also sovereign. How and when can occupying powers withdraw yet remain confident that their interests will be secure?

Conditions for Successfully Ending an Occupation

Before an occupying power withdraws, it must satisfy two conditions to improve the chances of long-term success. These conditions are consistent with the security-oriented goals that occupying powers usually have when they embark on an occupation. First, the occupying country must identify an independent, indigenous, and reliable government to which it can return power. Ideally, the government will be supportive of the long-term interests of the occupying power, so that there is a low probability of future tension between the occupiers and the territory it formerly occupied. If the occupying power is unable to locate such a government, then withdrawal is only likely to unleash instability, and such instability may only precipitate future reintervention by the occupying power.

Second, while returning sovereignty, the occupying power must take steps to guarantee that the occupied territory will be both secure and nonthreatening after the occupation ends. Recall that the benefits of occupation must persist beyond the formal end of the occupation in order for it to be considered successful. Security guarantees can take the form of a military alliance or, in some cases, direct military aid. Newly independent, postoccupation states are likely to need assistance in stabilizing their countries and ensuring that predatory states do not try to take advantage of any instability. At the same time, occupying powers must be wary of providing too much military capability to a postoccupation state, as those capabilities may be viewed as threatening by other neighboring states. Thus, the responsibility of an occupying power cannot simply end when the occupation ends.

When these two conditions are met—a stable indigenous government and security guarantees—occupying powers can successfully withdraw. As discussed in the preceding two chapters, these conditions are more likely to be met when the occupation is undertaken with a favorable threat environment. Successful occupying powers that have benefited from a propitious threat environment and cooperative strategies of occupation find it easier to establish a stable government and cement security ties with the occupied territory. A commonly perceived external threat leads a postoccupation government to welcome the protections offered by its erstwhile occupier and the occupying power to offer protection so that its occupation efforts will not have been for naught. Less favorable threat conditions force an occupying power to rely on coercive occupation strategies that inherently make the creation of a reliable and stable government more difficult and make an occupying power reluctant to offer postoccupation security guarantees.

The Occupation Dilemma

Occupying powers that struggle to achieve their goals in the occupied territory and face an unfavorable threat environment are likely to face an unwelcome dilemma. An unfavorable threat environment not only lessens the likelihood of success, it also makes it more difficult for the occupying power to consider withdrawal. Both the occupying power and the occupied population want an occupation to end, but the occupation dilemma makes it hard for an occupying power to withdraw successfully. This dilemma typically unfolds in three stages.

In the first stage, occupying powers underestimate the difficulty of the occupation tasks confronting them. In order to rally support for an occupation, leaders of the occupying power may purposely misrepresent the challenge of the occupation, or they may mistakenly overestimate their ability to win over an occupied population. Even in the ultimately successful case of the U.S. occupation of Japan, U.S. leaders underestimated the tasks before them, believing that the occupation would last no more than two or three years.[1] Occupying powers may enjoy an initial "honeymoon period" immediately after the invasion during which some of the occupied population is grateful for the assistance of the occupying power and other segments of the population are not yet organized to resist the occupation. This honeymoon period only further delays recognition of the challenges of occupation that need to be addressed if success is to be accomplished.

In the second stage, despite the growing commitment of the occupying power, the challenges of occupation only multiply instead of diminish. The costs of occupation grow, and the citizens of the occupied territory become increasingly resentful of the presence of the occupying power. The honeymoon period that occupying powers may have enjoyed in the initial stage makes it more likely that occupying powers will enter this second stage with great optimism, but any initial welcome begins to obsolesce as the occupation grows longer. Simultaneously, the occupied territory becomes increasingly dependent on the occupying power, and the occupying power becomes economically and politically entrenched in the occupied territory, making it more difficult for the power to consider withdrawal. While the nationalist impulses of the occupied citizens push for withdrawal, pragmatic needs require the occupying power to stay. For example, the American occupation of Haiti was extended largely because of the perceived responsibility of Washington to protect American investments in Haitian bonds and the critical role of American capital in the Haitian economy.[2]

In the third and final stage, the occupying power faces the dilemma of a failing occupation. On the one hand, the occupying power can choose to cut its losses and evacuate the occupied territory. By doing so, the occupier relieves itself of the burden of occupation, but its goals may be left unachieved, subsequent reoccupation may prove necessary, and reputation costs may be incurred. On the other hand, the occupying power can choose to stay the course and remain in the occupied territory. When occupations go poorly and withdrawal appears infeasible, occupying powers may alter the goals of the operation from temporary occupation to either colonialism or annexation. This alternative is likely to generate more resentment, more cost, and less success. Unfortunately for suffering occupying powers, occupations that get going on the wrong track are difficult to reverse and turn into successes. Stay or go, the occupying power has failed.

The occupation dilemma captures a paradox that afflicts unsuccessful occupations. A defining feature of occupation is that both the occupying power and the occupied population want the occupation to end, but when an occupation struggles, bringing it to an end only becomes more difficult. The more unsuccessful an occupation is, the more difficult it is to locate an acceptable way to terminate the occupation.

The Occupation Dilemma in Cuba, Egypt, and Japan

To evaluate this argument, I present three case studies that illustrate the challenge of ending an occupation: the U.S. occupation of Cuba between 1898 and 1902, the British occupation of Egypt between 1882 and 1954, and the U.S. occupation of Japan from 1945 until 1952.

The cases of Cuba and Egypt make for an interesting comparison since they were, in fact, so often compared at the time. The *London Chronicle* noted about the U.S. position in Cuba, "The President is naturally compelled to add that until complete tranquility prevails in the island, and a system of government is inaugurated, the military occupation will be continued. We shall not be thought discourteous or cynical if we remark that this is precisely the language that successive British Governments have maintained about Egypt, with a result known to the world, and an omen which is certainly not inapplicable."[3] Joseph Chamberlain, the British colonial secretary, observed, "The United States now finds itself [in Cuba] in much the same position as ourselves in Egypt. We are bound to put down rebellion, and we shall stay there until we do."[4] And Secretary of War Elihu Root himself noted that U.S. goals in Cuba were similar to British goals in Egypt: "retire and still maintain her moral control."[5] Yet the occupations of Cuba and Egypt proceeded in very different ways: whereas the United States withdrew prematurely from Cuba, Great Britain overstayed its welcome in Egypt. These two case studies demonstrate the difficulties introduced by both horns of the occupation dilemma.

The third case, the U.S. occupation of Japan after World War II, illustrates an occupying power that devised a successful withdrawal strategy. In 1952, the United States returned sovereignty to a reliable indigenous Japanese government while also providing guarantees that ensured Japanese security at the same time that Japan's ability to threaten its neighbors was curtailed. A favorable threat environment in this case enabled a timely and successful withdrawal.

The U.S. Occupation of Cuba, 1898–1902

United States interest in Cuba grew throughout the nineteenth century as economic ties brought the two neighbors together. In particular, the growth of the

Cuban sugar industry led to increasing American interest in the Cuban economy. Even though Spain held political control of Cuba, by 1860 the United States was buying 62 percent of Cuban exports compared to only 3 percent by Spain.[6] In the 1890s, a U.S.–Spain reciprocity treaty opened Cuba to American exports, leading to a doubling of U.S. exports to Cuba.

In February 1895, a separatist insurrection against Spanish rule began in Cuba. Cuban landowners lamented the possible success of the insurrection and appealed to U.S. president Grover Cleveland to intervene in order to prevent the emergence of an independent Cuba that would lack a stable government. One Cuban planter wrote, "The worst thing that could happen to Cuba would be independence."[7]

Washington was sympathetic to the landowners. Cuban independence, it was argued, would invite instability and violence in Cuba, undermining U.S. economic interests on the island. Cleveland and Richard Olney, his secretary of state, set out to convince Spain to adopt a political solution that would placate nationalist Cubans with some measure of autonomy, resolving the tension in Cuba without U.S. military intervention. Olney wrote to the Spanish minister Enrique Dupuy de Lôme, "What the United States desires to do is to cooperate with Spain in the immediate pacification of the island on such a plan as, leaving Spain her rights of sovereignty, . . . shall yet secure to the people of the island all such rights and powers of local self-government as they can reasonably ask."[8]

Spain eventually responded with a series of measures, including a new constitution and the installation of a liberal government in January 1898. These reforms, however, neither satisfied those Cubans who sought full independence from Spain nor those loyal to Spain who feared for their livelihood under a new autonomous Cuban government.[9] Cuban *insurrectos* interpreted the Spanish reforms as a sign of Spanish weakness. General Calixto García, a leader of the Cuban rebels, argued, "I regard autonomy only as a sign of Spain's weakening power and an indication that the end is not far off."[10] Far from ending the insurgency, the signs of a Spanish willingness to negotiate only encouraged the rebels to muster their troops.

On February 15, 1898, the tension over Cuba intensified when the U.S. battleship *Maine* mysteriously blew up in Havana harbor, killing 250 Americans. Though the cause of the explosion on the *Maine* was unclear, many in the United States assumed that Spain was responsible and began to prepare for war. On March 27, U.S. president McKinley issued an ultimatum to Madrid demanding an armistice until October, an end to resettlement programs in Cuba, permission for the United States to distribute relief supplies in Cuba, and acceptance of President McKinley as a mediator in the dispute. In return, Washington promised to use its "friendly offices to get insurgents to accept the plan."[11] By April 10, Spain had agreed to the ultimatum and the Spanish governor general Ramón Blanco had ordered all of his forces to stop fighting, but the Cuban insurgents did not accept the armistice as the end of their struggle. To the contrary, the *insurrectos* saw the Spanish-American agreement as an opportunity finally to achieve their independence. "In order to suspend hostilities, an agreement is necessary with our Government and this will have to be based on independence," General García insisted, "More than ever before, the war must continue in force."[12]

GOALS AND MEANS

Military intervention now appeared the only way to prevent an independent Cuban government led by the *insurrectos*. On April 11, McKinley sent a message to Congress requesting authorization to intervene militarily in Cuba. McKinley argued that intervention was necessary for four reasons: (1) to end misery and death, (2) to protect the lives and property of U.S citizens in Cuba, (3) to end the injury done to U.S trade and commerce by the Cuban struggle, and (4) to end the expense to the U.S. government resulting from the enforcement of the neutrality laws and the protection of its citizens in the danger area.[13]

What McKinley proposed was a "neutral intervention" intended both to protect the Cubans from the Spanish and to limit instability caused by possible Cuban independence. The proposed intervention met opposition from the Cuban lobby in the United States and from the U.S. Congress. Both groups objected because of the possibility that a U.S. intervention would lead inexorably to U.S. annexation of Cuba. Gonzalo de Quesada, a leading Cuban exile in the United States, asserted, "We will oppose any intervention which does not have for its expressed and declared object the independence of Cuba."[14] Congressional opponents to the administration's planned intervention insisted that the United States recognize a provisional government in Cuba as a way of renouncing any intention of annexing Cuba. To reassure his critics, McKinley pointedly eschewed annexation, "I speak not of forcible annexation for that cannot be thought of. That, by our code of morality, would be criminal aggression."[15]

Ultimately, congressional approval was granted to the intervention but only after the Teller Amendment was added to the resolution approved by the Senate.[16] The amendment stated "that the United States hereby disclaims any disposition or intention to exercise sovereignty, jurisdiction, or control over said island [Cuba] except for the pacification thereof, and asserts its determination when that is accomplished to leave the government and control of the island to its people."[17] The Teller Amendment served to assuage the concerns of both Cubans seeking independence and the antiannexationists in the United States. As I will discuss below, however, the amendment also remained ambiguous, most notably with regard to the definition of "pacification."

With congressional approval in place, the U.S. intervention in Cuba began in June. General William R. Shafter commanded an expeditionary force of eighteen thousand men that was received peacefully by the Cuban *insurrectos*. Through the summer of 1898, the Americans and the Cubans were uneasy allies. The Cubans were grateful for U.S. assistance, and the Americans relied heavily on Cuban assistance in landing their troops on shore. But the American honeymoon period would be short lived. The Cubans saw themselves as fighting for their own country, while the U.S. forces were not particularly fond of the Cubans. Stephen Crane, writing for *New York World*, observed that "both officers and privates have the most lively contempt for the Cubans. They despise them."[18] By mid August, the Spanish-American War had come to a close with a decisive U.S. victory. Attention now turned to the postwar fate of Cuba.

The prevailing sentiment in the United States was that Cuba was not prepared for self-governance following the war. The war of liberation took a costly toll on Cuba. Between 1895 and 1898, 300,000 of Cuba's prewar population of 1.8 million were killed.[19] Cuba emerged from the war with enormous debt: $400 million in a country with a declared property value of only $139 million.[20] By 1900, only 3 percent of Cuba's 28 million acres of farmland were being cultivated.[21] Politically, General S. B. M. Young concluded, "The insurgents are a lot of degenerates, absolutely devoid of honor or gratitude. They are no more capable of self government than the savages of Africa."[22] Major George M. Barbour, the U.S. sanitary commissioner in Santiago de Cuba, added, the Cubans "are stupid, given to lying and doing all things in the wrong way. . . . Under our supervision, and with firm and honest care for the future, the people of Cuba may become a useful race and a credit to the world; but to attempt to set them afloat as a nation, during this generation, would be a great mistake."[23] Thus, Spain had been expelled, political instability was bubbling beneath the surface, and the country was economically devastated. Annexation was an unlikely option for the United States since, among other things, that would transform Cuban debt into American debt.[24] The only available option for the United States appeared to be to occupy the country until it was ready for independence.

In July, McKinley directed Leonard Wood, the commander of the army of occupation in Cuba, to announce "that we come not to make war upon the inhabitants of Cuba, nor upon any part or faction among them, but to protect them in their homes, in their employments, and in their personal and religious rights. . . . Our occupation should be as free from severity as possible."[25] In general, the United States was driven by concerns about the security of its interests in Latin America, especially from potential threats from Europe and political instability within Cuba.

To ensure that the United States did not exploit Cuba economically, the Senate passed the Foraker Amendment to the army appropriations bill in March 1899. The Foraker Amendment demanded that "no property franchise, or concessions of any kind whatever, shall be granted by the United States, or by any other military or other authority whatever in the Island of Cuba during the occupation thereof by the United States." Foraker's great concern was that extensive U.S. economic involvement in Cuba would preclude American withdrawal from the island. Economic penetration, Foraker argued, would mean "that the United States will not get out of Cuba in a hundred years."[26]

In December, McKinley instructed John Brooke, who was to become the first commander of the military government in Cuba in January 1899, that the authority of the military government in Cuba would continue "until such time as the people shall have established a firm and stable government of their own, capable of performing its international obligations. The government to be maintained under this authority by you on behalf of the United States is not in the interest or for the direct benefit of this country, but in the interest and for the benefit of Cuba and those possessed of rights and property in that Island."[27] "Until there is complete tranquility in the island and a stable government inaugurated," McKinley asserted, "military government will continue."[28] General Brooke subsequently proclaimed, "The object of the present Government is to give protection to the people, security to person and property, to restore confidence, to encourage the people to resume the pursuits of peace, to build up waste plantations, to resume commercial traffic, and to afford full protection in the exercise of all civil and religious rights."[29] Beyond those generalities, however, Brooke was able to offer few specific plans for the military government.[30] One of Brooke's subordinates, General James H. Wilson, the military governor of the Matanzas and Las Villas provinces, recalls, "When I asked Brooke as I did frequently that year, what our government's policy and ultimate purpose were in that it was doing, in short, what was the law under which we were acting, he frankly confessed that he did not know, 'except by induction.'"[31]

CONDUCT OF THE OCCUPATION

With little clarity about specific objectives or how to achieve them, the U.S. military government's first initiative was to attempt to demobilize the Cuban liberation army, which consisted of approximately forty thousand men.[32] McKinley dispatched Roger Porter as a special envoy to negotiate directly with General Máximo Gómez, a leader of the Cuban revolutionary army and no fan of the U.S. occupation. "Ours is the Cuban flag," Gómez declared, "The one for which so many tears and so much blood have been shed, and the one that will be run up if, setting aside spurious and selfish passions and guided only by the good of the country . . . we unite in order to bring to an end this unjustified military occupation."[33]

Without any pressing external threat aside from the United States, Cubans did not see the need for U.S. occupation. As in other cases of military occupation, the initial threat environment of the occupation of Cuba greatly influenced the ability of the United States to accomplish its goals. Perfecto Lacosta, chairman of the Havana committee, lamented, "For years we have suffered only to see, at this hour, our emotions changed from pleasure at the departure of the Spaniards to apprehension at the arrival of the Americans."[34] The United States intervened in Cuba largely in support of Cuban nationalism, so it is hardly surprising that Cuban nationalism was anything but defeated in 1898.

Porter eventually managed to convince Gómez that the American occupation of Cuba was temporary, and by late February, Gómez had accepted an offer of $3 million to disband the army. "The United States," Gómez exulted, "has intervened only for the pacification of Cuba and the establishment of a stable independence government and . . . it does not intend to exercise any control or sovereignty over Cuba."[35] Gómez came to view cooperation, rather than confrontation, as the most effective way for ending the occupation. In January 1899, he called on Cubans to "aid in every pacific method" the accomplishment of peace and security, so that the occupation would come to an end.[36]

Following the dissolution of the Cuban army, the situation on the island quieted during the summer of 1899. This is not to suggest that Cubans were satisfied with being occupied, but they had adopted Gómez's advice that the best way to end the occupation was to cooperate with the United States. Strikes remained common in Cuba, including, for example, a strike by between four thousand and eight thousand workers on September 24. In late November and early December, protests and rallies erupted around Cuba at the rumor that the United States was contemplating replacing the military government in Cuba with a more colonial-style, civil government.[37] In general, though, widespread revolt and insurgency were absent from the U.S. occupation of Cuba.

Meanwhile, General Brooke was increasingly the subject of criticism by his own subordinates as dissatisfaction with the lack of progress in the occupation emerged. In July, General Leonard Wood wrote to Theodore Roosevelt that he found General Brooke's leadership "discouraging and disgusting."[38] Of Brooke's attempts to restore old Spanish legal customs, Wood wrote, "Nothing more idiotic can be imagined than the attempt to establish a liberal government under Spanish laws."[39] By the end of 1899, it was clear that Brooke's leadership of the military government was foundering, and as a consequence, in December, Brooke was replaced by Wood. McKinley instructed Wood, "I want you to go down there to get the people ready for a Republican form of government. . . . We want to do all we can for them and to get out of the island as soon as we safely can."[40]

Unlike Brooke or McKinley, Wood favored the eventual annexation of Cuba. This annexation would be by "acclimation" following a period of benevolent rule by the United States. Wood's biographer, Hermann Hagedorn, writes, "Forcible annexation he had refused to consider, annexation by guile he had effectively opposed; but annexation by acclimation had been his dream from the beginning."[41] Wood's priorities, therefore, were to ensure that Cuba would be governed by leaders who would support a continuing U.S. presence in Cuba and eventually annexation by the United States. Wood remained confident that the Cubans would ultimately prefer to annex themselves to the United States rather than becoming independent.[42] Rather than attempting to coerce the Cubans, the United States should now turn to strategies of accommodation and inducement. Secretary of War Elihu Root agreed, "It is better to have the favors of a lady with her consent, after judicious courtship, than to ravish her."[43] As predicted in the previous chapter, however, accommodation and inducement are difficult strategies to implement successfully in the face of an unfavorable threat environment.

AN ATTEMPT AT ACCOMMODATION

The first notable steps in the accommodation strategy were the holding of popular elections and movement toward the reduction of the overall American presence in Cuba.[44] Wood insisted, "We have got to trust them with the handling of affairs under our supervision and in this way teach them."[45] United States leaders recognized, however, that popular elections in Cuba could be dangerous for U.S. interests. The majority of Cubans favored independence, and open elections might very well lead to the election of an anti-American government. Wood claimed that open elections "would be fatal to the interests of Cuba and would destroy the standing and influence of our government among all thinking intelligent people in the island. . , . Giving the ballot to this element means a second edition of Haiti and Santo Domingo in the near future."[46]

The challenge for Wood and the occupation administration was to ensure that the Cuban "better classes"—meaning the white, landed bourgeoisie—would control the government. The U.S. strategy was to facilitate the formation of a Cuban political coalition that could survive and protect U.S. interests after U.S. withdrawal.[47] Thus the United States attempted to co-opt influential Cuban leaders by offering lucrative positions in the Cuban civil government to former Cuban generals.[48] Wood explained to Root, "These men [Gómez's supporters] have a great influence with the army and great influence among the people."[49]

If elections were to be held, the only way to guarantee that the victors in the election were the candidates that the United States favored was to restrict suffrage within Cuba. The final electoral law, approved on April 18, 1900, limited the franchise to those who were literate, owned property worth $250 in U.S. gold, or served in the Cuban army prior to July 18, 1898 and were honorably discharged.[50] Using questionable logic, Root suggested that opposition to such restrictions was limited to those who did not warrant a vote in any case. "I think it fair," Root wrote, "that proposed limitation is approved by the best, and opposed only by the worst or the most thoughtless of the Cuban people."[51] The implication of this law was that two-thirds of all adult Cuban males were excluded from the franchise. Despite the law, however, the National Party, which opposed the continuation of the U.S. occupation, was victorious in June municipal elections.

THE OCCUPATION DILEMMA IN CUBA

As if the disappointing election results were not enough, other events conspired in the summer of 1900 to push the United States to begin to look for a way to end its occupation of Cuba. Most notably, the ongoing difficulties in the Philippines and the outbreak of the Boxer Rebellion in China distracted both Washington and General Wood's attention. United States resources were now being stretched, and Wood longed to go where there was the potential for combat. Added to this was a controversial embezzlement scandal in the Cuban postal system.[52] Finally, the impending U.S. presidential elections compelled American leaders to do whatever they could to keep the Cuban situation quiet.[53] As historian David Healy writes, "The circumstances of the past months—the postal scandals [in Cuba] and the near-rebellion of Congress, the imminence of the elections of 1900, the embarrassments in the Philippines, Wood's ambition to play a role in the China expedition—had succeeded at last in bringing the administration, the Congress, and the occupation generals into a temporary agreement in favor of early action in Cuba."[54]

Before any U.S. withdrawal, however, a stable government had to be created that would guarantee U.S. interests on the island. For Wood, then, the next step in Cuba was to be the holding of a constitutional convention in the fall to constitute the government and determine the nature of Cuba's relationship with the United States. Like the elections before them, this constitutional convention was an attempt to accommodate Cuban nationalists. Elections for delegates to the convention were held on September 3. Once again, to Wood's dismay, the nationalist elements in Cuban society were victorious in elections that had less than 30 percent turnout.

On January 31, 1901, the Cuban convention published a draft of the Cuban constitution, and within two weeks, on February 11, the Cuban constitution had been adopted. While not thrilled with the document, Secretary Root wrote, "It contains no features which justify the assertion that a government organized under it will not be the one to which the United States may properly transfer the obligation for the protection of life and property under international law, assumed in the Treaty of Paris."[55] The issue of what Cuba's future government would look like had been solved, but the remaining question was about the role that the United States would play in Cuba and when the occupation of Cuba would come to an end. The increasing costs of the U.S. operations in the Philippines, in particular, made it difficult for the United States to sustain both operations, so U.S. leaders started consciously envisioning a strategy for ending the occupation of Cuba.[56]

In February 1901, Wood and Root exchanged letters on the state of affairs in Cuba. Wood wrote to Secretary Root, "It is my opinion that at the next municipal elections we shall get hold of a better class of people. If we do not, we must choose between establishing a central American republic or retaining some sort of control for the time necessary to establish a stable government.... All Cubans want independence as a matter of sentiment but all the thoughtful ones are very much in doubt as to the success of an independent government."[57] On February 9, Secretary Root responded with a lengthy dispatch to Wood summarizing his position. According to Root, "It would be a most lame and impotent conclusion if, after all the expenditure of blood and treasure by the people of the United States for the freedom of Cuba, and by the people of Cuba for the same object, we should ... be placed in a worse condition in regard to our own interests than we were while Spain was in possession, and the people of Cuba should be deprived of that protection and aid from the United States which is necessary for the maintenance of their independence."[58]

Root then proceeded to establish his conditions for U.S. withdrawal. First, Cuba must not make any treaty with any other foreign power that conferred special rights on that other power. Second, the United States must be granted the right to intervene in the event of domestic instability in Cuba. Third, Cuba must lease the United States land for naval stations. Fourth, and finally, Cuba must reaffirm all of the acts of the U.S. occupation authority.

Root's ideas were soon to be codified in the Platt Amendment, which was introduced in the Senate on February 25, 1901.[59] The amendment set out eight conditions that the Cuban government had to accept in order to authorize the president to end the occupation of Cuba. Most famously, Article III granted "that the government of Cuba consents that the United States may exercise the right to intervene for the preservation of Cuban independence, the maintenance of a government adequate for the protection of life, property, and individual liberty, and for the discharging the obligations with respect to Cuba imposed by the treaty of Paris on the United States, now to be assumed and undertaken by the government of Cuba."[60] For Washington, the Platt Amendment represented a way out. That is, the United States needed to protect its interests, most importantly from the prospect of European interference, but it had little interest in a permanent occupation of the island.[61] Root later wrote, "You can not understand the Platt Amendment unless you know something about the character of Kaiser Wilhelm the Second."[62] Within the United States, many were opposed to the seemingly annexationist overtones to the Platt Amendment.[63] Nevertheless, after a short debate over the conditions under which the United States might intervene in Cuba in the future, the Platt Amendment was passed by the Senate on February 27 and by the House of Representatives on March 1. On March 2, President McKinley signed the army appropriations bill, with the Platt Amendment attached, into law.

If the Platt Amendment represented a necessary guarantee to the United States, it represented a denial of long-sought sovereignty to many Cubans, who believed that it violated the pledge that the United States had made in the Teller Amendment.[64] Salvador Cisneros Betancourt, former provisional president of Cuba, lamented, "Such an order [as the Platt Amendment] if carried out, would inflict a grievous wrong on the people of Cuba, would rob them of their independence for which they have sacrificed so much blood and treasure, and would be in direct violation of the letter and purpose of the solemn pledge of the people of the United States to the world as consigned in the [Teller Amendment]."[65] Cuban efforts to reverse or amend the Platt Amendment were, however, to fail. Secretary Root made it clear, "No constitution can be put into effect in Cuba and no government can be elected under it, no electoral law by the Convention can be put into effect, and no election held under it until they have acted upon this question of relations in conformity with this act of Congress."[66] The United States now faced the occupier's challenge of locating reliable local allies to whom it could return sovereignty over the island.

American leaders evaded Cuban concerns by relying on the ambiguous language of pacification in the original Teller Amendment. In this interpretation, the Platt Amendment could be viewed as part of the effort to pacify Cuba and ensure stability there.[67] To assuage Cuban concerns about the Article III right to intervention, Root cabled Wood, "You are authorized to state officially that in view of the President the intervention described in the third clause of the Platt Amendment is not synonymous with intermeddling or interference with the affairs of the Cuban Government."[68] A Cuban delegation traveled to Washington in late April in search of revisions of the Platt Amendment, or, if that failed, at least

American commitments to trade reciprocity after the occupation concluded. Ultimately, several prominent Cuban leaders, including Tomás Estrada Palma and Máximo Gómez relented and endorsed the Platt Amendment.[69] After failing to convince the United States to modify the treaty, the constitutional convention approved the relationship between the United States and Cuba as stipulated in the Platt Amendment on June 12.

The approval of the Platt Amendment turned the key on the process of U.S. withdrawal from Cuba. The amendment managed simultaneously to satisfy those who wanted to see an end to the occupation and those who still hoped that Cuba would ultimately be annexed to the United States. Those who favored annexation thought that the Platt Amendment was only a temporary interruption in the drive toward "annexation by acclimation" by the Cubans. Wood wrote privately to Theodore Roosevelt on October 28, 1901, "There is, of course, little or no independence left Cuba under the Platt Amendment."[70]

Elections for both a parliament and a president were scheduled for before the end of 1901, and the occupation was scheduled to end when the new president was inaugurated on May 20, 1902. The two major candidates for president were Tomás Estrada Palma, who supported cooperation with the United States, and Bartolomé Masó, who ran primarily on a platform of opposition to the Platt Amendment. When the United States exerted its influence on the election in the fall by favoring election supervisors who supported Estrada Palma, Masó's supporters accused the United States of meddling in their election. Masó withdrew from the election in protest, leaving Estrada Palma as the unopposed candidate for president. On May 20, the first U.S. occupation of Cuba officially came to an end when Tomás Estrada Palma was inaugurated president of Cuba and American troops began to withdraw.

Considerable optimism attended the end of the first U.S. occupation of Cuba. General Wood wrote, "The work called for and accomplished was the building of a republic . . . in short, the establishment, in a little over three years, in a Latin military colony, in one of the most unhealthy countries in the world, of a republic modeled closely upon the lines of our own great Anglo-Saxon republic."[71] In 1904, President Theodore Roosevelt wrote hopefully, "If every country washed by the Caribbean Sea would show the progress in stable and just civilization which . . . Cuba has shown since our troops left the island, . . . all questions of interference by this Nation with their affairs would be at an end."[72]

United States optimism about Cuba was, however, ill-founded. Beginning in 1904, the political system that the United States created during the occupation began to unravel. The United States had withdrawn from Cuba too early, before political institutions could be stabilized and before a reliable Cuban military could be created to ensure stability on the island.

The troubles that would eventually precipitate U.S. reintervention on the island began with the national Congress elections in February 1904. The elections were fraught with corruption and fraud—"a farce represented with less shame than in the times of the colony."[73] When the Congress opened in April, the populist Liberals refused to attend, preventing the Congress from achieving its required quorum. A compromise was eventually reached in September, but not before the damage had been done to the fledgling Cuban political system.

With the controversial congressional elections behind them, the attention of the Cuban people and their political leaders now turned to the forthcoming presidential elections of 1905. Estrada Palma reluctantly agreed to run again as the candidate of the Moderate party in the elections scheduled for December. The former general José Miguel Gómez headed up the Liberal ticket, opposing the Platt Amendment and continued U.S. influence in Cuba. By the fall of 1905, accusations of fraudulent voter registration were rampant throughout Cuba, and in October, the Liberal party announced that it would boycott the elections scheduled for December. Elections went forward, however, with the Moderates unsurprisingly enjoying an overwhelming victory. The Liberals, who included among their ranks most of the leaders of the now defunct revolutionary army, were effectively excluded from power.

As Estrada Palma was inaugurated for his second term on May 20, 1906, the Liberals began to plan their revolt against the government, forming a Central Revolutionary Committee that included four ex-generals of the Cuban revolutionary army. Over the course of the summer, they assembled a force of twenty-four thousand rebels facing government opposition consisting of no army, about six hundred artillerymen, and three thousand dispersed rural guards.[74] In early September, Estrada Palma refused to consider any compromise with the Liberals and sporadic fighting began throughout Cuba.

As the crisis in Cuba developed, both Liberals and Moderates expected the Platt Amendment would lead the United States to come to their rescue. On the one hand, the Liberals interpreted Article III of the Platt Amendment as mandating that the United States would intervene to protect "life, property, and individual liberty." Given the fraudulent elections of 1904 and 1905, the Liberals calculated that the United States must intervene to ensure legitimate elections that the Liberals would surely win. From Estrada Palma's perspective, the Platt Amendment guaranteed that the United States would intervene to protect the constitutional government of the Moderates.

Both sides were counting on U.S. intervention, but the United States itself was quite reluctant to intervene. President Theodore Roosevelt vented, "At the moment, I am so angry with that infernal little Cuban republic that I would like to wipe its people off the face of this earth. All we have wanted from them was that they would behave themselves and be prosperous and happy so that we would not have to intervene. And now, lo and behold, they have started an utterly unjustifiable and pointless revolution and may get things into such a snarl that we have no alternative [but] to intervene."[75] Roosevelt recognized that the Estrada Palma government that the United States created had "almost no support among the Cubans; it had taken no steps in advance which would enable it to put down the crisis with nerve and vigor."[76]

Roosevelt, however, found himself in a difficult position. Not only was the United States legally committed through the Platt Amendment to ensuring stability in Cuba, but U.S. interests would also be in danger were civil war to break out in Cuba. At the same time, the president had little desire to reoccupy Cuba, especially considering the resources that the continuing campaign in the Philippines was consuming.[77] On September 6, TR summarized his difficult position, "On the one hand, we cannot permanently see Cuba a prey to misrule and anarchy; on the other hand I loathe the thought of assuming any control over the island such as we have over Puerto Rico and the Philippines. We emphatically do not want it; and . . . nothing but direst need could persuade us to take it."[78]

Events in Cuba were about to force Roosevelt's hand. Estrada Palma reiterated his desire for U.S. intervention a week later when he acknowledged that he could not "prevent rebels from entering cities and burning property" nor could he "protect North American lives and property."[79] Roosevelt dispatched Secretary of War William Taft and the Assistant Secretary of State Robert Bacon to Havana to enter negotiations toward a peaceful solution, but little progress was made. Estrada Palma responded only by threatening to resign, which would necessarily precipitate a U.S. intervention. On September 25, Roosevelt made a final plea to Estrada Palma, "I adjure you for your own fair fame not to so conduct yourself that the responsibility if such there be for the death of the Republic can be put at your door."[80] Three days later, however, Estrada Palma and his Vice President Domingo Méndez Capote resigned, leaving Cuba with no government. On September 29, two thousand U.S. marines landed in Cuba and undertook the second occupation of Cuba. Again, the United States was in control of Cuba, not to relinquish it again until 1909.

EVALUATING THE OCCUPATION OF CUBA

The first occupation of Cuba failed to meet either of the prerequisites for successfully ending an occupation. Neither a reliable indigenous government nor effective security guarantees were in place when the United States left in 1902. Instead, the United States left behind an unstable government without a military sufficient to prevent opposition attacks. As a result, the United States was forced to reoccupy Cuba in 1906. Even after the United States withdrew again in 1909, instability persisted in Cuba with yet another U.S. intervention in 1912. Lieutenant Colonel Robert Bullard predicted at the end of the second occupation, "The US will have to go back. It is only a question of time."[81] Thus, in terms of achieving its goal of political stability, the first occupation of Cuba was a failure.

The occupation of Cuba is an example of how an occupation can fail in the long-term without a costly insurgency. From early on, Cuban nationalists adopted a strategy of cooperating with the United States in order to produce a U.S. withdrawal rather than violently resisting. General Gómez concluded, "To fire a single shot in our fields would be to prolong indefinitely the realization of our ideals and satisfy the desires of our enemies because the resolution of [April 1898] says that the government of the Island will not be turned over to us until peace has been assured."[82] The United States convinced many Cuban leaders that the self-restraining pledge that the United States issued through the Teller Amendment would be fulfilled. The end result, though, was that the United States withdrew from Cuba prematurely before stable political and security institutions had been created.

The first U.S. occupation of Cuba vividly demonstrates the pressures that occupying powers encounter when a favorable threat environment is absent. First, from the perspective of the occupied Cuban population, the occupation was not seen as valuable or necessary but rather as an impediment to the achievement of Cuban national aims. One American army officer reported as early as August 1898 that Cubans "had no love for the Americans" and that "they expressed a willingness to participate" in a subsequent conflict between Cubans and the United States.[83] General Máximo Gómez observed, "None of us thought that [peace] would be followed by a military occupation of the country by our allies, who treat us as a people incapable of acting for ourselves, and who have reduced us to obedience, to submission, and to a tutelage imposed by force of circumstances."[84] Another general, Pedro Pérez, was even blunter, "I am willing to continue the fight for another thirty years, if necessary. The Cuban army has not fought for annexation or American control of our affairs. Our fight has been for independence, and the army will not be satisfied with anything else."[85] Put differently, there was no security threat to the Cuban nationalists that generated a desire for an extended occupation. The greatest threat to Cuban independence came from the U.S. occupation itself. Americans, on the other hand, mostly seemed to believe that the Cubans should be nothing but grateful for American assistance.[86] This despite the conclusion of a Senate mission to Cuba in March 1900: "It can be said of all classes in Cuba that they are looking to the establishment of an independent government, a Cuban republic."[87]

In the United States, the value of the occupation was also questioned. Cuba held geostrategic value to the United States, and Washington was concerned about the continuing European presence in the Caribbean, especially the perceived growth of German ambitions.[88] The threat posed to Cuba was, however, outweighed by other geostrategic priorities.[89] Events in Asia, in both China and the Philippines, pushed the United States to consider the prompt withdrawal from Cuba.[90] In the absence of a compelling enough third-party external threat to Cuba's survival, the United States encountered significant pressure to end the occupation of Cuba.

The occupation of Cuba also demonstrates the problems raised by the occupation dilemma and the premature withdrawal that often results. The successful completion of occupation goals takes time and without the luxury of that time, the United States withdrew too early, without having created sustainable political and security institutions. Elihu Root expressed his frustration at the simultaneous pressures to withdraw from Cuba from Congress and from Cubans, "We desire as soon as possible to be relieved from the burden and annoyance of their government. . . . I think we are in great danger of finding ourselves in a very awkward and untenable position."[91] At the same time, Wood feared that premature U.S. withdrawal would lead to a "great stampede" because of the absence of an effective government.[92]

The United States went through all three stages of the occupation dilemma: an initial optimism about accomplishing relatively modest goals, growing entrenchment in the occupied territory's society, and finally a dilemma about whether to prolong the occupation or withdraw. Louis Pérez Jr., captures the essence of this dilemma, "As 1900 drew to an end, the United States found itself in possession of an island that it could neither fully retain nor completely release, confronting the imminent ascendancy of the very political forces that the intervention had been designed to contain."[93] As a result of the pressure to withdraw and the subsequent premature evacuation, the United States left behind critical weaknesses that made it likely that the occupation would fail.

First, the political institutions created by the United States were unstable and not given the time to solidify and stabilize. Although an American-style constitution was adopted, elections in Cuba were plagued by fraud and boycotts that delegitimized the Cuban political system. As William Howard Taft observed prior to taking over as military governor in 1906, "The truth is that the Cuban government has proven to be nothing but a house of cards."[94] By leaving too early, the United States only made it more likely that the new Cuban government was going fail.

Second, the United States did not provide the necessary security guarantee. Even though the Platt Amendment ostensibly provided security, it actually undermined the stability of the postoccupation Cuban government. During its period of occupation, the United States did not create a responsible and reliable Cuban national army that could maintain security after the United States withdrew. The Cuban army had fought a long and bloody war against Spain and then was bought out of existence when the American occupation began.[95] All that was left behind to maintain security in Cuba was a small rural guard of approximately three thousand poorly trained Cubans. Moreover, this rural guard was a product of the American occupation, and therefore, lacked legitimacy as a Cuban national army.[96] The United States was forced to reoccupy Cuba when it recognized that the Cuban military itself was going to be incapable of stopping the larger rebel force from successfully overthrowing the Moderate government.[97]

Third, the U.S. withdrawal under the Platt Amendment was designed to fail. As was anticipated by some U.S. senators, the Platt Amendment created a perverse incentive for groups to agitate in order to precipitate a U.S. intervention. Senator Joseph Foraker of Ohio warned, "If we adopt this amendment . . . [it] would seem to invite intervention. . . . It seems that instead of having a restraining influence it would have an exciting influence and that the very result the committee evidently sought to accomplish would be defeated and the opposite would be the result."[98]

Foraker's worry was prescient. In 1906, both the Liberals and Moderates expected that the Platt Amendment would force the United States to come in and rescue them. If the Platt Amendment was, in fact, designed to foster the future annexation of Cuba, these plans too backfired. When the United States was forced to reintervene in Cuba in 1906, all ambition of annexing Cuba was lost in the United States.[99] While there is no guarantee that a longer occupation would have created stable and sustainable Cuban political institutions, it is clear that the U.S. withdrawal in 1902 was premature and only bred further instability on the island.

The British Occupation of Egypt, 1882–1954

The British entered Egypt in 1882 with a desire to restore order and withdraw as quickly as possible. Shortly after the occupation began, however, British authorities recognized that if they withdrew there was a significant chance that British interests in Egypt would be unsafe and that the anti-European nationalists in Egypt might succeed in gaining power. As a consequence, the British gradually became ensconced in Egypt. Afaf Lufti Al-Sayyid concludes, "Between the years 1882 and 1907 England made nearly one hundred and twenty declarations and pledges of its intention to evacuate Egypt, and at the same time, initiated actions, each of which established its power in Egypt more securely."[100] Ending the occupation became unthinkable, and occupation transformed into colonialism. A strategy initially described as "rescue and retire" had turned into a strategy of "rescue and reside."[101] The British confronted a classic occupation dilemma. Unlike the United States in Cuba, Great Britain responded to the dilemma by extending a failing occupation.

I focus on the initial period of the occupation from 1882 until 1907 when the occupation was run primarily by Evelyn Baring (elevated to the peerage as the first earl of Cromer in 1892). By the end of Cromer's tenure, the British presence had transformed from a military occupation into a colonial venture.

GOALS AND MEANS

Years of growing European consternation over the leadership in Egypt culminated in the British occupation of Egypt in the summer of 1882. Egypt had acquired nearly 100 million pounds of debt in order to finance construction of the Suez Canal, and European bondholders and their governments were concerned about the ability of the Egyptian government to repay that debt. With the completion of the canal in 1869, the strategic significance of Egypt increased enormously. Were Egypt and the canal to fall into unfriendly hands, the British would have been deprived of the most expeditious route to its colonies in Central and South Asia.

In the mid 1870s, Great Britain and France attempted to gain more control over Egyptian finances and the maintenance of Egypt's debt. In the summer of 1875, over the objections of Liberal leader William Gladstone, the British purchased 176,602 shares (a 44% interest) in the Suez Canal Company from the Egyptian khedive Ismail for 4 million pounds.[102] Within a year after the British bought the canal shares, Ismail accepted the advice of the French and formed the Caisse de la Dette Publique, a commission composed of European ministers that was to manage Egyptian finances and the repayment of European bondholders. Still rivals, Britain and France were now jointly in control of the Egyptian debt.

Three years later in 1879, a nationalist movement began to emerge in Egypt. Under the leadership of Colonel Ahmed Urabi, the movement sought to end the favoritism toward Circassian officers within the Egyptian military.[103] In September 1881, Urabi's group issued a series of specific demands: they wanted all of the Egyptian ministers to be dismissed, a new parliament to be convened, and the size of the army increased to eighteen thousand men. Witnessing the tumult in Egyptian politics, Gladstone declared that "anarchy would not be permitted in Egypt."[104] Foreign Secretary Granville added that the only circumstance that would lead to British intervention in Egyptian affairs would be "a state of anarchy."[105]

On January 6, 1882, London and Paris issued a joint note affirming their support for the Egyptian khedive Tawfiq and his opposition to any nationalist movement. The note was delivered in the form of instructions to the British and French representatives in Cairo. In part, it read, "I have accordingly to instruct you to declare to the Khedive that the British and French Governments consider the maintenance of His Highness on the throne, on the terms laid down in the Sultan's *firman* and officially recognized by the two Governments, as alone able to guarantee, for the present and future, the good order and development of general prosperity in Egypt in which France and Great Britain are equally interested."[106] In early February, leaders of the Egyptian nationalists went to the khedive and demanded a change in government. Auckland Colvin, the British controller in Egypt, remarked, "I think we are rapidly approaching a state of affairs which differs little, if at all, from anarchy."[107]

The immediate cause of the British intervention in Egypt was the outbreak of riots in Alexandria on June 11, 1882. Several hundred people were either injured or killed in the riots, including at least fifty Europeans who were killed. The riots were immediately blamed on Urabi's nationalist movement, although historical perspective has muddied the waters of who was responsible for the riots.[108] Recalling Gladstone's standard for intervening in Egyptian affairs, Lord Dufferin, the British ambassador to the Ottoman Empire, observed, "It is no exaggeration to say that during the last few months absolute anarchy has reigned in Egypt."[109]

In early July, Prime Minister Gladstone authorized the British admiral on the scene, Admiral Beauchamp Seymour, to issue an ultimatum to the Egyptian nationalists to cease building fortifications in the port of Alexandria.[110] On July 11, the day after a final ultimatum was issued, the British fleet bombarded Alexandria. Urabi and his followers set Alexandria aflame and withdrew to the town of Tel el-Kebir. A small British force was dispatched from Cyprus to restore order in Alexandria, and Tawfiq, recognizing the precariousness of his position, placed himself under the protection of Admiral Seymour.

Following the bombardment, the British attempted to rally an international force to help settle the situation in Egypt. Both the French and the Turks were, however, reluctant to intervene in Egypt. The British, then, faced a choice: either pursue Urabi and attempt to end his rebellion themselves or withdraw and likely see Egypt again descend into chaos. By late July, the House of Commons had approved a credit of 2.3 million pounds to support an expeditionary force in Egypt.[111]

On August 11, a British expeditionary force of approximately thirty thousand troops under the command of General Garnet Wolseley arrived in Alexandria. Wolseley's troops pursued Urabi to Tel el-Kebir, where they decisively defeated the nationalist forces.[112] Without much forethought, the British now found themselves in control of Egypt. Urabi and his nationalist followers had been routed, and the khedive owed his continuing authority to the British intervention. The occupation of Egypt had begun.

The objectives of the British occupation of Egypt remain a matter of some debate. Some argue that the intervention was fought primarily on behalf of bondholders.[113] When it became clear that the position of the khedive was not secure, London felt it necessary to intervene to protect its financial interests. A second possible motive focuses on strategic priorities. The British were determined to maintain access to the Suez Canal, which provided a quicker route to British colonies in South and Central Asia than the longer voyage around the Cape of Good Hope.[114] Eighty-nine percent of the shipping through the Suez Canal was British.[115] London was greatly concerned by the prospect that the canal could come under the control of either Egyptian nationalists or France.[116] Speaking to the House of Commons, Charles Dilke, the Foreign Office spokesman in the House of Commons, identified both a commercial and a political interest in the canal as it was the "principal highway to India, Ceylon, the Straits, and British Burmah, where 250,000,000 people live under our rule."[117]

Prime Minister Gladstone was initially quite reluctant to undertake the occupation of Egypt. As leader of the Liberal Party, Gladstone urged Britain to refrain from further imperialism and endorsed a general policy of encouraging national self-determination.[118] In rejecting a potential occupation of Egypt, Gladstone wrote that the occupation would produce "a great empire in each of the four quarters of the world, and with the whole new or fifth quarter to ourselves, we may be territorially content, but less than ever at ease."[119] Gladstone also thought that imperialism would unnecessarily antagonize Britain's rivals in Europe. In the same 1877 article, Gladstone predicted, "My belief is that the day, which witnesses our occupation of Egypt, will bid a long farewell to all cordiality of political relations between France and England."[120]

Gladstone was skeptical of both of the justifications for the British intervention in Egypt. The prime minister maintained that the British could survive even if the Suez Canal was blocked off, as the British had a readily accessible route around the Cape of Good Hope. As he commented, it "seems to be forgotten by many that there is a route to India round the Cape of Good Hope."[121] Gladstone had opposed the British purchase of additional canal shares in 1875 precisely because it might commit the British to intervention on behalf of bondholders.[122] In early 1882, Gladstone seemed to endorse the agenda of the Egyptian nationalists, "'Egypt for the Egyptians' is the sentiment to which I should wish to give scope and could it prevail it would I think be the best, the only good solution for the 'Egyptian question.'"[123] Or, as Gladstone elsewhere declared, "An indefinite occupation would be absolutely at variance with all the principles and views of Her Majesty's Government, and the pledge they have given to Europe."[124] Finally, on August 10, 1882, Gladstone answered a question about his intentions in Egypt in the House of Commons, "I can go so far as to answer the honourable gentleman when he asks me whether we contemplate an indefinite occupation of Egypt. Undoubtedly, of all things in the world, that is a thing which we are not going to do."[125] Ultimately, Gladstone reconciled himself to intervention by distinguishing the rebellious Urabist movement, which had to be defeated, from his more general wish that Egypt govern itself.[126] Still, Gladstone maintained, "It is madness to suppose that we can undertake the Government of Egypt . . . a Mahometan country, in the heart of the Mahometan world, with a population antagonistic to Europeans."[127]

Gladstone was not the only British leader who was skeptical of the intervention. Edward Malet, the British consul general in Egypt at the time of the intervention, expressed his skepticism at the proposed intervention, "I trust there may be a way out of the difficulty, for I own to having repugnance to a war engaged on behalf of bondholders and which would have for effect to repress the first attempt of a Musselman country at Parliamentary Government. It seems unnatural for England to do this."[128]

Yet by the fall of 1882, the British had indeed invaded and occupied Egypt. From London's perspective, there appeared to be few alternatives. If Britain did not take control, then either a military dictatorship under Urabi or an unstable monarchy under Tawfiq was likely to be the outcome.[129] The real question was what were the British to do with Egypt now that it was under their control and how could Britain establish the conditions that would allow for its withdrawal. Gladstone came to accept that the occupation might be necessary, and in fact, he idealistically argued that "there is reason to hope that when the incubus which now afflicts her is removed, and a reign of law is substituted for that of military violence, something may be founded there which may give hope for the future . . . a noble thirst may arise for the attainment of those blessings of civilized life which they see have been achieved in so many countries in Europe."[130]

CONDUCT OF THE OCCUPATION

The British did not enjoy a favorable threat environment when they first entered Egypt. No threat appeared graver to Egyptian nationalists than the threat of European, either British or French, colonialism. To develop a plan for managing the occupation of Egypt and the resistance that they might face, London dispatched Lord Dufferin to Egypt in November 1882.

In early February 1883, Dufferin reported back to London on what he had found. In general, he suggested that the British should "content ourselves with a more moderate role, and make the Egyptians comprehend that instead of desiring to impose on them an indirect but arbitrary role, we are sincerely desirous of enabling them to govern themselves."[131] Dufferin's report, however, posed a dilemma to the British government. Gladstone was anxious to evacuate Egypt as quickly as possible, leaving "Egypt for the Egyptians," but Dufferin's report suggested reforms that simply could not be accomplished in a short period of time.[132] Already, the contours of the occupation dilemma were becoming apparent.

To undertake the occupation of Egypt, Gladstone's government turned to Evelyn Baring to be the new consul general to Egypt in the summer of 1883. Baring had extensive experience as a proconsul, having served in the British administration in India, and in Egypt, where he was a commissioner on the Caisse de la Dette Publique in the late 1870s.[133] Baring's instructions were to implement the reforms suggested in Lord Dufferin's report, but he was also encouraged to conclude the occupation in months, not years.[134]

Like the Liberal leaders in London, Baring initially resisted a lengthy occupation of Egypt. Once stability had been restored in Egypt, Baring favored retiring "from the scene as soon as we could do so with dignity."[135] Three main issues, however, confronted Baring when he arrived in Egypt and precluded a hasty end to the occupation.

First, to the south in Sudan, the Mahdist movement—a messianic Muslim religious movement inspired by Muhammad Ahmad—was growing in strength and posed an increasingly serious threat to Egyptian security. Stability in Sudan could not be attained without extending the British military intervention, but such an intervention would only further ensconce the British in northern Africa. In the fall of 1883, Colonel William Hicks and his army were sent to Sudan to destroy the Mahdists. Instead, however, both Hicks's army and the rescue mission of General Charles Gordon were destroyed.[136] Unable to defeat the Mahdists, the British now had to offer protection to the khedive in Cairo or face the prospect of religious nationalists taking over in Egypt.[137] By early January 1884, Baring wrote to Foreign Minister Granville, "I do not think there is the smallest chance our getting away in a shorter time [than five years]."[138]

Second, Egyptian finances were unstable. When the occupation began in 1882, the total debt of Egypt equaled nearly $100 million pounds. In the first few years of the occupation, little relief was offered for the Egyptian debt, and the House of Commons grew reluctant to approve anymore expenditures on Egypt, especially after the debacle in the Sudan.[139] Finally, in London in March 1885, an agreement was reached to restructure Egyptian finances, including an international loan of 9 million pounds.[140] By 1889, Egypt had achieved financial solvency, representing one of the great successes of the British occupation.

Finally, the British recognized that they could not withdraw from Egypt unless a reliable government was in place. Anti-European Egyptian nationalism had been suppressed in 1882, but the khedive was a weakened British puppet in the aftermath of the intervention. As Baring argued in 1886, "I do not say that our occupation of Egypt need last for ever. It may be that at some future time we may be able to withdraw. The country is too civilized and too closely connected with Europe to be able to fall back in the tranquil oriental barbarism of former days. But it is not civilized enough to walk by itself."[141] Throughout the 1880s, Baring found it increasingly difficult to consider withdrawal from Egypt because he was unconvinced that the Egyptians were capable of stable self-rule.[142]

Thus, Baring soon recognized that none of the three goals of security, solvency, and stability could be accomplished in a manner that would allow the occupation to end in months rather than years. In a classic expression of the occupation dilemma, Baring wrote, "Two alternative policies were open to the British Government. These were, first, the policy of speedy evacuation; and, secondly, the policy of reform. It was not sufficiently understood that the adoption of one of these policies was wholly destructive of the other."[143]

THE "VEILED PROTECTORATE"

In 1885, the liberal government of William Gladstone was replaced by a conservative government under Lord Salisbury. Salisbury was ideologically more inclined to support the expansion of the British Empire, but even he was not in favor of a sustained British presence in Egypt. In particular, Salisbury was skeptical of the British occupation of Egypt because of the damage that it had done and could do in the future to British relations with France, which he saw as far more important to the overall direction of British grand strategy. Salisbury also recognized that the British occupation was not particularly popular with many Egyptians or with many Britons, for that matter.[144] On taking over as prime minister, he wrote, "Relief from our hated presence is the one benefit we have to offer."[145]

While hoping for withdrawal, Salisbury also appreciated the strategic significance of Egypt, so he sought a way that Britain could evacuate Egypt while still maintaining control over access to the Suez Canal. Alluding to geopolitics, Baring argued, "Getting out of Egypt is a very different problem than getting out of Afghanistan."[146] In 1886, Baring further warned, "All I say is that we certainly cannot withdraw at present, and that it would be the highest degree imprudent to fix any time at which we would engage to withdraw."[147]

Salisbury resolved to seek a diplomatic agreement with other European powers that would protect British interests in Egypt while facilitating a withdrawal. The prime minister dispatched Sir Henry Drummond Wolff to Turkey with a mandate to find a diplomatic solution. Drummond Wolff was to "secure for this country the amount of influence which is necessary for its own Imperial interest, and, subject to that condition, to provide a strong and efficient Egyptian government, as free as possible from foreign interference."[148] Salisbury also instructed Drummond Wolff to attempt to use Egypt as a bargaining chip in Britain's larger diplomatic game with Europe. Britain should get something from the rest of Europe were it to agree to withdraw from Egypt.

In May 1887, the Drummond Wolff Convention was preliminarily agreed to between Britain and the Ottoman Empire. The convention called for the withdrawal of British troops within three years as long as there was no threat to Egyptian security and stability either from internal or external sources. In addition, should such a threat arise after Britain withdrew, the convention stipulated that both Britain and the Ottoman Empire reserved the right to reoccupy the country to restore stability. The convention not only called for approval by Britain and the Ottoman Empire, but also by the five other major European powers—Germany, France, Austria-Hungary, Russia, and Italy. Creatively, Salisbury argued that if the other five European powers refused to sign the convention, then that would constitute an external threat to Egypt, and Britain's obligation to withdraw from Egypt would be abrogated.[149]

Baring offered his congratulations to Drummond Wolff on agreement to the convention. "We must now try and set on its legs a machine that will work after we go," Baring wrote to Drummond Wolff.[150] France and Russia, however, immediately objected to the terms of the convention, especially the right of intervention reserved by the British, and placed heavy pressure on Constantinople to do the same. By the summer of 1887, the convention had fallen apart.

The British reacted to the failure of the Drummond Wolff Convention by tightening their control over Egypt. This was to become the British pattern in Egypt: any trouble would be met with tighter controls that only made it more difficult for the British to contemplate withdrawal. As time went on, the British simply fell deeper into the occupation dilemma, unsatisfied with an extended occupation but unable to locate a satisfactory withdrawal strategy. London concluded that it could not trust Paris, St. Petersburg, or Constantinople, so it must remain in Egypt to ensure the security of its interests there.[151] Salisbury lamented, "I heartily wish we had never gone into Egypt. Had we not done so we could snap our fingers at all the world."[152]

The prime minister remained convinced that Britain's ambitions in Egypt should be modest. "Interference with the internal government [of Egypt] is no part of our political aim and should only be practiced so far as the higher dictates of humanity require. . . . I do not believe in the plan of moulding the Egyptians to our civilization."[153] Baring, meanwhile, recognized the difficulty of the task confronting the British: the only way to secure British interests was to prevent future revolution within Egypt, but the only way to prevent revolution was by extending the occupation. If the Egyptians were not yet ready to govern themselves, then the British must remain. As Salisbury declared in August 1888, "The moment we are satisfied that [a stable and secure regime] exists, we shall gladly relieve ourselves of an unnecessary burden."[154]

By the end of the 1880s, Britain had consolidated its indirect rule over Egypt. In an effort to placate any remaining nationalist Egyptians, the British administration applied a relatively light touch while also trying to win over the Egyptian population with a strategy of inducement that was evident in a series of economic reforms. Baring sought to eliminate corruption in the Egyptian political system and abolish the corvée system of forced labor.[155] All of this, Baring thought, would satisfy the Egyptian nationalists while allowing the British to continue their occupation. In Baring's view, "It would be difficult for me to exaggerate the total want of capable native administrators—there are none."[156] As Baring wrote to Salisbury, "Until a race of Egyptians has arisen far more competent than any which now exists, the evacuation of the country by the British Army would be attended with very grave risks."[157] By the end of the 1880s, Baring observed, "The main argument [for continuing the occupation] is based on the incapacity of the ruling classes in this country. I am more and more struck with this the longer I remain here. . . . The more I look at it, the more does the evacuation policy appear to be impossible under any condition."[158] The paradox, of course, was that Baring's reforms and increasing authority over Egypt prevented the emergence of an effective Egyptian governing class.[159]

By the end of the 1880s, Egypt had become a "veiled protectorate of uncertain extent and indefinite duration for the accomplishment of a difficult and distant object."[160] Not only did Baring believe that the situation required that the British remain in Egypt, but he also maintained that the Egyptians welcomed the occupation, "I do not believe that there are a dozen people in the country who really wish us to go."[161] The British had emerged out of the first hopeful phase of the occupation dilemma and entered the second phase wherein withdrawal becomes difficult to fathom as the occupying power becomes more essential to the survival of the occupied territory.

THE RETURN OF EGYPTIAN NATIONALISM

Unlike some other cases of occupation, the British occupation of Egypt encountered little sustained violent resistance from the occupied population. In the face of an unfavorable threat environment, British forces squashed the Egyptian nationalist movement in their initial 1882 intervention. With the exception of some passive resistance to the British occupation, aggressive demonstrations of nationalism were absent in Egypt in the 1880's, providing the British with a window of opportunity to implement an inducement strategy in the shape of a series of economic reforms.[162]

Baring's attempt at inducement, however, had two flaws. First, although the British did implement improvements in the Egyptian irrigation system, the common Egyptian peasant saw little benefit. As Robert Tignor concludes, "During 30 years of occupation there was the continued growth of large estates, the continued impoverishment of the small peasantry by the reduction of landholdings, and the loss of proprietary rights."[163] Second, material reward was not sufficient to satisfy the Egyptian population. Egyptians wanted to be able to govern themselves, and the British showed few signs of allowing this type of self-determination. Baring himself eventually recognized that the economic improvements in Egypt had not brought much reward in the form of improved governance or social services.[164]

In the 1890s, Egyptian nationalism awoke from its decade-long doldrums. Nationalist sentiment in the media, among religious leaders, and among students began to grow in strength. Groups gathered in salons to discuss their nationalist ambitions and opposition to the continuing occupation.[165] The earlier nationalist slogan of "Egypt for the Egyptians" was revived and open opposition to British control of Egypt increased. The nationalist leaders disagreed among themselves about how best to pursue independence from Britain, but what they all shared was opposition to the continuation of British rule in Egypt.[166]

When Khedive Tawfiq died in January 1892 and was replaced by his son Abbas, an eighteen-year-old who was studying in Vienna at the time of his father's death, Egyptian nationalism received an additional impetus. Whereas Tawfiq owed his survival as the leader of Egypt to the British, Khedive Abbas II was soon to challenge British authority in Egypt. Abbas was intent on taking advantage of signs that Britain was growing tired of the occupation in order to push for a complete restoration of Egyptian sovereignty. For example, Gladstone had declared in October 1891 that the occupation was "burdensome and embarrassing" to England, and the British press reported that London was less inclined to intervene in Egyptian domestic matters than it had been previously.[167]

Within a year, relations between Baring—now elevated to Lord Cromer—and Abbas were in crisis. Problems initially arose over Abbas's attempt to replace the ailing prime minister Fahmy with the nationalist Tigrane. Though Abbas's attempt was ultimately rebuffed, Cromer was forced to compromise, leading to increasing concern about the independence that the new khedive was exhibiting. "The young Khedive is evidently going to give a great deal of trouble," wrote Cromer to the foreign minister Rosebery, "He is an extremely foolish youth. It is difficult to know how to deal with him. I think he will have to receive a sharp lesson—the sooner the better."[168]

Sensing trouble, Cromer wired to London to request an increase in the number of occupation troops. As Cromer wrote to Rosebery on January 20, "The system under which Egypt has been governed for the last ten years has broken down. It was always very artificial and unsatisfactory and the wonder is that it has lasted so long. I cannot carry it on successfully any longer. You will have to choose between going backwards or forwards, i.e., either asserting yourself more strongly or retiring from the country."[169] What had "broken down" was the British strategy of indirect rule over a population that was increasingly nationalistic. That same day, January 20, hostile demonstrations against the British and in favor of the khedive broke out in Cairo. Cromer now called for more assertiveness—more coercion—in order to control the increasing nationalist agitation in Egypt. Gladstone, again prime minister, was skeptical, "I would as soon set a torch to Westminster Abbey as send troops to Egypt."[170]

Once again, faced with the prospect of an ignominious withdrawal or prolonging a difficult occupation, the British opted to extend and intensify their control over Egypt. Despite Gladstone's reluctance to continue the mission in Egypt, Rosebery, on behalf of Cromer, was able to convince the cabinet to dispatch an additional battalion of British infantry to Egypt.[171] With an antagonistic khedive, Cromer argued that Britain must "assert ourselves much more strongly than heretofore."[172] In addition to the increase in British troops, Cromer responded to the surge in nationalist activity in Egypt by asserting more control over the political situation in Egypt. British advisers, who had limited their involvement to being observers under Tawfiq, were now required to be consulted on any proposals being considered by the ministers of Justice, War, and Public Works.[173] In addition, the British asserted control over the Egyptian higher education system from where they feared young Egyptian nationalists would emerge.[174] Again, in the face of trouble, the British only tightened their authority over Egypt.

Over the course of the next year, two additional crises called the British occupation strategy into question. First, in the fall of 1893, the Egyptian government for the first time asked the British to leave and refused to continue paying for the British army of occupation as they had been since the occupation began in 1882. As Cromer reported to Rosebery, "For the first time an Egyptian Government, backed by the Legislative Council, has publicly and officially declared that they want us to go . . . under the inspiration of an inexperienced and headstrong boy of no particular talent who probably would not be able to maintain himself in power for six months without our assistance."[175]

Second, on a tour of Egyptian frontier posts, the khedive remarked to Herbert Kitchener, the British commander of the Egyptian army, "To tell you the truth, Kitchener Pasha, I think it is disgraceful for Egypt to be served by such an army."[176] Kitchener immediately insisted that Abbas apologize for his affront to the British Army, but he refused. On hearing of the incident, Cromer capitalized on the khedive's words to call for forceful action against the Egyptian leader. Cromer wrote, "This was the opportunity for which I had been waiting . . . the Khedive richly deserved to be punished."[177] Rosebery offered a thinly veiled threat that such behavior by the khedive could result in British annexation of Egypt, and London authorized Cromer to demand that Abbas issue a commendation of the British army. Recognizing the seriousness of the threat from London and the prospect that British public opinion might support more assertive action in Egypt, Abbas eventually submitted to the British demands.[178]

The crises of 1893–94 had two consequences. First, the British reaction to the crises demonstrated the coercive response of London to increasing Egyptian nationalism. Sir Reginald Wingate, governor of Sudan, wrote that the British had created a "huge Frankenstein"—Egyptian nationalism—"and now we must do our best to stifle the monster."[179] Although the British did not resort to force to control demonstrations in 1893, the latent coercive threat of British annexation of Egypt was used to cow the Egyptian opposition.[180] Second, the crises only hardened the divide between the British and the Egyptian nationalists. Cromer told Rosebery of "the sullen hostility of the whole Government; British officials are being practically boycotted and so are natives with sympathies with England."[181] In response, the British dismissed the Egyptian nationalists as a small minority that they would not engage, while the Egyptian nationalists only became more discouraged about the prospects for genuine self-rule in Egypt.[182] Abbas's initial attempt to stand up to the British occupation administration had been put down by Cromer, but this did not mean that Egyptian nationalism had again been extinguished.

THE OCCUPATION DILEMMA IN EGYPT

Cromer consistently responded to the occupation dilemma by attempting to exert an even stronger hold on Egyptian society. At the end of 1905, however, the Liberal Party regained power in Britain, making Cromer's position in Egypt precarious. Three events then combined in 1906 to prompt London to consider a fundamental change in its policies in Egypt. First, in March, a small detachment of Turkish troops was observed in the small village of Taba, on the Sinai Peninsula. Cromer was bothered by the apparent Turkish encroachment toward the Suez Canal, but the Turkish move received the support of both the khedive and the Egyptian nationalists and appeared to challenge British authority in Egypt.[183] Second, on the heels of the Taba crisis, an unprecedented strike broke out among Egyptian law students espousing nationalist ambitions. The students only backed down after Cromer intervened to mediate between the students and the director of the law school.

Third and most significantly, the Dinshaway incident in June raised alarm both in Egypt and, more important, in London about the fate of the occupation. The Dinshaway incident began when a detachment of British army officers stopped for a rest outside of the village of Dinshaway. The officers began pigeon-shooting, leading to an altercation between the officers and the villagers. One British officer ultimately died as a result of the injuries suffered in the dispute. The British response to the Dinshaway incident was quite severe. A special tribunal was established to prosecute the villagers for the murder of the British officer. On June 27, following a dubious trial of fifty-two men, twenty-one were convicted with four men sentenced to hang. Shortly thereafter, the executions were carried out publicly in Dinshaway.[184]

The Dinshaway incident had significant implications for the ongoing British presence in Egypt. The disproportional response of the British to the incident demonstrated to many that the British were more interested in sending a message to any potential opponents of the occupation than in meting out just punishment. In the wake of the incident, the first Egyptian political parties— the *Ummah* Party, National Party, and the Constitutional Reform Party—were founded. Again, far from extinguishing antioccupation nationalism, the reaction to the Dinshaway incident was a catalyst for further nationalist agitation, much of it directed against the khedive himself with whom the nationalists had now grown dissatisfied.[185] Finally, the seemingly unfair special tribunal at Dinshaway raised grave concerns in Britain about the direction of the occupation.[186] Was this really the way that "liberal" Victorian imperialists were going to behave?[187]

In May 1907, Lord Cromer departed Egypt and was replaced by Eldon Gorst.[188] Responding to the deteriorating relations of the last year of the Cromer era, Gorst adopted a more cooperative approach toward Egyptian nationalism. Rather than discounting nationalism as the views of a small minority, as Cromer had done, Gorst resolved to repair relations with the khedive and, thereby, attempt to satisfy the Egyptian nationalists. Cooperation with the khedive, however, was not the way to appease many Egyptian nationalists. Egypt's nationalists were, in fact, disappointed that the khedive appeared now to be willing to compromise with the new British administration.[189]

Gorst died in the summer of 1912 and was replaced by Herbert Kitchener. The more liberal policies of Gorst were abandoned, especially with the arrival of World War I. In 1914, Egypt formally became a protectorate of Great Britain in anticipation of its strategic significance in World War I. In 1919, Egyptian nationalism asserted itself in its most violent form yet with a successful revolution that was followed by negotiations toward a meaningless form of Egyptian independence.[190] Only in 1936 did the British finally agree to a treaty creating an independent Egypt that was a member of the League of Nations. As part of this treaty, however, Great Britain was entitled to retain troops in Egypt and the Suez Canal to protect its interests. Finally, in 1954—seventy-two years after it began as an occupation intended to be short and limited—the British withdrew completely from Egypt.

EVALUATING THE OCCUPATION OF EGYPT

The British occupation of Egypt demonstrates the difficulty with judging whether an occupation succeeded or failed. On the success side of the ledger, one could include the strategic value of maintaining control over the Suez Canal. Access to the canal was one of the initial justifications for the intervention in 1882, and control over Egypt was strategically valuable in both World Wars.

On the negative side, the occupation was both costly and lengthy. The Egyptians themselves were initially forced to pay the costs of supporting and supplying the British troops in Egypt, but the British were responsible for managing the Egyptian debt when they occupied the country. The British parliament became increasingly wary of further expenditures in Egypt. Baring wrote to Childers, the chancellor of the exchequer, "The main question . . . is this—who is to be sacrificed, the bondholders or the English taxpayers? You will either have to reduce the rate of interest on the debt or bear the expense of the army. The alternatives are exceedingly unpleasant, but they have to be faced."[191]

In terms of length, the initial British goal was to "rescue and retire" from Egypt. Intervene quickly, restore the power of the khedive, and withdraw the troops. Within a decade, however, the British presence in Egypt had transformed into a permanent occupation. It took seventy-two years, until 1954, for the final British troops to withdraw from Egypt. If the British were sincere in their goal of short occupation—and there is every reason to believe that Gladstone especially was sincere—then the length of the occupation must be deemed a considerable failure.

The British had to stay so long in Egypt because their goal of restoring political order in Egypt was easier said than done. As Robinson and Gallagher write, "The occupation had to go on because it was the only way of retaining supremacy and keeping the lid on the unresolved internal crisis."[192] London did not want to withdraw from Egypt only to face reintervention shortly thereafter. If a primary British goal was to create a stable and sustainable political system that allowed the British to withdraw in a timely manner, then this too must be considered a failure of the occupation.

Finally, one must ask whether there were reasonable alternatives to the British occupation. The Egyptians did face significant financial and governance problems in the early 1880s that could not have been easily resolved.[193] Where there was a failure was not necessarily in the decision to intervene, but in the supposition that the goals of occupation could be achieved quickly or easily. British historian Niall Ferguson maintains that the British never actually intended to carry out a short-term occupation of Egypt.[194] In his view, the repeated declarations of intentions to withdraw were "willful hypocrisy" on London's behalf. To the contrary, the evidence indicates that Gladstone was genuinely intent on foregoing any further British imperialism, but once in Egypt, the British, like other occupiers, were inexorably pulled into more and more control of the territory.

The threat environment in Egypt was not conducive to occupation success. There was no external threat to Egypt perceived by both sides. While the British intervention was initially motivated, in part, by concerns about control of the Suez Canal and a potential French threat to the canal, the Egyptians were most interested in their own national self-determination. While Egyptian nationalism was quiet for much of the 1880s, it returned in the 1890s.

As for British occupation strategies, in the absence of effective coercion, Britain's more cooperative strategies failed in the 1890s when Egyptian nationalism was resurgent. Cromer was hopeful that an inducement strategy could improve the welfare of Egyptians, and they then would remain peaceful in the face of continued occupation.[195] Cromer's inducement strategy, however, had two fatal flaws. First, while Cromer's reforms did improve the economic condition of much of Egypt, these economic benefits did not trickle down to common Egyptians.[196] Instead, most of the benefits were captured by the wealthy, landed class within Egypt. In 1908, a Turkish diplomat observed to a British colleague, "Look at Egypt—since you have been there you have made millionaires but you haven't raised the *fellaheen* [peasants] one bit."[197] Second, as anticipated by my theoretical argument above, economic benefits were not sufficient to squash the self-determination goals of Egyptian nationalists. Nationalists were unwilling to suppress their nationalist desires for the sake of elusive economic benefits.

British attempts at political accommodation also failed in the absence of effective coercion. The British style of indirect rule inhibited significant reform and created confusion about political authority within Egypt.[198] Any political leaders who demonstrated an independent or rebellious streak was summarily dismissed from power. As Michael Doyle persuasively argues, the British political strategy was to balance cooperation with those willing to collaborate while avoiding antagonizing Egyptian nationalists.[199] This strategy succeeded during the 1880s when Egyptian nationalism went dormant but was increasingly difficult to sustain in the 1890s when it became more assertive. When the more nationalist Abbas replaced the subordinate Tawfiq in 1892, the British responded by tightening their grip on Egyptian society. Far from quieting the Egyptian population, this increased control over Egypt only motivated the nationalists.

In the face of an unfavorable threat environment, success in the occupation of Egypt would have required additional British coercion, but the British mostly abstained from the use of military force. Early in the occupation, Baring seemed to be inclined toward more coercive tactics. "Give me 2,000 men and power to settle matters between the English and Egyptian governments, and I will guarantee that in twelve months there shall not be a British soldier in Egypt, and that the country is put in such a position as to render it very improbable that any Egyptian question will be raised again for many years to come at all events."[200] London demurred, however, and was reluctant to endorse such a coercive strategy for controlling Egypt. After the new khedive assumed the throne in 1892, the British clamped down on society, but they refrained from the use of extensive violent force other than the latent threat of annexation. When the British did try and use force to control Egyptian nationalism, as at Dinshaway, the use of coercion only further agitated the nationalists.[201] The use of more aggressive, coercive tactics might have defeated nationalist resistance, but the danger is that unsuccessful strategies of coercion would only have exacerbated resistance.[202] As Al-Sayyid argues, "perhaps had the British ruled Egypt in a more brutal manner, had there been more than one [Dinshaway] incident, the revolution might have come earlier."[203] Unless the British were willing to commit substantially more resources and troops to Egypt—which was unlikely given the geopolitical priorities of the British at this time—it is doubtful that a strategy of violent coercion would have enabled the British to accomplish their goals more expeditiously.

One puzzle, however, remains: why did the occupation of Egypt last for seventy-two years? The transformation of the British occupation of Egypt from a short-term occupation into an extended, colonial stay conforms with the occupation dilemma model. Recall that in the first phase of this dilemma, the occupying power enters the occupied territory unjustifiably optimistic about their capabilities to achieve their occupation goals in a timely manner. Resistance to the occupation may also be relatively weak in this initial "honeymoon period" as nationalists watch closely to gauge the true intentions of the occupying power. In the case of Egypt, William Gladstone initially believed that a short occupation could achieve the goals that he set for Egypt. Gladstone's colonial secretary Joseph Chamberlain claims, "In the early stage of our occupation we were all desirous of a speedy evacuation and believed that the conditions which we had down would be accomplished in the course of a year or two at the outside."[204] The commitment to a short occupation enabled the prime minister to reconcile his rejection of explicit colonialism with the need to intervene in Egypt to protect British strategic and economic interests.

In the second phase of the dilemma, the occupying power becomes increasingly entrenched in the occupied territory. The power becomes a great benefactor of its chosen political leader, and the economic interests of the occupying power in the occupied territory grow. In Egypt, much of the 1880s fit into this second phase. The Egyptian khedive was dependent on protection from the British, and the khedive, in turn, was fairly pliant. The British meanwhile took on Egyptian debt as well as investments in extensive infrastructure projects and financial reform that made it increasingly difficult for the British to contemplate withdrawal.

Finally, in the third phase an occupying power faces a difficult dilemma. In this phase, the occupying power recognizes that the goals of the occupation have not been achieved in the quick manner that they initially thought would be possible. Not only does the nationalist population of the occupied territory begin to resist the occupation, but domestic support for the occupation begins to erode. The occupying power must decide between withdrawing from the occupied territory with its goals unaccomplished and potentially having to reintervene in the future or continuing the occupation despite the prospect of nationalist resistance and the growing costs—both of sustaining the occupation and domestic political costs.

By the early 1890s, the third phase of occupation had begun in Egypt. With the resurgence of Egyptian nationalism after the death of Tawfiq, the British recognized that their presence in Egypt would essentially need to be permanent if they were going to protect their interests there. If the British had withdrawn, they conceivably would have lost all that Cromer had worked to establish in the previous ten years. If they stayed, however, they faced the prospect of increasingly strident nationalist opposition. In 1896, Cromer presented to Salisbury a laundry list of reasons why the British garrison needed to remain in Egypt:

(1) Elements of disorder and confusion abound
(2) The incapacity of the Egyptian governing classes
(3) The arbitrary disposition of the khedive
(4) The unreliability of a Moslem army officered by Christians
(5) Very ignorant and credulous population
(6) A host of incompetent and corrupt place-hunters
(7) A debased and unreasonable European population influenced by international rivalry and under no proper legal control
(8) A formidable foe on the frontier[205]

This was thirteen years after the occupation began! In fact, the British opted to stay, and nationalist resistance to the British occupation did increase, though full-fledged revolution did not occur until after World War I. Once World War I began, withdrawal became inconceivable as control over the Suez Canal became a strategic priority. In the first few decades of the occupation of Egypt, the British were never able to create a stable and secure government to which it could return power and withdraw. As a consequence, London faced a choice between withdrawing with its interests insecure or prolonging an unpopular occupation.

The case of the British occupation of Egypt illustrates one horn of the occupation dilemma: when an occupying power chooses to sustain a struggling occupation. As A. G. Hopkins concludes, "Britain had important interests to defend in Egypt and she was prepared to withdraw only if conditions guaranteeing the security of those interests were met—and they never were."[206] In 1896, the director of Naval Intelligence issued a confidential "Memorandum on Naval Policy Viewed under the Existing Conditions": "The advantages of holding the Suez Canal are bound up in the question of Egypt and need not be dwelt upon—but it may be said that if there was no Suez Canal, it would not be long before there was no India."[207] Even though this occupation certainly was not a complete failure, the occupation did not progress at the pace or in the manner that British leaders envisioned. Instead, the British were forced to maintain a continuing presence in Egypt. As Baring wrote to Lord Goschen in February 1890, "Many have come here with evacuation on the brain. I have not yet known a single case in which the disease has not been cured."[208]

The U.S. Occupation of Japan, 1945–1952

The occupation of Japan was arguably the most successful occupation in modern history. In less than seven years, the United States managed to transform Japan from an enemy into a reliable ally with a rapidly growing economy. Even more striking is that the Japanese, fire-bombed and then subjected to two atomic weapon attacks by the United States, accepted the occupation and cooperated in U.S. efforts to rebuild their country.

Why were the Japanese people willing to suppress their nationalist desires in deference to the American occupation, and why was the United States willing to pay the enormous cost of occupying and rebuilding Japan? My answer to both questions revolves around the threat environment confronting Japan at the end of World War II. The Japanese leadership recognized that the United States offered them valuable protection against the threat of Soviet-inspired communism. Leaders in Washington simultaneously identified Japan as a critical node in their strategy of containing the Soviet Union. This favorable threat environment allowed the United States to pursue a successful occupation strategy that focused more on accommodation and inducement rather than coercion. Finally, I ask why the United States was able to end the occupation of Japan in a successful manner? Unlike in other cases, the United States satisfied the two conditions for successful withdrawal in the case of Japan. First, the United States located a stable and reliable indigenous government to which it could return power, but, second, at the same time, the United States ensured that Japan would be both secure and nonthreatening to its neighbors. A propitious threat environment facilitated a timely and successful withdrawal by encouraging the United States to guarantee Japan's security.

GOALS AND MEANS

On August 15, 1945, a week after the second atomic weapon exploded over Nagasaki, Emperor Hirohito announced to his people that Japan had lost the Second World War. A few weeks later, on September 2, General Douglas MacArthur, representatives of nine other allied powers, and representatives of the Japanese military and government signed the instruments of surrender officially ending World War II.

As supreme commander of the Allied Powers, General MacArthur inherited the destruction left by World War II and undertook the occupation of Japan. The initial goals and liberal objectives of the occupation were delineated in three significant documents prepared in the summer and fall of 1945. First, the Potsdam Declaration, issued by the leaders of the United States, the United Kingdom, and China at the conclusion of the Potsdam Conference on July 26, 1945, called for the unconditional surrender and subsequent occupation of Japan, rejected any intention to "enslave" the Japanese people, and pledged that the occupying forces would be withdrawn from Japan "as soon as these objectives have been accomplished and there had been established in accordance with the freely expressed will of the Japanese people a peacefully inclined and responsible government."[209]

The second document, "United States Initial Post-Surrender Policy for Japan," identified two major goals for the U.S. occupation of Japan: prevent Japan from ever again becoming a menace to the United States or the security of the world and bring about the establishment of a "peaceful and responsible government." To achieve these ends, Japan's sovereignty would be limited to four major islands and assorted minor islands, the defeated nation would be disarmed and demilitarized, the Japanese people would be encouraged to respect certain human rights and individual liberties, and Japan would be permitted to establish a prosperous, but peaceful, economy.[210]

The "Initial Post-Surrender Policy" delineated four specific reforms that indicated the liberal spirit of the early occupation period. First, all proponents of militant nationalism in Japan should be excluded from the postwar government of Japan. Second, the occupation authority should encourage the establishment of a free labor movement. Third, the large banking and industrial conglomerates, the *zaibatsu,* that dominated the Japanese economy should be dissolved. Fourth, the occupation authority should permit the Japanese population to initiate any modifications in their form of government that they saw fit. The role of MacArthur and his staff was not to support any specific Japanese government, but rather to utilize whatever government was in place to achieve the larger goals of the occupation. At the same time that the initial policy statement was issued, General MacArthur was granted the explicit authority to implement reforms at his discretion: "Since your authority is supreme, you will not entertain any question on the part of the Japanese as to its scope."[211]

The third formative document, the "Basic Initial Post-Surrender Directive to Supreme Commander Allied Powers for the Occupation and Control of Japan" (also known as JCS 1380), was issued by the Joint Chiefs of Staff in conjunction with the State-War-Navy Coordinating Committee (SWNCC) on November 3, 1945. JCS 1380 offered even more detailed advice to General MacArthur on how to administer the occupation. Perhaps the most important provisions limited American involvement in the economic rehabilitation of Japan: the United States would not be responsible for rebuilding the Japanese economy, strikes were to be allowed unless they threatened the occupation forces, and imports were strictly limited to supplies needed in order to "prevent widespread disease or civil unrest as would endanger the occupation forces or interfere with military operation."[212]

MacArthur recognized the opportunity before the United States in Japan. "If we exert that influence in an imperialistic manner, or for the sole purpose of commercial advantage, then we shall lose our golden opportunity," wrote MacArthur. "But if our influence and our strength are expressed in terms of essential liberalism, we shall have the friendship and the cooperation of the Asiatic people far into the future."[213] While he noted the advice of those back in Washington, he also quickly developed his own priorities in the occupation: "First, destroy the military power. Punish war criminals. Build the structure of representative government. Modernize the constitution. Hold free elections. Enfranchise the women. Release the political prisoners. Liberate the farmers. Establish a free labor movement. Encourage a free economy. Abolish police oppression. Develop a free and responsible press. Liberalize education. Decentralize political power. Separate the church from state."[214] MacArthur's vision for Japan was ambitious: a liberal and neutralized Japan was to take the place of the conservative and militaristic Japan that had caused World War II in the Pacific.

CONDUCT OF THE OCCUPATION

MacArthur quickly went to work on achieving his goals. Directives 1 and 2 of the occupation authority called for the demobilization and disarmament of the Japanese military.[215] By the middle of October, less than two months later, MacArthur declared that Japanese forces had completed their demobilization and "ceased to exist as such."[216] On September 10, only days after the instruments of surrender had been agreed to, MacArthur issued Supreme Commander of the Allied Powers Instruction (SCAPIN) 16, which decreed that "there shall be an absolute minimum of restrictions upon freedom of speech."[217] SCAPIN 244, issued on November 6, called for the dissolution of the massive holding companies in which Japan's economic power had become concentrated.[218] On December 15, SCAPIN 448 abolished the state-sponsored Shinto religion.[219]

All of these steps were, however, simply precursors to the comprehensive constitutional reform that MacArthur envisioned. MacArthur hoped to accommodate Japanese nationalism by retaining the emperor in some role while providing Japan with a new, liberal constitution. As early as October 11, MacArthur met with Shidehara Kijuro, the Japanese prime minister, to inform him of five reforms that MacArthur would insist on and that would require rewriting the constitution. These reforms aimed to enfranchise women, encourage labor unions, institute a more liberal educational system, eliminate fear of the government in Japanese society, and promote a wider distribution of economic wealth.[220]

Perhaps the most important issue to be addressed in the new constitution was the role of the emperor in the new Japanese state. Among American policymakers there was an active debate between the old Japan hands, who believed that the imperial institution was critical to Japanese society, and the China hands, who advocated for the elimination of the emperor and the complete democratization of Japan.[221] The emperor himself opened up the possibility of reforming his role in Japanese society in his January 1, 1946, "Declaration of Humanity." In this rescript, drafted in cooperation with the American occupation authorities, Hirohito dispelled the mythological basis of the emperor's rule: "The ties between us and our people have always stood upon mutual trust and affection. They do not depend upon mere legends and myth. They are not predicated on the false conception that the Emperor is divine, and that the Japanese people are superior to other races and fated to rule the world."[222] By admitting that his power was not divine, the emperor permitted constitutional reform that would modify, but not completely eliminate, his role in the Japanese government. General MacArthur welcomed the emperor's rescript, "The Emperor's New Year's statement pleases me very much. By it he undertakes a leading part in the democratization of his people."[223]

On March 6, 1946, General MacArthur presented a first draft of the new constitution to the Japanese cabinet for consideration.[224] The constitution reflected the three goals that MacArthur hoped to achieve: maintaining the emperor in a symbolic role, disarming the Japanese state, and ending the feudal land system that had predominated in Japan.[225] Most notably, Article 9 of the proposed constitution called for the abolishment of war as "a means of settling disputes with other nations."[226]

A month later, a new Diet was elected to consider the new constitution. The Diet's debate over the constitution centered around the role of the emperor in the new constitution and the controversial Article 9 provision. Ultimately, the Diet overwhelmingly approved the new constitution with a vote of 421 to 8 in the House of Representatives and a vote of 298 to 2 in the House of Peers (which, in essence, was voting to abolish itself).[227] On November 3, the emperor promulgated the new constitution in a rescript confirming the approval of the Diet and "rejoic[ing] that the foundation for the construction of a new Japan has been laid according to the will of the Japanese people."[228] Six months later, the new Japanese constitution came into effect.

THE EMERGING SOVIET THREAT

At the same time that the new Japanese constitution was being adopted, larger geopolitical considerations began to have a direct effect on the conduct of the occupation. As in the simultaneous case of the Western occupation of Germany, the growing cold war tension between the United States and the Soviet Union granted additional significance to the occupation of Japan. Prior to 1947, the U.S. occupation was dominated by a series of liberal policies—including labor and land reforms, war crimes trials, and dissolution of the *zaibatsu*—aimed at fostering liberal democracy in Japan.[229] But, beginning in 1947, the liberal reform policies of the early occupation period with an emphasis on demilitarization and democratization began to recede.

In place of the early liberal policies, the "reverse course" policy of the United States sought to rebuild Japan and keep it out of the Soviet orbit.[230] In February 1948, 325 companies had been designated for possible reorganization under the anti-*zaibatsu* provisions of the constitution, but by April, the decision was made to exclude almost all of these companies from consideration. John Dower quotes a supporter of the economic deconcentration program, "Facts of the last war faded … and conjectures on the next war took their place."[231] This was the essence of the transition taking place in U.S. policy toward Japan: economic deconcentration, punishment of war criminals, and even democratization were being put on hold in deference to the geopolitical importance of Japan in the Cold War struggle with the Soviet Union. As John Dower retells, "*Until 1947*, leftists as well as liberals commonly regarded the overwhelmingly American occupation force as an army of liberation, and the notion of achieving a 'democratic revolution' under the eagle's wing was so widespread as to become an instant cliche."[232] As part of the Truman Doctrine commitment to preventing the spread of communism, President Truman recognized that, like Germany, Japanese recovery must be supported as a bulwark against Soviet expansion.[233] Economic recovery and prosperity in Germany and Japan had to be encouraged or else the expenses of occupation would drain American resources and likely leave economic chaos in both countries. Economic chaos, in turn, would make these societies vulnerable to the spread of communism. Once again, the threat environment in Japan at the time made success in Japan imperative for the United States.

George Kennan emerged as the most vocal advocate of reenergizing the Japanese economy as part of a global grand strategy of containment. For Kennan, balancing against the Soviet Union on the Eurasian land mass was "unthinkable as long as Germany and Japan remain power vacuums."[234] The State Department's Martin Report of March 1947 emphasized the need to reinvigorate Japan's economy in order to rebalance the emerging dollar gap in East Asia.[235] In April 1947, the Joint Chiefs of Staff concurred with Kennan that Japan was of particular importance in the struggle with the Soviet Union. Of "all the countries in the Pacific area," the JCS argued, "Japan deserves primary consideration for current United States assistance designed to restore her economic and military potential."[236] The SWNCC also agreed, issuing SWNCC 360, which proposed a massive aid program to Japan to assist in its economic recovery.[237]

MacArthur's own position differed from that being advanced by Kennan and others in Washington. The supreme commander still hoped that the liberal reforms of the early occupation could be salvaged in Japan, and he ultimately sought the creation of an independent, neutral Japan—the "Switzerland of the Pacific"—that would be surrounded by a ring of American bases.[238] MacArthur understood that the occupation of Japan could not go on indefinitely without inviting Japanese resistance. In March 1947, the Supreme Commander of the Allied Powers (SCAP), therefore, introduced the possibility of reaching a peace agreement with Japan with or without Soviet involvement. "The time is now approaching," MacArthur told press correspondents, "when we must talk peace with Japan."[239] Such an agreement would have allowed Japan to get back on its own feet while allowing the United States to retrench. For most in Washington, however, too much uncertainty remained about the policies that an independent Japan would pursue toward the Soviet Union.[240]

On October 4, 1948, President Truman approved NSC 13/2, one of the earliest products of the newly formed National Security Council.[241] NSC 13/2 was primarily the work of George Kennan, who visited Japan in February and March of 1948, met with MacArthur three times during his visit, and reported his recommendation in what was to become NSC 13/2 on his return. The document included twenty policy prescriptions for the occupation of Japan in the emerging context of a Soviet-American cold war. For example, Kennan was troubled by SCAP's purging of approximately 200,000 people from political and military positions, finding it to be arbitrary and ineffective for achieving long-term U.S. aims.[242] Kennan further suggested that after the concerns of maintaining Japanese security, the next priority should be rebuilding the Japanese economy. All of Kennan's reforms were directed at limiting the potential for communism to find a foothold in Japanese society while simultaneously preparing Japan for independence without rushing toward a hasty peace agreement.[243]

INDUCEMENT AND ACCOMMODATION IN JAPAN

In the threat environment of the emerging cold war, the United States could rely primarily on cooperative strategies of inducement and accommodation. Accommodation took the form of constitutional reform and an independent Japanese government. Inducement came in the form of steps to rebuild the industrial Japanese economy. To aid in the reconstruction of the Japanese economy, Joseph Dodge, a Detroit banker, was dispatched to implement a new economic program for the stagnant Japanese economy. Dodge arrived in Tokyo with an aggressive plan to balance the Japanese budget, stabilize prices, and generally improve Japanese productivity.[244] The American strategy of redeveloping Japanese industry was a classic inducement strategy that was aided by the preexisting industrial infrastructure within Japan. Economic development was important to success in Japan, mostly because it eased the implementation of strategies of inducement. This strategy of inducement, in turn, reinforced the positive initial threat environment.

The "Dodge Line" brought the Japanese budget and inflation under control and encouraged industrial growth within Japan. Most important, the Dodge Line was representative of a string of policies in 1948 and 1949 that gradually moved Japan even further away from the New Deal reforms that had characterized the early occupation and further toward the cold war policies that epitomized the later occupation. On May 12, 1949, SCAP essentially canceled the reparations obligations of Japan against the wishes of other Asian and allied powers.[245]

The economic reconstruction of Japan was a true win-win for the United States. Not only would it relieve the costs of occupation that were burdening the United States, but it would also create a strong Japan that could aid in balancing against the Soviet Union. During the summer of 1947, the SWNCC concluded that if the United States did not support Japanese recovery "[it would inevitably] result in a breakdown, gradual or precipitous, that would represent a complete loss in the American investment in a stable, democratic, and peaceful Japan and would seriously jeopardize the U.S. program for worldwide economic recovery and political stabilization."[246]

A series of political reforms—a strategy of accommodation—also were a part of the reverse course. First, by 1948, the war crime tribunals in Tokyo had become an afterthought. Similar to the denazification effort in Germany, the occupation administration in Japan lost interest in assigning blame for the events of World War II and turned its attention to ensuring the allegiance of Japanese leaders in the cold war against the Soviet Union.[247] In fact, some of those Japanese leaders who had initially been purged from the political system were "depurged" and invited back into the political process in the service of fighting communism.[248]

Along with the abandonment of war crimes tribunals came the "red purge" of any communist influences in Japanese society and, in particular, Japanese labor unions. The occupation administration increasingly embraced conservative Japanese politicians who could be relied on to cooperate in American efforts in the emerging cold war. On June 6, 1950, MacArthur instructed Prime Minister Yoshida Shigeru, "I direct you to make the necessary administrative measures to remove and exclude the full membership of the Central Party of the Japanese Communist Party from public service and render them subject to the prohibition, restrictions and liabilities of my directive of Jan. 4, 1946 and their implementing ordinances."[249]

In December 1949, the National Security Council issued a lengthy summary of the situation in Japan. NSC 48, "The Position of the United States with Respect to Asia," recognized the essential role of Japan in the doctrine of containment.[250] NSC 48 advocated the expansion of Japan's economic presence in Asia as a way of ensuring that the whole of Asia, including Japan, would remain outside of the communist sphere of influence. With the likelihood of making inroads into China decreasing, the United States should instead attempt to create a "great crescent" that would stretch from Japan down to Southeast Asia and India.[251]

END GAME AND THE ABSENCE OF THE
OCCUPATION DILEMMA IN JAPAN

The question of when to end the occupation was directly tied to the question of Japanese rearmament. Extending the occupation could provoke dissatisfaction among the Japanese people that could eventually manifest itself in a move toward communism. At the same time, the military and most of the diplomatic corps agreed that it was still premature to consider a permanent peace treaty with Japan and a subsequent end to the occupation. Japan was simply too critical to the containment of the Soviet Union to entrust it with independence.[252] Further, an independent Japan was likely to be a rearmed Japan. Yoshida initially resisted efforts to force Japan to rearm, arguing that Japan could not afford rearmament, the Japanese people were opposed to remilitarization, and rearmament would antagonize Japan's neighbors.[253]

The Korean War was a critical moment in the evolution of the occupation of Japan for three reasons. First, the war provided a stimulus to the Japanese economy. United States military procurements provided a lucrative market for Japanese manufactured goods. Second, in July 1950, the process of Japanese rearmament began. Only two weeks after North Korea invaded South Korea, MacArthur sent a letter to the Japanese leadership asking that a seventy-five-thousand-man reserve be added to the Japanese police force and eight thousand men be added to the Japanese maritime force.[254] Despite his initial apprehension, Yoshida ultimately accepted limited rearmament, and he came to embrace the presence of U.S. bases in Japan as a means for ending the occupation.[255] The Japanese leadership welcomed protection against "Soviet intimidation," but it did not want the occupation to go on indefinitely and rearmament was a critical step toward ending the occupation.[256]

Third, the Korean War provided the impetus for finally ending the occupation of Japan. With Japan now rearming and the occupation becoming, in Secretary of State Dean Acheson's words, a "diminishing asset," a permanent peace treaty now seemed plausible.[257] The government in Tokyo was reliably anticommunist and pro-American. If properly structured, a peace agreement would cement Japan's presence in the U.S. sphere of influence, mitigate Japanese anxiety about recovering its independence, and alleviate other Asian countries' concerns about potential Japanese rearmament. Any treaty with Japan would, however, have to include both provisions for Japanese rearmament and permanent basing rights for the United States in Japan.

In San Francisco in September 1951, forty-nine nations initialed instruments of peace for Japan. Japanese independence was formally restored without any acceptance of war guilt, though Japan was required to pay reparations and relinquish some of its territory.[258] Simultaneous to the general instruments of peace, Japan signed security agreements linking it with the United States, Australia, and New Zealand. On April 28, 1952, all of these agreements officially went into force, and Japan reclaimed its sovereignty. The formal occupation of Japan was over. Japan had regained its sovereignty with the termination of the occupation, but simultaneously, Japan was enmeshed in a series of security treaties that would protect both Japan and its neighbors.

EVALUATING THE OCCUPATION OF JAPAN

By any standard, the occupation of Japan was a success. Within a decade of its defeat, Japan had been rebuilt into a functioning democracy with one of the world's fastest growing economies.[259] In addition, Japan was safely protected under the U.S. nuclear umbrella, and the United States could count Japan, its erstwhile bitter enemy, as a trusted ally. The occupation was undoubtedly costly, but the cost was justified in light of the occupation's accomplishments. Finally, the United States managed to terminate the occupation of Japan in a way that left Japan both sovereign and secure in the short- and long-term.

Why was the occupation of Japan so successful? Despite the high costs of occupation, 81 percent of Americans in 1948 agreed that the United States should maintain its commitment of troops in Japan.[260] An external threat—the threat of Soviet-sponsored communism—is key to explaining the success of the occupation of Japan. This threat environment sustained Japanese and U.S. interest in the occupation and allowed the United States to rely primarily on cooperative strategies, rather than coercion, to manage the occupation.

On the Japanese side, there is only limited direct evidence of the Japanese people's views of the occupation.[261] Instead, we can induce through other evidence that the Japanese were supportive of the occupation. First, the Japanese held very positive views of General MacArthur. Theodore Cohen, who served as chief of the occupation's Labor Division for part of the occupation, reports that MacArthur was viewed as a "hero" for keeping the Russians out of Japan.[262] John Dower writes, "Japanese at all levels of society embraced the new supreme commander with an ardor hitherto reserved for the emperor and commonly treated [General Headquarters] with the deference they had until recently accorded their own military leaders."[263]

Second, through elections, the Japanese people expressed their preference for political parties with more conservative agendas and in opposition to the Communist Party.[264] With a brief exception from June 1947 until February 1948, the Japanese Diet was dominated by conservative parties. Even during that exception, the socialist party was able to form a government only with a plurality, not a majority, of seats. Throughout, the Communist Party of Japan never amassed any significant support within Japan. In short, unlike in southern Korea where a common external threat was not perceived, in Japan, the United States found a population that shared its opposition to Soviet-inspired communism.

The third piece of evidence that suggests that the Japanese were at least toler-
ant of the occupation was the absence of any popular resistance to the occupation. Even in the face of significant malnourishment in Japan during the first
winter of the occupation, there was basically no violent resistance of which to
speak. Later, MacArthur was able to squash the budding labor movement in
Japan without violent reaction, and the antiwar movement in Japan that objected
to Japanese involvement on either side of the Cold War was unable to prevent the
emerging U.S.–Japanese alliance.[265] Undoubtedly, the latent threat of U.S. coercive violence likely had something to do with Japanese quiescence, but the evidence also suggests that the Japanese, in John Dower's words, "embraced defeat."

The Japanese leadership also saw the value in a U.S. occupation that guaranteed Japanese security against a communist threat.[266] Conservative prime minister Yoshida Shigeru writes in his memoirs, "The native Communists are not
strong enough to [bring off a coup d'état], but had Soviet forces been permitted to enter Hokkaido, there can be no doubt that Hokkaido would today have
another East Germany or North Korea, and Japan would have been divided. . . .
For preventing this, if for nothing else, the Japanese people have abundant reason
to be grateful to General MacArthur."[267]

The level of destructiveness caused by World War II also contributed to occupation success by making Japan seem particularly vulnerable to communist infiltration. Close to 3 million Japanese military personnel and civilians were killed
in the war from a 1941 population of 74 million. An additional 4.5 million soldiers were left wounded at the end of the war. Sixty-six of Japan's cities were heavily bombed over the course of the war with 65 percent of all residences destroyed
in Tokyo, 57 percent in Osaka, and 89 percent in Nagoya. Economically, Japan
lost an estimated quarter of its prewar national wealth during the course of the
war, and rural living standards declined to 65 percent of prewar levels with urban
living standards falling even more precipitously to 35 percent of prewar levels.[268]
As in postwar western Germany, the United States was able to offer much-needed
resources to the devastated Japanese society. Early in the occupation, the United
States increased the food ration of the Japanese people in order to prevent
widespread starvation, which American leaders feared would make communism
attractive.[269]

The influence of the emerging cold war on the occupation of Japan is even
clearer from the perspective of the United States. United States political and
military leaders appreciated the strategic importance of Japan from early in
the occupation. Even before the war had concluded, U.S. and British intelligence warned of the Soviet threat to control the resources of Northeast Asia.[270]
George Kennan's enunciation of the grand strategy of containment only amplified the significance of controlling Japan. Few U.S. leaders feared a direct Soviet

invasion of Japan; instead, the fear was that communism would infiltrate its way into Japanese society and that Japan would eventually ally itself with the Soviet Union.[271] In order to prevent communism's spread in Japan, the United States eventually came to the conclusion that the Japanese economy would have to be rebuilt, the occupation of Japan would have to end, and Japan would have to be included in America's emerging network of alliances.[272]

The most telling evidence of all is the manner in which U.S. occupation policy traced the evolution of the Cold War. As the confrontation with the Soviet Union became clearer, the commitment of the United States to keep Japan out of the Soviet orbit became stronger. The more liberal, New Deal reforms of the early occupation were abandoned in favor of steps that would strengthen the Japanese economy and ensure American control over Japan's defense policies. The occupation of Japan was a costly endeavor for the United States, and only the looming threat of the Soviet Union justified the continued expenditure.

The favorable threat environment also allowed the United States to pursue an effective strategy of occupation. In the absence of violent opposition, the occupation authority could refrain from coercion and rely instead on a combination of inducement and accommodation to win the favor of the Japanese people. These strategies, in turn, reinforced the sense in Japan that the greatest threat to their eventual national self-determination was not the United States.

In terms of inducement, in more than six years of occupation by tens of thousands of troops, the United States provided $2 billion in food, fertilizer, petroleum products, and raw materials for industry.[273] As for accommodation, the United States allowed the introduction of a new constitution that explicitly recognized a role for the emperor in the new Japanese state. No longer was the emperor to be the political leader of Japan, but MacArthur hoped to, in the words of John Dower, create a "usable emperor."[274] If the emperor had been excluded from the new constitution, then MacArthur feared that "it is quite possible that a minimum of a million troops would be required which would have to be maintained for an indefinite number of years" in order to control the outrage of the Japanese people.[275] Accordingly, and in deference to Japanese nationalism, the emperor's culpability for war crimes committed during World War II was never seriously examined.[276]

In Japan, the United States managed to avoid the occupation dilemma by returning sovereignty to the Japanese people in a timely manner and enmeshing Japan in security treaties that provided for Japan's defense and limited its ability to threaten others. Even so, these two goals were not accomplished nearly as easily or quickly as some had hoped. When the occupation of Japan began, most American leaders, including General MacArthur, believed that the occupation could and should be concluded in less than three years.[277] In the end, the occupation lasted over twice that long because the United States would not consider withdrawal from Japan until it was clear that American interests had been secured in Asia.

From early in the occupation, U.S. leaders faced pressure to end the occupation and avoid the rising costs of the operation. In late September 1947, Under Secretary of the Army William Henry Draper Jr. told reporters in Japan that the prime objective of the occupation of Japan would now be "to reduce the costs to the American taxpayer."[278] Roger Buckley argues that the shift in occupation policy beginning in 1947 was the product of increasing domestic pressure on President Truman to lower the costs of the occupation.[279] In 1947 alone, the costs of maintaining the occupation troops in Japan was $370 million.[280] Yet the United States continued to pay the costs of occupation until 1952. As the threat environment hypothesis predicts, it was a sense of external threat to American interests that made the costs of occupation acceptable and, therefore, made an extended occupation palatable.

By May 1949, leaders in Washington had further begun to recognize that the continuation of the occupation, with little end in sight, might endanger the very purpose of the occupation. Dean Acheson warned that an indefinite occupation would not only continue to cost the United States, but it would also make Japan "easy prey to Commie ideologies."[281] General MacArthur himself argued that most occupations could only persist for a limited period of time before they began to suffer problems. Or as he observed, "After about the third year, any military occupation begins to collapse of its own weight."[282]

The favorable threat environment surrounding the occupation of Japan allowed the United States to avoid the occupation dilemma. The absence of coercion in Japan eased the process of locating an independent, reliable government to which the United States could return sovereignty without having to worry about the long-term consequences. A heavier reliance on coercion, especially following the destruction of World War II, would have left lingering animosity in the wake of the occupation. The presence of the Soviet threat also guaranteed the long-term U.S. commitment to Japanese security. By withdrawing and relinquishing sovereignty, the United States was relieved of the difficulties of occupation, but by tethering Japan to a series of security agreements with both it and Japan's neighbors, the United States was able to withdraw confident that its mission of protecting its interests, in both the short- and long-term, had been accomplished.

Despite its success, it would be incorrect to argue that the occupation of Japan was easy. The occupation was expensive and required the deployment of hundreds of thousands of troops in Japan. Prime Minister Yoshida, who was a strong advocate of close relations with the United States, joked that GHQ—General Headquarters—should actually stand for "go home quickly."[283] Nationalism in

Japan was not extinguished by World War II; instead, it lay dormant in the wake of the destruction incurred during the war. To conclude the occupation, then, the United States led the effort to combine a restoration of sovereignty with simultaneous security guarantees that protected Japan and reassured Japan's neighbors that the country would not again pose a threat to Asian security.

Conclusion

Ending an occupation is the final difficult challenge that all occupying powers face. In this chapter, I have argued that successful occupying powers satisfy two critical conditions before they end an occupation—restoring sovereignty to a reliable indigenous government and ensuring the security of the occupied territory. Unsuccessful occupying powers are likely to confront a dilemma between withdrawing prematurely or prolonging a costly, but unsuccessful, occupation. Further, a favorable threat environment makes it more likely that an occupying power will achieve these conditions for successfully ending an occupation whereas an unfavorable threat environment makes it more likely that an occupying power will fail to achieve its goals and confront the occupation dilemma.

The three cases I presented in this chapter capture the nature of the challenge of ending an occupation. In Cuba, the United States withdrew prematurely in 1902. In Egypt, the British prolonged an occupation that was originally intended to be quite short. In Japan, the United States managed to craft a successful withdrawal strategy.

In this chapter and the previous two, I have developed my argument for why occupations succeed or fail, how different strategies of occupation can influence outcomes, and when occupying powers can successfully conclude an occupation. In the next chapter, I consider an alternative argument that focuses on multilateralism as a key to occupation success.

WHO OCCUPIES

Multilateralism and Military Occupation

Multilateralism might be conducive to occupation success for two reasons. First, according to a prominent argument, it is increasingly accepted that states must use military force in a multilateral manner in order to be viewed as legitimate.[1] Legitimacy, in turn, makes it more likely that a state or group of states will be able to accomplish their goals without significant opposition. For instance, the eminent historian of the occupation of Japan, John Dower, argued that the U.S.– led occupation of Iraq would be less successful than the occupation of Japan because the occupation of Iraq lacked the legitimacy that multilateralism and UN approval might provide.[2] In the context of occupation, this argument suggests that occupations that are multilateral and have the approval of the United Nations are more likely to be successful in contemporary international politics. When an occupation is viewed as legitimate, not only do other states support the occupation but the occupied population is more likely to see the occupation as appropriate. Second, multilateralism may benefit an occupation because it allows for burden-sharing within an occupation. If one of the challenges of occupation is the expense of the occupation, then multilateralism can defray the cost of occupation among several countries and make it sustainable for a longer period of time. Both of these arguments generate a simple hypothesis: if an occupation is multilateral, it is more likely to succeed. The cases of the UN occupations of East Timor and Kosovo below provide an opportunity to evaluate this hypothesis.

Contrary to this basic hypothesis, I argue that the advantages of multilateralism for the purposes of military occupation have been overstated. First, occupied populations and potential occupying powers most often judge an occupation based on its effects on security and self-determination, not its legitimacy. The legitimacy granted by the UN imprimatur on an occupation appears to have had no great influence on the occupations of East Timor or Kosovo. Second, multilateralism does offer the benefit of burden sharing, but burden sharing also introduces disadvantages. Most important, multilateral participation in an occupation also entitles participants in an occupation to a say in the goals and means of the occupation. When occupying powers disagree, it can make it more difficult to achieve short- and long-term occupation success.

In short, multilateralism alone cannot overcome the challenges of nationalism that make occupation so difficult. Multilateralism can help alleviate some of the challenges that occupying powers face in sustaining an occupation, but not without also introducing some of the challenges of managing multilateral occupations. The commitment of occupying powers to end an occupation in a timely manner may appear more credible when an occupation is multilateral and carried out under U.N. auspices. In the end, though, whether or not a population accepts a multilateral occupation continues to depend on whether the occupation offers protection from some other external threat, and whether or not occupying powers maintain interest in a multilateral occupation depends on the strategic goals at stake and the costs of sustaining the occupation.

Evidence on Multilateralism and Occupation

De facto UN occupations of East Timor and Kosovo began in the same year, but they have had differing outcomes. The United Nations faced particularly propitious circumstances in East Timor that augured success there. In Kosovo, on the other hand, the United Nations confronted the type of threat environment that has hindered other non–UN occupations.[3] Though the United Nations may, in fact, confer legitimacy on occupations, the case of Kosovo demonstrates that this legitimacy is often not sufficient to overcome the nationalism that remains at the heart of a population's objection to occupation.

The UN Occupation of East Timor, 1999–2002

The chronology of events that culminated in an independent East Timor began in 1974 when the government of Portugal announced that all of its colonial territories were entitled to self-determination. Lisbon's announcement unleashed a civil war in East Timor between those who favored independence and those who supported annexation to Indonesia. Despite the protests of the United Nations, Indonesia proceeded to invade East Timor, and on July 17, 1976, annexed it as its twenty-seventh province.

Until 1998, the United Nations exerted pressure on Indonesia to allow East Timorese self-determination, but to no avail. Finally, an opportunity for transforming Indonesia's relationship with East Timor arose in May 1998 when the long-time Indonesian president Suharto was forced to leave office and was replaced by B. J. Habibie. In June, Habibie announced that he would be willing to allow East Timor considerable autonomy within the Indonesian state. Under increasing pressure from Australian prime minister John Howard, Habibie went even further in January 1999 when, in what has been called the "second option," he indicated that the East Timorese population would be given the option to choose between autonomy within Indonesia or complete independence.[4]

In response to indications that East Timor was going to be able to choose its path forward, pro-Indonesian militias incited violence in the spring of 1999. On April 6, a pro-Indonesian militia with the support of the Indonesian military attacked two thousand refugees sheltering from the violence in the Catholic church in Liquiçá. Though the precise death toll remains uncertain to this day, it is believed that as many as sixty people were killed in the Liquiçá massacre. The East Timorese were outraged by the mounting Indonesian violence in East Timor. Xanana Gusmão, one of the leaders of the National Council of Timorese Resistance (CNRT), authorized the East Timorese militia group Falintil "to undertake all necessary action in defense of the population of East Timor against the unprovoked and murderous attacks of armed civilian groups and the [Armed Forces of the Republic of Indonesia]."[5]

The increasing violence in East Timor lent urgency to ongoing tripartite negotiations between Indonesia, Portugal, and the United Nations. On May 5, an agreement was signed in New York between foreign ministers Ali Alatas of Indonesia and Jaime Gama of Portugal with United Nations Secretary General Kofi Annan standing by as a witness. The agreement called for strict controls on armed militias on all sides and the redeployment of the Indonesian military. In addition, a date of Sunday, August 8, was set for the "popular consultation" on the future of East Timor.

GOALS AND MEANS

As part of the May 5 agreement, the United Nations pledged to establish a mission to ensure the peaceful and successful conduct of the popular consultation. A little more than two weeks later, the secretary general presented his proposals for a United Nations Mission in East Timor (UNAMET). UNAMET was to be a political, not a peacekeeping, mission, staffed with fifteen political officers, twenty-eight professionals appointed to regional offices, four hundred volunteers serving as district electoral officers, nine public information officers, 275 police, and 271 administrative and support staff. Indonesia was unlikely to accept a large UN military presence in East Timor, so despite concerns about the deteriorating security situation in the province, only fifty military liaison officers were added to the UNAMET team. On June 11, UNAMET was formally established by the UN Security Council.

As the vote on East Timor's status approached, violence again surged in East Timor. A core group of interested powers, including Australia, Japan, New Zealand, the United Kingdom, and the United States, warned Jakarta that it must control the violence preceding and during the election, but efforts to increase the military capabilities of UNAMET before the referendum failed. Concern continued to grow about not only the violence attending the election, but also the potential for a large number of refugees if the East Timorese were to vote for independence.

After an initial delay, on August 30, East Timorese went to the ballot boxes with an impressive 98.6 percent of the registered electorate casting their votes. The elections were interrupted only by sporadic violence, but the same could not be said for the postelection period. On September 4, the election results were announced: 21.5 percent had voted for autonomy within Indonesia while 78.5 percent had voted for independence by voting against any autonomy arrangement. The election results opened the floodgates to violence in East Timor. In an operation known as "Clean Sweep," anti-independence militias first targeted foreigners who might be witness to their atrocities before laying waste to whatever there was to destroy in East Timor. UNAMET pulled its staff back from regional offices to the capital of Dili before most of the UNAMET staff was evacuated altogether on September 10.

Meanwhile, pressure was intensifying for the international community to intervene militarily to stop the violence that the Indonesians were clearly incapable or unwilling to stop on their own. Despite appeals from great powers such as the United States and regional powers such as Australia, the Indonesians steadfastly refused to admit an international peacekeeping force into East Timor. Secretary General Annan warned, "If [Indonesia] refuses [to accept an outside force], it cannot escape responsibility for what could amount, according to reports reaching us, to crimes against humanity."[6] Finally, in the face of mounting pressure and the risk of significant international political and economic consequences, President Habibie announced on September 12 that he would allow an international intervention to restore order in East Timor.

Three days later, on September 15, the United Nations Security Council authorized the formation of the International Force for East Timor (INTERFET) in UN Security Council Resolution 1264.[7] By September 20, the first elements of an Australian-led multinational force consisting of twelve thousand troops began to arrive in East Timor with the mission of restoring peace and security in East Timor. At the same time, Indonesian authorities recognizing that they had now lost control over East Timor began to withdraw from their erstwhile province, leaving a vacuum of civilian authority in the region.

CONDUCT OF THE OCCUPATION

To fill this vacuum, the United Nations formed a temporary government in East Timor. On October 25, the Security Council approved the United Nations Transitional Administration in East Timor (UNTAET) in UN Security Council Resolution 1272.[8] UNTAET was to oversee the transition of East Timor from an Indonesian state to independence. When the final elements of the Indonesian government left on October 30, the United Nations remained as the interim holder of East Timorese sovereignty. The UN occupation of East Timor had begun.

By February 2000, INTERFET troops had been phased out of East Timor as UNTAET took over complete control of East Timor. A year later, in March 2001, UNTAET announced that the elections for the first East Timorese representative assembly would be held on August 30, exactly two years from the popular consultation on independence. Peaceful elections produced a victory for Fretilin, the former East Timorese resistance party. Finally, on May 20, 2002, the Democratic Republic of East Timor was officially founded with the long-time East Timorese leader Xanana Gusmão as the first East Timorese president. Though a small UN security force—the United Nations Mission in Support of East Timor (UNMISET)—remained in East Timor for three years after independence was officially declared, the UN occupation of East Timor had come to an end.[9]

EVALUATING THE OCCUPATION OF EAST TIMOR

The United Nations mission in East Timor has largely been a success. Although East Timor is far from a prosperous society today, the UN's accomplishments in East Timor must be weighed relative to the alternatives. Without the intervention of the United Nations, uncontrolled militia violence in East Timor could have led to a conflict of genocidal proportions. In less than three years of occupation, the United Nations facilitated democratic elections in East Timor while assisting in the management of a large-scale internal refugee problem.

A propitious threat environment can best account for UN success in East Timor. The East Timorese population mostly agreed on the external threat posed by Indonesia.[10] Seventy-eight percent of the East Timorese population voted for independence from Indonesia and were left helpless by the violence that followed the referendum on August 30, 1999. Thus, the East Timorese were willing to suppress their strong nationalist feelings in the short-term if the United Nations could offer them protection from the external threat posed by Indonesia.[11]

Not only was there an initial external threat, but the sense of threat was exacerbated by East Timorese vulnerability. A *Washington Post* story in May 2002 described postconflict East Timor as an "unimaginable apocalyptic ruin."[12] As much as 70 percent of East Timorese infrastructure was destroyed by the end of the September 1999 militia rampages.[13] More than 75 percent of East Timor's nearly 900,000 residents were displaced by the violence. The United Nations promised assistance in rebuilding from that ruin in a way that the East Timorese could not have done on their own.[14] Even better from the East Timorese perspective, the United Nations had not inflicted this damage, so the difficulty of being occupied by one's conqueror was obviated.

Given a favorable threat environment, the United Nations could mostly refrain from coercion in favor of policies of accommodation and inducement. From its inception, all parties involved understood that the UN presence in East Timor was meant to be transitional to independence.[15] United Nations pledges to establish an independent, sovereign East Timor were inherently more credible than any individual state's pledge might have been. The East Timorese never had to fear that they were permanently going to be denied their sovereignty by the United Nations. As Anthony Goldstone summarizes, "The vast majority of East Timorese living in the territory regarded the UN intervention as essentially benign, at worst as an uncomfortable interregnum that was the necessary precursor to independence."[16] By making this end goal of independence perfectly clear to the East Timorese population, the United Nations was able to avoid much of the unrest that afflicts other occupations.

To even more credibly communicate its intentions to the East Timorese, the United Nations engaged in a strategy of attempting to accommodate East Timorese nationalism. Initially, UNTAET encountered a fair amount of criticism for the seemingly slow pace of the operation and the lack of involvement by the local population.[17] Leaders of the CNRT, the most significant coalition of political parties opposed to the Indonesian presence in East Timor, called for disobedience against the United Nations and contemplated a unilateral declaration of independence.[18] Recognizing this as early as November 1999, Sergio Vieira de Mello, the transitional administrator, urged the creation of "a participatory, inclusive process that involves the Timorese, their representatives, in particular the CNRT, that has a pre-eminent role to play in decision-making."[19] Vieira de Mello agreed in April 2000 to the appointment of East Timorese deputies to the regional administrations under international control.[20] Still, in May, CNRT vice president and Nobel peace laureate José Ramos-Horta asked Kofi Annan to remove all UN district administrators by August and to set a fixed date for the UN's departure.[21] According to Ramos-Horta, "There was a sense of frustration, a lack of faith in UNTAET. This was because of their inability to involve the East Timorese, their inability to come forward with a roadmap, a plan. We saw time going by and no Timorese administration, no civil servants being recruited, no jobs being created."[22]

By mid 2000, even the United Nations had largely worn out its welcome in East Timor. Vieira de Mello noted that the population now sensed that "UNTAET is on a separate path from the East Timorese."[23] In December 2000, Timorese cabinet members complained that they were being "used as a justification for the delays and the confusion in a process which is outside our control. The East Timorese Cabinet members are caricatures of ministers in a government of a banana republic. They had no power, no duties, no resources to function adequately."[24] Increasingly, the continuing UNTAET presence in East Timor was questioned at all levels of East Timorese society.[25] Anicetto Guterres Lopes, a leading East Timorese politician and later the chairman of the East Timorese Commission for Reception, Truth, and Reconciliation, expressed his views that UNTAET had been going on for too long and should be terminated quickly.[26] In his new year's speech for 2001, Gusmão called for the political empowerment of the Timorese and a relatively quick end to the international administration of East Timor.[27] UNTAET responded by gradually turning more authority in the country over to local Timorese and taking credible steps toward the creation of an independent, sovereign East Timor.[28]

The United Nations effectively complemented its policy of political accommodation with a strategy of inducement. The international community invested more than $2 billion in East Timor to aid in reconstruction and foster cooperation from the East Timorese population.[29] With a favorable threat environment, the United Nations was able to craft an effective occupation strategy that relied on accommodation and inducement while minimizing the use of coercion.

MULTILATERALISM IN EAST TIMOR

The United Nations entered East Timor with a large mandate and unclear directions on how to accomplish that mandate.[30] Simon Chesterman suggests that the UN role in East Timor can be thought of as "benevolent foreign autocracy."[31] By examining this case, we can assess the importance of the UN imprimatur to the success or failure of this type of operation. Some have argued that the legitimacy conveyed by UN authorization can attract more international involvement and convince an occupied population to accept occupation.[32]

In East Timor, however, it is difficult to disentangle the legitimacy benefits of United Nations involvement from the practical benefits and credibility lent by that involvement. It was the credibility of the United Nations pledge to withdraw in relatively short order that convinced the East Timorese that they were not facing another extended occupation in the aftermath of Portuguese colonialism and Indonesian annexation.[33] Even with the credibility of the United Nations, however, the population of East Timor grew impatient with the UN presence. As beneficial as UN involvement may ultimately have been, multilateralism also came with practical difficulties as the United Nations suffered from an inability to coordinate all of the various agencies and organizations involved in the reconstruction of East Timor.[34]

The United Nations experience in East Timor is certainly worthy of praise, and it is a notable success in the history of military occupation.[35] However, it also enjoyed unusually advantageous circumstances. Peter Galbraith, who directed UNTAET political affairs from January 2000 until the summer of 2001, notes, "We were given Mission Possible. The mission was completely congruent with people's wishes. We had adequate security resources."[36] Scott Gilmore, a Canadian diplomat who served in UNTAET, concludes, "It's hard to think of another case of nation-building that would be as easy as this one."[37] Not only was East Timor relatively small, but the population is relatively homogeneous and desirous of protection from Indonesia. Add in the vulnerability of East Timor to the Indonesian threat and the credibility of the United Nations pledge to withdraw, and it is unsurprising that the United Nations was relatively successful in East Timor.[38]

A favorable threat environment also enabled the United Nations to avoid the occupation dilemma of either withdrawing too early or prolonging a stagnant occupation. The United Nations was able to establish a stable and secure government while continuing to offer security assistance to that government even after it was functional. The United Nations neither left too early, nor stayed too long.

Even as the United Nations enjoyed certain successes in East Timor, however, the outbreak of riots in East Timor in May 2006 raised the question of whether the United Nations did, in fact, leave East Timor too soon. Withdrawing forces quickly has the advantage of placating nationalist populations, but it introduces the danger of recurring instability if forces leave too soon. In fact, José Ramos-Horta has admitted, "For the immediate future, we need a special police force . . . that is a rapid-reaction force to stop riots, hooligans, looting."[39] And former UN secretary general Kofi Annan understandably asked, "There has been a sense that we tend to leave conflict areas too soon. . . . We've been in Cyprus for ages, we've been in Bosnia, Kosovo. Why do we often try to leave other areas after two or three years?"[40] Thus, while the initial verdict on the occupation of East Timor is positive, the long-term consequences of the UN intervention in East Timor remain uncertain.

The UN Occupation of Kosovo, 1999–Present

In contrast to the UN's success in East Timor, the threat environment in Kosovo contributed to UN difficulties there. Contrary to the expectations of the multilateralism argument, the presence of the United Nations in Kosovo has done little to defuse the population's unhappiness with being occupied. Kosovo faced both an internal division between Serbs and Albanians and an external threat from Serbia that has only been perceived by the Albanian population within Kosovo. Given this unfavorable threat environment, the United Nations would have had to pursue a more effective strategy of coercion in order to succeed. Instead, the United Nations pursued a wrong-headed "standards before status" policy in Kosovo that has only fed Kosovar nationalism and resistance to the continuing presence of the United Nations.

The contemporary conflict in Kosovo can be traced to Yugoslav president Slobodan Milošević's efforts to restrict the autonomy of the province within the Yugoslav federation. In response, during the 1990s, the Kosovo Liberation Army (KLA) emerged as an insurgent army of resistance against Serbian control of the province. Milošević and the Serb-dominated Yugoslav army responded with a concerted effort to suppress Kosovar Albanian nationalism and, in particular, the KLA. In March 1999, after the failure of negotiations at the French palace of Rambouillet, NATO initiated air strikes against Serbia in an effort to force Serbian military elements out of Kosovo and allow negotiations to identify an acceptable status for Kosovo. On June 3, after more than two months of intense NATO bombing, Milošević capitulated to NATO's demands to end the war over Kosovo.

GOALS AND MEANS

United Nations Security Council Resolution (UNSCR) 1244 of June 10, 1999, first addressed the postwar status of Kosovo by calling for the establishment of an international civil presence in Kosovo under the control of a special representative of the UN secretary general. The UN presence was charged with facilitating the political, economic, and social reconstruction of Kosovo. Most controversially, 1244 simultaneously recognized the continuing territorial integrity of the Federal Republic of Yugoslavia while also assigning the civil administration the task of "promoting the establishment, pending a final settlement, of substantial autonomy and self-government in Kosovo." As commentator Timothy Garton Ash has correctly observed, UNSCR 1244 simultaneously called for "virginity and motherhood."[41]

The administration created in Kosovo was composed of the UN Mission in Kosovo (UNMIK) together with a NATO-led Kosovo Force (KFOR). The tasks of UNMIK were further divided into four "pillars": an interim civil administration (under the control of the special representative of the UN secretary general), a humanitarian affairs pillar (led by the UN High Commissioner for Refugees), a pillar for reconstruction (led by the European Union), and a pillar for institution building (coordinated by the Organization for Security and Cooperation in Europe).[42] KFOR was tasked with supporting the UN mission by providing security in Kosovo, which largely entailed preventing ethnic Albanian violence against the remaining Serb minority.

On June 11, the day after UNSCR 1244 passed the Security Council, Secretary General Kofi Annan named Sergio Vieira de Mello as the Acting Special Representative for Kosovo. By the end of July, the United Nations had essentially occupied Kosovo. The first UNMIK regulation proclaimed, "All legislative and executive authority with respect to Kosovo, including the administration of the judiciary, is vested in UNMIK and is exercised by the Special Representative of the Secretary General."[43]

CONDUCT OF THE OCCUPATION

UNMIK faced a number of short-term challenges when it first began its work in Kosovo. Kosovo confronted both an internal threat to its security in the form of tension between Serbs and Albanians and an external threat posed by Serbia that was perceived by the Albanian population. This threat environment, combining an internal threat and a disputed external threat, was not conducive to occupation success. Despite an agreement to demobilize, the Kosovo Liberation Army continued to operate throughout the province. Approximately 1 million Kosovar Albanians had been displaced before and during the war, and after the war, many Kosovar Serbs were forced to leave their homes in Kosovo.

While UNMIK and KFOR struggled to manage these short-term challenges, the larger issue looming on the agenda was the final status of Kosovo. Kosovar Albanians believed that they had fought and won a war of liberation against Serbia, and it was not the prerogative of the United Nations to deny them their independence. On the other hand, the United Nations had also made a commitment to maintaining the territorial integrity of the Federal Republic of Yugoslavia. Any premature movement toward Kosovar independence might precipitate a renewal of violent conflict.

In December 1999, UNMIK took its first valuable step toward allowing Kosovar Albanians to govern themselves. An agreement between three Kosovar Albanian leaders—Hashim Thaci, Ibrahim Rugova, and Rexhep Qosja—and UNMIK created a Kosovo-UNMIK Joint Interim Administrative Structure and an Interim Administrative Council.[44] These shadow institutions would, for the first time since UNMIK had assumed control over the territory, enable indigenous input into governance decisions.[45]

Over the next three years, however, Kosovo would continue to be plagued by sporadic violence and increasing Kosovar Albanian impatience with the unwillingness of the United Nations to allow Kosovo to have its independence. Some progress was made in the direction of self-rule. In October 2000, municipal elections were held, and a year later, in November 2001, Kosovars elected their first regional assembly in nearly a decade after a May 2001 agreement on a Constitutional Framework for Provisional Self-Government. In February 2002, Kosovar Albanian leaders agreed on a coalition government with Ibrahim Rugova as its president. Finally, in June 2002, the Kosovar provisional government was sworn into office. Still, however, the United Nations had not moved toward any resolution of the final status of Kosovo either within the Federal Republic of Yugoslavia or as an independent state.

Michael Steiner, a German who took over as the special representative of the secretary general in Kosovo in February 2002, initiated the most significant step toward the consideration of Kosovo's ultimate status.[46] In April 2002, Steiner introduced an idea that would come to be known as "standards before status." That is, before the final status of Kosovo could be considered, Kosovo would have to demonstrate that it had achieved certain standards of economic and political development. Steiner eventually presented benchmarks in eight specific areas that Kosovo needed to address: functioning democratic institutions, rule of law, freedom of movement, returns and reintegration, economy, property rights, dialogue with Belgrade, and the form and function of the Kosovo Protection Corps. If, and only if, Kosovo made progress toward implementing these standards, would the United Nations consider a final resolution of Kosovo's status.[47]

In March 2004, demonstrations against the lack of progress toward self-determination in Kosovo turned into riots as nationalist Albanians directed their violence against not only Serbs, but also against symbols of the UNMIK presence, including the UN's iconic white vehicles.[48] Once again, nationalism proved to be the greatest impediment to extended foreign occupation, whether by the United Nations or a single foreign power. By the time the riots ended, nineteen were dead, more than nine hundred were injured, hundreds of homes, public buildings, and churches were destroyed, and forty-five hundred people were displaced. As

James Traub wrote in the *New York Times,* by this point, "The Kosovars were sullen because they were sick and tired of international tutelage."[49] Søren Jessen-Petersen, who took over as the special representative of the secretary general in Kosovo in June 2004, remarked, "There was a sense after the March riots [in 2004] that we had to accelerate the process and simplify standards implementation, not to reward violence but because to keep this place in limbo for much longer would be rather risky."[50]

Finally, in October 2005, Kai Eide, the special envoy of Secretary General Annan, presented a report to the secretary general affirming that Kosovo had made sufficient progress on the standards so that negotiations on final status should begin. The October 2005 decision to move toward final status negotiations was not so much a recognition of extensive progress in Kosovo as it was a recognition that the existing UN policy was not succeeding.[51]

EVALUATING THE OCCUPATION OF KOSOVO

The international intervention into Kosovo stopped the ethnically motivated warfare being perpetrated by Belgrade in Kosovo. For this, NATO, in particular, deserves much credit. Unfortunately, the verdict for the postwar international occupation of Kosovo is less positive.[52] As Simon Chesterman concludes, "Kosovo was stillborn as a political entity. As long as its final status remains undecided, its political development will continue to be undermined by uncertainty."[53] Eight years after the war in Kosovo ended, the political future of Kosovo remains unresolved, ethnic tensions persist, and the de facto occupation in Kosovo has become a semipermanent fixture in Kosovar society.[54] The United Nations has not yet faced a severe occupation dilemma in Kosovo because the costs of the continuing presence there is divided among many wealthy countries, but pressures certainly have been felt to end the international presence in Kosovo before stable institutions and security have been created. Although one must be careful not to offer a premature final judgment on the international effort in Kosovo, at this point, it is hard to reach an overly positive conclusion.

Even with the legitimacy granted by the United Nations, the occupying force ran into the opposition of nationalist Kosovars who impatiently awaited their independence. After the war in Kosovo, there was no commonly perceived external threat from which UNMIK and KFOR could offer protection. While the threat from Serbia persisted, inside Kosovo, the greatest instability stemmed from continuing tension between ethnic Albanians and ethnic Serbs.[55] As expected, an internal threat to the coherence of the occupied territory undermined the occupation even as part of the population perceived an external threat from Serbia and welcomed the protection offered by KFOR.

Both Kosovar Albanian and Serbian nationalism remained strong even after the war in 1999. Far from forcing the Kosovars to reconsider their nationalism, the war unleashed Albanian nationalism and set it off against remaining Serb elements within Kosovo. As early as October 2000, Ibrahim Rugova, the first president of the provisional government in Kosovo, declared, "I am for straightforward, formal recognition of Kosovo, better now, when KFOR and UNMIK are here. Today or tomorrow—for me, better today."[56] In September 2002, Sadik Halitjaha, president of the Association of War Veterans of the KLA, said, "I never thought that we'd come to the stage of protesting against [UNMIK]. We never thought we would say goodbye by throwing stones at them, and we hope we don't have to."[57] And as Bajram Redenica, executive director of the Society of War Invalids of the Kosovo Liberation Army, lamented in September 2004, "This isn't what we fought for, to be half-free."[58] Similar to southern Korean nationalists after World War II, Kosovar Albanians felt much more liberated than defeated in the wake of the 1999 war. They longed for independence not a further denial of sovereignty.

An unfavorable threat environment forces occupying powers to employ coercion in order to succeed, but UNMIK and KFOR reacted slowly to the residual ethnic violence after the war against Serbia ended in June 1999. A more effective strategy of coercion may have stifled some of this animosity, but, instead, it was allowed to fester and only further complicate the process of building an independent Kosovo.[59] Most infamously, when riots erupted in March 2004, KFOR was unprepared and slow to respond to the potentially dangerous fighting. More generally, for the United Nations, a concerted strategy of coercion is often inconsistent with its mission and may not be supported by all the member states participating in a mission.

In terms of a strategy of inducement, Kosovo has benefited from an extraordinary amount of financial support, but UNMIK suffered from delays in providing much-needed resources to the Kosovar population.[60] Further, UNMIK required the coordination and management of numerous different international organizations, which inevitably delayed the delivery of economic and humanitarian aid to the population.[61] By the end of 2002, Kosovo had received more than $2 billion in international aid, yet that aid could not solve the political desire for independence among Kosovo's nationalist population. Inducement was premature without an effective prior strategy of coercion to control the potential for violence. In addition, much of the rebuilt economy of Kosovo was not sustainable as it was dependent on the continuing expenditures of the large international presence in Kosovo.[62]

UNMIK also chose a poor strategy for accommodating Kosovar nationalism.[63] The strategy of "standards before status" only frustrated the population, especially since the ambitious standards seemed unachievable.[64] As Kai Eide reported in November 2004, "The current 'standards before status' policy lacks credibility."[65] A wiser strategy might have been the converse: status before standards. With a guarantee that a final status of independence awaited them, the Kosovar population may have been more willing to engage in the process of building institutions that would satisfy the standards requirements.[66] Instead, as the occupation progressed, the Albanian population only grew more and more frustrated with a continuing occupation that had no certain end date and with a minority population that seemed to be the primary hindrance to independence.[67]

As a consequence of the combination of an unfavorable threat environment and poor occupation strategies, the Albanian population of Kosovo has been consistently pushing for an end to the occupation, and the countries participating in the occupation have begun to grow tired of what now seems to be a permanent mission.[68] UNMIK, facing the dilemma of an occupying power that has overstayed its welcome but which cannot withdraw because of the instability that might introduce, is now searching for a way out of Kosovo.[69] In short, the United Nations has been unable to realize either of the two conditions that are necessary for a timely termination of an occupation: returning sovereignty to a stable and secure indigenous government and ensuring the security of the occupied territory after the occupation ends.[70]

MULTILATERALISM IN KOSOVO

The Kosovo case vividly demonstrates that not even the legitimating approval of the United Nations can placate a nationalist population. When demands for sovereignty and international legitimacy butt up against one another, demands for sovereignty tend to prevail.[71] As Eide wrote in the fall of 2004, "The international community in Kosovo is today seen by Kosovo Albanians as having gone from opening the way to now standing in the way. It is seen by Kosovo Serbs as having gone from securing the return of so many to being unable to ensure the return of so few."[72] This case also reveals how disagreement among members of the Security Council, illustrated best by Russia's staunch opposition to Kosovo's independence, can paralyze a multilateral UN occupation.

One instructive element of the Kosovo case is the differing receptions afforded to UNMIK as opposed to KFOR. While NATO is in Kosovo to provide security and has been effective at doing so, the United Nations is responsible for the challenging political dimensions of state-building. The method in which this mission has been divided allows one to disaggregate the views of people within Kosovo with regard to this mission. Unsurprisingly, KFOR is far more popular than UNMIK among the Kosovar population. Since November 2002, the percentage of the population satisfied with KFOR has consistently been greater than 80 percent, making it, along with the Kosovo Police Service, the most popular institution within Kosovo. UNMIK, on the other hand, has received the lowest satisfaction scores, with less than 40 percent satisfied and going as low as approximately 20 percent. As expected, Kosovar Albanians embrace the security that KFOR can provide against a potentially revanchist Serbia, but they long for the sovereignty that they view UNMIK as withholding.[73]

Comparing the Occupations of East Timor and Kosovo

What can be learned by comparing the cases of East Timor and Kosovo? The two cases share much in common: they both occurred around the same period of time; both occupations had the approval of the United Nations; and both territories were relatively small former provinces within much larger and complicated countries. Yet the occupation of East Timor is commonly cited as one of the UN's successes while judgments of the United Nations in Kosovo are far more reserved. There are two major explanations for this variation in outcomes.

First, whereas the population of East Timor valued the protection that the United Nations could offer it from anti-independence militias, the population in Kosovo was divided in a way that precluded agreement on a common external threat. While Kosovar Albanians clearly saw Serbians as a threat from which NATO and the United Nations could protect it, Serbs in Kosovo had little desire to be a minority within an Albanian-controlled state. In addition, East Timor suffered from intense vulnerability in the wake of anti-independence militia violence that made UN protection even more desirable. Sergio Vieira de Mello, who was a prominent UN figure in both occupations, observed, "Unlike when we arrived in Kosovo, there was nothing here in East Timor. Everything had either been destroyed or stolen. We had to start from scratch."[74]

Second, the contrast between the strategies pursued in East Timor and Kosovo could not be any starker. In East Timor, the eventuality of Timorese independence was apparent from the day that the United Nations Transitional Administration in East Timor began its mission.[75] There was never any contemplation of returning East Timor to Indonesia or having East Timor remain a permanent UN mandate. Though they still grew impatient, East Timorese knew that political independence would be granted in a relatively short period of time. In Kosovo, the "standards before status" policy only delayed a decision on whether or not Kosovo would be independent, and the desire to balance Kosovar demands for self-determination with an instinct to maintain the territorial integrity of the Federal Republic of Yugoslavia led to a muddled UN approach in Kosovo.[76] Rather than satisfying the nationalist demands of the Kosovar population, the UN's approach only exacerbated the population's nationalist concerns.[77]

In sum, the presence of the United Nations may have contributed to UN credibility in East Timor, but there is little evidence that the legitimacy of the United Nations made the population much more patient with being occupied. Even in East Timor, the population grew anxious to see the United Nations depart. Occupied populations resist occupation, whether that occupation is by an individual country or by the United Nations. The only solution to this impatience is to offer protection and credible guarantees of future sovereignty. In East Timor, the United Nations accomplished this task. In Kosovo, they have not yet. The lesson here is not about the importance of UN involvement in occupations, but rather about the persistence of nationalist demands even in the presence of an internationally legitimated occupying force.

Conclusion

To be clear, multilateralism may be beneficial in some cases, but it is not a necessary or sufficient condition for occupation success, nor is legitimacy its primary benefit. Multilateralism is advantageous inasmuch as it reduces the costs of occupation and, thus, makes it easier for occupying powers to sustain a multilateral occupation. In addition, UN pledges that an occupation will be temporary appear more credible, though the case of Kosovo suggests that occupied populations will eventually even question the intentions of the UN. The two case studies presented suggest that the general argument about threat environment presented in this book can be extended to nation-building operations led by international organizations rather than by individual countries.

What about the effects of multilateralism on earlier historical occupations? In this chapter, I have not presented a table summarizing the effect of multilateralism across the entire data set of occupation. The argument about the emerging norm of multilateralism is an argument about an evolving, emerging, largely post–World War II phenomenon, so it would be unfair to expect the norm to have an influence in cases that predate the norm. Still, it is useful to examine how multilateralism affected some of the more prominent occupations in history. In the multilateral occupation of western Germany after World War II, disagreements among the Western allies actually impaired occupation success rather than fostered it. French opposition to any central government institutions in Germany slowed the process of zonal unification in western Germany.[78] Multilateral occupations may be valuable for burden sharing, but burden sharing also grants more states a say in the direction of an occupation, which can impair progress.

As for John Dower's example of Japan cited at the beginning of this chapter, while the general notion of a postwar occupation of Japan was viewed as legitimate by other states, the conduct of the occupation itself was viewed quite skeptically by many states, including close American allies. Although the occupation of Japan was ostensibly multilateral, it was, in practice, a unilateral U.S. operation and legitimacy had little to do with its success.[79] General MacArthur was openly contemptuous of any outside influence on his powers as supreme commander. Not only was the Soviet Union excluded from occupation decision making for geopolitical reasons, but even the British were routinely ignored by the U.S occupation administration.[80] The British Commonwealth initially deployed a force of forty thousand in the occupation under Australian command, but by October 1946, the decision had been made to begin the withdrawal of those troops. The British had become disaffected with American unilateralism and, especially, its determination to rebuild the Japanese economy in ways that might be damaging to the British export economy.[81] Even though the multilateral Far Eastern Commission (FEC) was created in late 1945 with the purpose of advising the occupation, MacArthur acted to undercut its authority, including the introduction of a new constitution for Japan in the spring of 1946 before the FEC had a chance to evaluate it.[82]

The occupation of Japan was multilateral in name only.[83] A favorable threat environment, not the perceived legitimacy of the occupation, enabled success in Japan. In fact, all of the other powers that were supposed to play a part in the reconstruction of Japan resented the unilateral assertion of authority by the United States, but they were powerless to stop it. Japan's neighbors, meanwhile, welcomed the occupation primarily because of the material security benefits it provided. Namely, the occupation guaranteed that they no longer needed to fear unconstrained Japanese militarism.[84] In sum, advocates of multilateralism have overstated the benefits of the legitimacy that multilateralism may bring to an occupation. Multilateralism may offer some benefits to occupying powers, but it does not resolve the fundamental political challenges of military occupation.

THE FUTURE OF MILITARY OCCUPATION

"A year ago we liberated them from the Fascist Monster, and they still sit there doing their best to smile politely at us, as hungry as ever, more disease-ridden than ever before, in the ruins of their beautiful city where law and order have ceased to exist. . . . The days of Benito Mussolini must seem like a lost paradise compared with this." The prolific British travel writer Norman Lewis, serving as an intelligence officer in occupied Italy, wrote these words on September 23, 1944.[1] The allied occupation of Italy ultimately succeeded, but one can easily imagine these same words being written about a number of historical occupations that have failed. States often embark on military occupation with the promise of delivering a better, more secure future for both themselves and the occupied population, yet so often they fail to accomplish their goals. This book has attempted to explain why so many military occupations throughout history have failed to achieve their goals.

The contemporary U.S.–led occupation of Iraq has heightened both scholarly and lay interest in the subject of military occupation. Despite this interest, the field of international relations has not provided an explanation for why some military occupations succeed whereas others fail.

Why Military Occupations Succeed or Fail

To succeed, military occupations require both time and resources. The longer and more costly an occupation becomes, however, the more likely it is that the occupation will meet resistance from both the occupied population and the occupying power. Occupying powers may enjoy a brief honeymoon period when they begin an occupation, but occupied populations soon grow weary of being under the control of a foreign power. Lengthy occupations are likely to meet nationalist resistance as any initial welcome obsolesces. Occupying powers, meanwhile, often would prefer to spend their limited national resources elsewhere, and long and costly occupation is likely to generate domestic opposition. Successful military occupiers must convince both the occupied population and their own population to accept a lengthy and costly occupation. Occupying powers that are unable to accomplish these tasks are likely to meet resistance that will make it more difficult to achieve the goals of the occupation. More often than not occupying powers cannot accomplish these tasks, which explains why occupations fail more often than they succeed.

The key to occupation success is the threat environment in which an occupation is undertaken. When the occupied population perceives that an external power poses a greater threat to its self-determination than the occupying power itself, then the population will welcome the protection offered by the occupying power. For the occupying power, an external threat motivates the power to maintain its commitment to the occupation of a territory in which it has already invested considerable resources. Following this logic, occupations are more likely to succeed when the occupied territory is geopolitically significant rather than on the periphery of the international system. When the most significant threat to an occupied territory is internal—among groups within the territory—then an occupation is more likely to fail. Internal divisions make it improbable that the entire population will value the protection offered by a foreign occupying power.

As I demonstrated in chapter 2, the threat environment also affects the strategies that occupying powers pursue, and those strategies, in turn, affect the threat environment. When occupations initially confront an unfavorable threat environment, coercion is a necessary, but not sufficient, strategy for occupation success. Coercion, however, runs the risk of alienating the occupied population and exacerbating an already poor threat environment. When occupations initially enjoy a more favorable threat environment, occupying powers can mostly refrain from coercion and rely instead on cooperative strategies that reinforce a beneficial threat environment and are more likely to lead to the conditions for successfully ending an occupation.

Occupying powers face one final difficult decision: the choice of when to end an occupation. Occupations are defined, in part, by their intentionally temporary nature. Occupying powers eschew annexation and colonialism and seek to end the occupation at the earliest possible moment while still accomplishing their goals. To successfully withdraw, occupying powers must accomplish two tasks. First, they must return sovereignty to a legitimate, indigenous, and reliable government, and second, they must ensure that the occupied territory will be secure and nonthreatening after the occupation concludes. Such a combination allows the occupying power to withdraw with confidence that instability will not force it to reintervene.

Occupying powers that cannot accomplish these two tasks face a dilemma of either withdrawing too early from an occupation or prolonging an unwelcome occupation. Occupations that end prematurely may only invite further instability and later reoccupation. Occupations that go on too long lead to opposition from the occupied population and dissatisfaction among the occupying power's population. The threat environment also affects the ability of occupying powers to achieve the prerequisites for successful withdrawal. A favorable threat environment facilitates the creation of a stable, reliable, and secure postoccupation government by cementing a strong relationship between the occupying power and the occupied population. By contrast, occupying powers that have had difficulty throughout an occupation and are in an unfavorable threat environment are more likely to find it difficult to accomplish the two prerequisites for successfully ending an occupation and, thus, are more likely to find themselves in the occupation dilemma.

The Post–September 11 Occupations

Since September 11, 2001, the United States has led the invasions of Afghanistan and Iraq and undertaken differing types of occupations in both countries. Some might argue that there is little to be learned from cases of occupation that occurred as much as almost two centuries ago. According to this argument, the occupations of today are different in terms of objectives, methods, and context, so there are few lessons to be learned from, for example, the U.S. occupation of Cuba in 1898 or the multilateral occupation of western Germany after World War II.

To the contrary, I will argue that the same challenges of occupation that have historically made occupation difficult persist through these two cases, and the arguments presented earlier in this book are still relevant. In particular, the occupation of Iraq represented one of the most difficult threat environments for occupation that a state could encounter. The internal divisions within Iraq combined with the indecisive military victory made occupying Iraq particularly difficult. The occupation of Afghanistan has been moderately more successful, in large part, because the United States implicitly abandoned the goal of building an effective central state in Afghanistan. Afghanistan was never fully occupied and, thus, it provides a useful case for examining the consequences of choosing *not* fully to occupy a defeated state.

The Limited Occupation of Afghanistan, 2001

Within a month of the terrorist attacks on the United States of September 11, 2001, the United States launched a military invasion of Afghanistan. The immediate goals of the invasion were to topple the Taliban regime and disrupt al-Qaeda operations within Afghanistan.[2] For the longer term, the elimination of the Taliban regime required its replacement by a government that posed less of a risk to both U.S. security and regional stability.[3]

GOALS AND MEANS

Many Afghans initially welcomed the invading forces with the hope that the United States would end the tyranny of the Taliban and evict the foreigners that the Taliban had invited into the country.[4] In December 2001, the United Nations convened a conference of leading Afghan politicians and political groups in Bonn, Germany, to begin the process of reconstructing the country. The leaders agreed to form an interim authority with a chairman, who would govern Afghanistan until an emergency Loya Jirga (or tribal council) could be convened within six months. The emergency Loya Jirga would be charged with constructing a transitional administration that would hold power until a separate constitutional Loya Jirga could be held within eighteen months of the emergency Loya Jirga.

CONDUCT OF THE OCCUPATION

Annex I of the Bonn agreement also requested the assistance of the United Nations in authorizing an International Security Assistance Force (ISAF) that would help maintain security in Afghanistan and provide assistance in the training of a new Afghan military. United Nations Security Council resolution 1383 of December 6 endorsed the Bonn agreement, and UN Security Council resolution 1386 of December 20 authorized the formation of the ISAF.[5]

In the spring of 2002, the ISAF began its operations with eighteen participating countries and five thousand troops under British command. This ISAF force was separate from the U.S.–led coalition invasion force that continued to fight remnants of the Taliban regime and al-Qaeda within Afghanistan. Simultaneously, the United Nations created the UN Aid Mission in Afghanistan to address humanitarian needs and to assist in the reconstruction of the country.[6] In June, at the emergency Loya Jirga, Hamid Karzai, an ethnic Pashtun, was chosen as president of the Transitional Government that would remain in power until the Afghan constitution could be written at the constitutional Loya Jirga.

In October 2003, the United Nations authorized the extension of the ISAF mission, now under NATO command, beyond its previously limited mandate for Kabul. NATO subsequently expanded its military security mission and began participating in provincial teams that assisted in the reconstruction of the more remote regions of northern and western Afghanistan.[7] Still, by December 2003, thirteen of Afghanistan's thirty-two provinces were judged unsafe for UN humanitarian missions.[8]

The constitutional Loya Jirga met in Kabul in December 2003 to devise the new Afghan constitution.[9] Within a month, the constitution, complete with provisions for an executive, a legislature, and a judicial system, was ratified. After several delays due to concerns about security, Afghanistan's first democratic presidential elections were held in October 2004 with Karzai garnering the support of approximately 55 percent of the Afghan electorate and twenty-one of Afghanistan's thirty-four provinces. Two months later, Karzai was inaugurated as the democratically elected president of Afghanistan. Meanwhile, NATO continued its operations both around Kabul and through the provincial reconstruction teams, although locating the resources to support these operations became a growing problem.[10] Simultaneously, a separate U.S. force continued to seek out remaining Taliban and al-Qaeda elements within Afghanistan.

Since his inauguration, Karzai has led Afghanistan toward the next stage in the consolidation of its political system. In September 2005, the first parliamentary elections were peacefully held after yet more delays due to security concerns. Despite the elections, Afghanistan continues to face numerous problems, including a resurgent Taliban, the role of tribal warlords, and the dependence of the economy on illicit drug sales.

EVALUATING THE OCCUPATION OF AFGHANISTAN

Based on the initial threat environment, Afghanistan was an inauspicious choice for an occupation. Afghanistan is a multinational country divided both ethnically and geographically.[11] There was no external threat motivating the Afghan people as a whole to welcome the presence offered by the United States and its coalition partners. For the United States, there was a significant threat that motivated the continuing operation, but that threat was primarily internal in the form of the Taliban and remaining al-Qaeda elements.[12]

In the face of an unfavorable threat environment, NATO would have had to rely heavily on coercion to implement a successful occupation of all of Afghanistan. Instead, rather than creating a comprehensive occupation authority that attempted to control the entire country, ISAF pursued a more limited nation-building mission while the United States focused its efforts on fighting off those elements that were most threatening to it. The NATO operation in Afghanistan eschewed comprehensive nationwide occupation, and thereby, avoided the nationalist reaction that might otherwise be expected.

As a consequence, the Afghan central government remains weak as regional warlords continue to exert their authority. Efforts to curtail the trade of heroin out of Afghanistan have largely failed as the illicit drug trade continues to comprise 40 percent of the total Afghan economy.[13] The Afghan National Army, with approximately thirty-five thousand trained soldiers by early 2007, also remains relatively weak, with regional militias mostly providing security.[14]

The United States has complemented this strategy of accommodating regional warlords with an attempt to induce cooperation from the Afghan population, though there have been considerable delays in the delivery of aid to the Afghan people.[15] In addition, the amount of aid has been lower than comparable cases. In the two years after Karzai's inauguration, per capita aid to Afghanistan was less than one-tenth of the aid offered to Bosnia and Kosovo in comparable periods.[16]

Afghanistan is an interesting case precisely because it is a case where a comprehensive occupation could have been attempted, but another strategy was chosen instead. This overall approach has avoided large-scale resistance in the short-term, but may pose long-term dangers.[17] By allowing regional ethnic nationalisms to flourish in Afghanistan, the United States has avoided many of the traditional problems of occupation.[18] On the down side, however, this approach may delay the process of reconstruction in much of the country and leaves open the possibility of conflict in the remote regions that remain outside the control of a central government.[19] To entirely remake Afghanistan would have required a difficult comprehensive occupation that would have had to rely heavily on coercion to overcome the unfavorable threat environment of the occupation. Instead, the United States opted to allow regional warlords to retain power. Afghan public opinion remains mostly grateful that the Taliban was removed from power, though increasingly wary of the resurgence of violence and the slow pace of reconstruction.[20] If conflict does erupt within the remote provinces of Afghanistan or if the training of anti–U.S. terrorists resumes in the remote parts of the country, then this strategy of avoiding comprehensive occupation may ultimately leave U.S. interests insecure.[21]

The Occupation of Iraq

In March 2003, the United States led an invasion of Iraq that displaced the regime of Saddam Hussein. On May 1, President George W. Bush proclaimed an end to "major combat operations" and infamously declared "mission accomplished" despite an ongoing occupation of the country. More than four years later, nearly 150,000 U.S. troops remained in Iraq in an effort to stabilize the country and develop sustainable political institutions. In the process, U.S. military forces lost more than three thousand soldiers and spent hundreds of billions of dollars.

Contrary to the expectation of Vice President Richard Cheney that the United States would be greeted as liberators, not conquerors, when it entered Iraq, the U.S. occupation of Iraq was met by a violent and effective insurgency.[22] In this brief case study, I will argue that the U.S. occupation in Iraq was undertaken in an unfavorable threat environment.[23] As a consequence, the United States found it difficult to manage the coexisting nationalisms within Iraq. The Iraqi population, divided among itself, did not perceive an external threat greater than the occupying power itself, and the U.S. population has increasingly questioned the value of the occupation. Nor was Iraq particularly vulnerable to any external threat. In this sense, Iraq more resembled liberated southern Korea than defeated Japan. As a consequence of this unfavorable threat environment, the United States had difficulty implementing an effective strategy of occupation. Opposition to the occupation led to a reliance on coercion that did not succeed in quelling opposition to the occupation.

Finally, the United States faced a classic occupation dilemma. Both prolonging the occupation and ending the occupation appeared to be unattractive options. A successful withdrawal would have required returning basic sovereignty to Iraqis and ensuring the security of Iraq after withdrawal. Both of these conditions were impossible to accomplish. Before laying out this argument, I begin by briefly retelling the history of the occupation of Iraq.

GOALS AND MEANS

Resistance to the occupation of Iraq only grew in intensity over the summer and fall of 2003.[24] The insurgency was actually several different insurgencies, including displaced Baathists, Shiite citizens who longed for control over Iraq, and foreign insurgents affiliated with the international Jihadist movement. The initial administrator charged with overseeing the reconstruction of Iraq through the State Department's Office of Reconstruction and Humanitarian Assistance (ORHA), Jay Garner, was replaced in mid May with Paul Bremer, who became the head of the Coalition Provisional Authority (CPA).[25] The CPA

was charged with aiding in the rebuilding of the Iraqi economy as well as fostering the development of new political institutions. In addition, a new Iraqi army
.was to be trained to provide security so that coalition forces could eventually
withdraw.

American goals in Iraq were consistent with the security goals of other
occupations in history. The United States initially aimed to ensure that Iraq
did not have weapons of mass destruction and to replace Hussein's regime
with a government more friendly to American interests. The means for accomplishing this included aiding the Iraqi people in the creation of a representative democratic country. A democratic Iraq, liberated by the United States,
would be an important step in advancing U.S. interests throughout the Middle
East. Over time, the initial objective of creating a liberal democracy in Iraq
was replaced by a more modest goal of creating a functional government that
would allow the United States and its coalition partners to withdraw from the
country.[26]

CONDUCT OF THE OCCUPATION

In an effort to accommodate Iraqi concerns about self-governance, Bremer created the Iraqi Governing Council (IGC) in July 2003 to be composed of twenty-
five members, chosen by the CPA, and representative of the various groups across
Iraqi society. The IGC was meant to assuage Iraqi concerns about the unrepre-
sentative nature of the CPA. In the following months, however, violence in Iraq
and protests from the Iraqi Governing Council only increased.[27] The IGC wanted
the occupation to end and failed to see any U.S. plan for returning sovereignty to
an Iraqi government.

In an agreement of November 15, 2003, the United States took further steps
toward returning sovereignty to an Iraqi government. The agreement called for
the IGC to develop a transitional administrative law by the end of February 2004.
Basic sovereignty was to be returned to Iraq by June 30, 2004. Until national
elections for a constitutional convention and then a parliament could be held
in 2005, Iraq would be governed by an interim government selected through a
process of local caucuses. The IGC rejected the process of selecting the interim
government, but they were nonetheless encouraged by the agreement's recognition that sovereignty must be returned to an Iraqi government.

After arduous negotiations, the Transitional Administrative Law (TAL)
was finally signed on March 8, 2004. The TAL called for returning sovereignty
to a transitional government by June 30, 2004, holding elections in January 2005 for a transitional National Assembly, and the drafting of an Iraqi
constitution by fall 2005. That constitution would be ratified by the entire Iraqi

population before a final and permanent Iraqi government would be elected in December 2005.

The difficult issue still remained, however, of how the interim government scheduled to take power on June 30 would be selected. The influential Grand Ayatollah Ali al-Sistani vehemently objected to the proposed caucus system and insisted that the interim government be chosen by direct election. Such elections would favor the Shia majority of which Sistani is a part. The CPA, however, maintained that free and fair elections could not possibly be held in Iraq before the June deadline for returning sovereignty to an Iraqi government.

To break this deadlock, the CPA turned to the United Nations and its special envoy, Lakhdar Brahimi. United Nations involvement in Iraq had been limited since the bombing of the UN headquarters in Baghdad on August 19, 2003, that killed the highly regarded UN diplomat Sergio Vieira de Mello, but now a critical role had been identified for the United Nations. Brahimi considered a variety of options for selecting the new government until ultimately recommending that the interim government be appointed and filled primarily with technocrats who could serve as caretakers until a permanent constitution and government were in place.

In late May, the UN, the CPA, and the IGC met to consider who should be appointed as prime minister to assume power at the end of June. Eventually, the conference settled on a secular Shiite technocrat, Ayad Allawi. Following negotiations to ensure that all of Iraq's various political interests were represented, the full thirty-six member interim government was announced on June 1. On June 8, the UN Security Council unanimously adopted Resolution 1546, which recognized the legitimacy of the interim government, guaranteed the right of Iraq to its sovereignty, and authorized the continuation of the multinational force in Iraq to ensure peace and stability.[28]

Sovereignty was turned over to the transitional government on June 28, 2004. Scheduled elections were then held in January 2005 for a 275-member National Assembly that was tasked with writing an acceptable permanent constitution for Iraq. A coalition of Shiite political parties, the United Iraqi Alliance, won a plurality of the votes (48%) and subsequently selected Ibrahim al-Jafaari to be the new prime minister of Iraq. After difficult negotiations over power sharing in Iraq, the new constitution was ratified by referendum in October 2005.

Yet despite all of these apparent successes, Iraq continued to be a violent and unstable country. The Iraqi military remained unready to assume responsibility for the security of the country, so the coalition forces remained in place attempting to maintain order until the Iraqi military was adequately trained for the mission.

EVALUATING THE OCCUPATION OF IRAQ

The United States and its allies had considerable difficulty accomplishing their goals in Iraq. As Larry Diamond, who participated in the Coalition Provisional Authority, laments, "At every step, the United States and its allies would underestimate the force of Iraqi nationalism."[29] Arguably, U.S. interests have been hurt more than they have been helped by the invasion, and it remains unclear when and if a stable, unified Iraq will emerge from the violence that has engulfed the country. Displaced Sunnis are understandably concerned about whether their minority rights will be protected within a democracy run by the majority Shiite population, and the Shiite majority longs for the control they see as rightfully theirs.

In the case of the occupation of Iraq, there is no external threat that is seen by the entire population as a greater threat to Iraqi sovereignty than the occupying power itself. Even Bremer himself acknowledges this difference between the occupations of western Germany and Japan after World War II and the occupation of Iraq: "The vast majority of Iraqis were delighted to have Saddam and his henchmen thrown out, but few were happy to find a foreign, non-Muslim army occupying their country. And . . . with the Soviet Red Army occupying eastern Germany and Japan's northern offshore islands, the countries we had defeated in World War II had a strong motive to cooperate with us—nobody wanted the American Army replaced by the Red Army."[30] A significant percentage of the population has seen little value in the occupation and has rejected the continuing presence of foreign occupiers. Although a case could be made that Iran is an external threat to Iraqi sovereignty, a substantial portion of the Iraqi population views the U.S.–led occupation as a greater threat than Iran.[31] Others may point to the external threat posed by al-Qaeda, but it is unclear whether al-Qaeda represents a significant enough external threat to Iraqi sovereignty to motivate the Iraqi population as a whole to accept further occupation.[32]

The greater threat in Iraq is an internal one. Iraq is a society deeply divided between its Shiite, Sunni, and Kurdish populations.[33] Such a division, especially a politically charged one, is unlikely to produce agreement on which entity poses the greatest threat to self-determination. Some Iraqis have seen an internal threat that leads them to desire a continuation of the occupation. In a November 2003 poll conducted by the U.S. Department of State's Office of Research, 66 percent of Iraqis responded that the insurgent attacks indicated that coalition forces needed to remain in place in Iraq.[34] While somewhat encouraging, it is the other 34 percent of the population that has, in part, made the occupation so difficult. In November 2005, most Iraqis stated that they saw their life improving, but 50.3 percent maintain that the U.S.–led invasion of Iraq in 2003 was a mistake.[35] These internal divisions have only been exacerbated by the sense among many

Iraqis that they have been liberated, rather than defeated, and therefore should not be occupied.

The lack of an external threat has also hindered U.S. occupation efforts. Initially, the Bush administration mustered support for the invasion and occupation by pointing to the threat posed by terrorism and the supposed connections between Iraq and the al-Qaeda network. Over time, however, more and more Americans questioned whether the threat posed to Iraq by terrorists or others is worth the U.S. investment to protect that country. Whereas more than 60 percent of the American population approved of President Bush's handling of the invasion of Iraq, that support had dropped to 40 percent by March 2006.[36] The success of the Democratic Party in U.S. congressional elections in November 2006 was seen by most as a damning condemnation of the Bush administration's war strategy. Absent the perception of a significant threat to Iraq that warrants American involvement, pressures on the administration to withdraw from Iraq continued to mount.

The continuing opposition to the occupation, the lack of effective Iraqi security forces, and the absence of a compelling external threat from which Iraqis desired protection compelled the coalition forces to rely heavily on coercive techniques to try and suppress the insurgency. This unsuccessful strategy of coercion has only produced more opposition to the occupation and made it more difficult for the U.S.–led provisional authority successfully to engage in either accommodation or inducement. Efforts at accommodation were undone by the deep divisions within Iraqi society. Efforts at inducement were undermined by the difficulty of delivering resources and services to populations in the midst of the insurgency.[37]

When the United States did try to appease Iraqi nationalism, it was hindered by its mistakes and by the deep divisions within Iraqi society. Policies that favored one group within Iraqi society over another were met with opposition by out-of-favor groups. Any moves that were seen as favoring Shiite political elites were opposed by Sunni groups, and vice versa. The absence of a successful strategy of coercion in Iraq only contributed to the inability of the coalition to accommodate elites within Iraq. Even when the CPA tried to move toward Iraqi sovereignty, leaders like Sistani objected to the transition plans in the November 15, 2003, agreement.

In terms of inducement, the United States has allocated more than $250 billion to the occupation and reconstruction of Iraq thus far, but the insurgency has hindered the ability of the U.S. government to implement a policy of inducement.[38] Again, when the threat environment is unfavorable, coercion is a prerequisite for more cooperative strategies of occupation. As a consequence, reconstruction aid is mostly being delivered to those areas of Iraq that are already peaceful and supportive of the reconstruction assistance. Because of the continuing violence, areas where the insurgency continues have seen fewer funds delivered. The population in these areas has become increasingly skeptical of the ability of the United States to provide either security or jobs to the people.

The occupation of Iraq has evolved through the three phases of the occupation dilemma laid out in the previous chapter. In phase one, the occupying power is expected to underestimate the difficulty of the task of occupying another country. Either to generate domestic support, or because it does not yet understand the situation it has got itself in, the occupying power often underestimates the resources and time necessary for occupation success. A postinvasion honeymoon period may only reinforce mistaken ideas about the ease with which occupation can be undertaken. In the case of the occupation of Iraq, this first phase has become quite controversial. Whether willfully or not, the United States leadership suggested that the occupation of Iraq would be far easier and less costly than it has turned out to be. When General Eric Shinseki, chief of staff of the U.S. Army, testified in February 2003 that an occupation of Iraq would require "something on the order of several hundred thousand troops," the Bush administration promptly disagreed.[39] Within two days, Secretary of Defense Donald Rumsfeld declared, "It's not logical to me that it would take as many forces following the conflict as it would to win the war," and Deputy Secretary of Defense Paul Wolfowitz characterized Shinseki's estimate as "wildly off the mark."[40] By April 2003, the White House's Office of Management and Budget had requested only $2.5 billion for reconstruction in Iraq, less than 1 percent of what the actual costs have been. Extensive preparation by the State Department for the occupation was dismissed by the Department of Defense.[41] Instead, the U.S. leadership believed that the United States would be greeted as liberators, not occupiers. Secretary Rumsfeld infamously dismissed the initial looting after the invasion by stating that "freedom's untidy, and free people are free to make mistakes and commit crimes and do bad things. They're also free to live their lives and do wonderful things. And that's what's going to happen here."[42] This vision of the occupation helped to ensure domestic support for the invasion of Iraq.

In the second phase of the occupation dilemma, the tasks of occupation only increase, and the occupying power finds itself becoming more and more entrenched in the occupied territory. Withdrawal becomes difficult as the occupied territory grows dependent on the presence of the occupying power for both security and assistance in reconstruction. In Iraq, this second phase of the dilemma was evident only months after the occupation had begun. The United States could not consider withdrawal from Iraq because Iraq was entirely dependent on the presence of the occupying force for security.[43] In the absence of that security, Iraq was likely to descend into civil war, which was an unacceptable outcome for the United States.

Finally, in the third phase, the United States and its allies faced a classic occupation dilemma. Immediate withdrawal would relieve the occupying powers of the costs, both human and financial, of the occupation, but at the danger of a potential civil war in Iraq. Without the presence of the occupying powers in Iraq, the security situation in Iraq was only likely to deteriorate. On the other hand, however, the likelihood of long-term success in Iraq is low, given the inauspicious threat environment. As the costs of the occupation rise, domestic opposition to the continuing presence in Iraq is only likely to increase unless substantial and dramatic progress is made toward achieving peace and stability.

Theoretical Implications

The theory presented in this book has significant implications for wider theoretical debates about the use of force and the prospects for democratization in international politics.[44] One implication of the argument is that states should hesitate before using military force to reorder a foreign country.[45] Populations resist the implementation of political order by an occupying force, and the costs of occupation are likely to be high for the occupying power. The use of military force can be effective in many different contexts, but using force for the purpose of building political, economic, and social institutions is one of the more difficult tasks that states can undertake. Only the hubris of states allows them to think that they can easily reconstruct the institutions of another state that they have just conquered.[46] Reflecting on U.S. experiences in the 1990s, Anthony Lake, national security advisor to President Bill Clinton, acknowledged, "It is a dangerous hubris to believe we can build other nations. But where are our interests are engaged, we can help nations build themselves and give them time to make a start."[47] As the historian Roger Owen reflects on the British occupation of Egypt, "Once again, it is difficult to exaggerate the extraordinary, and misguided, ambition behind this exercise in what would now be called 'nation-building'. Even more striking than the unreality of the whole project is the megalomania involved."[48] Only this hubris can explain the continuing efforts of states to make occupation succeed despite the uninspiring track record of occupation. Given the dubious history of occupation, one might expect rational states to avoid the occupation of foreign territories, yet occupation continues.

More broadly, the argument in this book reinforces the lessons about prudence in the use of force that are at the heart of realist theory of international politics. I have argued that both military occupiers and occupied populations are driven by concerns about their security. Occupations are most likely to fail when the value of the occupation to their security is unrecognized by either the population or the occupying power. States must prudently use force, and they must be careful to use force only in response to genuine threats to their interests. In the absence of such threats, they are likely to lose interest in the costly and demanding tasks of occupation. Not surprisingly, then, occupation has typically been more successful when the occupied territory is geostrategically significant as opposed to occupations of territories on the periphery of the international system.

At the same time, the argument in this book raises questions about the place of coercion in the foreign policy of states. As I have argued, in an unfavorable threat environment, coercion is essential to a successful occupation. Coercion, however, often requires the use of ruthless military force. Theoretically, then, this book forces us to consider ways in which military force can effectively be employed by states to coerce occupied populations and what the challenges of using force in this way might be, especially for liberal democracies. If successful military occupation in an unfavorable threat environment requires the ruthless and costly use of coercion, is that a strategy that most states are willing and able to execute?

Finally, the argument in this book reminds us of the importance of structural factors in determining outcomes in international politics. The structural context of an occupation, including threats to the occupied territory, directly affects occupation outcomes and indirectly affects those outcomes by shaping the strategies available to occupying powers. Threats are not entirely structural, but they do have a structural element to them. Occupation outcomes, in other words, cannot be explained by looking only at the choices made by policymakers.

Policy Implications

Adopting a theoretical approach to the study of military occupation allows future analysts and policymakers to devise occupation strategies that are more likely to succeed. Rather than considering each occupation in an ad hoc manner, policymakers can look to deductive theory for guidance as to what factors are most important to consider before undertaking an occupation.

One of the common critiques made of the U.S.–led occupation of Iraq is that not enough planning was done for the occupation.[49] Undoubtedly, this is true, and the planning that was done was unfortunately often ignored. This criticism, however, misses a larger point. Being prepared for occupying a foreign country is certainly preferable to not being prepared, but the importance of local knowledge should not be overstated. In almost all of the cases considered in this study, including successful occupations, the occupying power's forces were ill-prepared for the task of occupation. For example, the British occupation of Egypt was conducted by "amateurs in government; they had only a modicum of training in the history and the cultures of the people they ruled."[50] These forces lacked local knowledge of politics, language, and custom, and they had little experience in military government or civilian administration. Local knowledge, in particular language skills, allows occupying forces to assess the particular challenges ahead of them once they arrive in a country they have occupied. Local knowledge is also essential to an effective strategy of political accommodation, which requires an understanding of the different elites in a defeated territory.

Deep, local knowledge must, therefore, be a priority of any future occupying power, but deep, local knowledge alone is not a recipe for occupation success. Even in cases where proconsuls were provided with local knowledge, such as at the Civil Affairs Training Schools that the United States established during World War II, and where the occupations ultimately succeeded, participants in the occupation lament how unprepared they were for the tasks in front of them.[51] The factors that make occupation difficult—nationalism and the impatience of occupying powers—are not primarily determined by local culture and cannot easily be addressed simply by understanding the nature of the society being occupied. The absence of planning does not explain *why* there has been so much opposition to the occupation of Iraq, nor why there was such little opposition in the famous successes in western Germany and Japan immediately following World War II. The insurgency in Iraq was not caused by an absence of planning, though a better-thought-out occupation strategy may have increased the likelihood of defeating the insurgency.

It has become equally common to blame failures in Iraq on an insufficient number of troops deployed to the country during the initial invasion and subsequent occupation. This claim is also certainly true, but it misses two key points. First, the correlation between troop strength and occupation outcome is weak. The prominent RAND study of American nation-building efforts analyzes the number of troops per capita and finds that the occupations of western Germany, Bosnia, and Kosovo had the highest number of troops per capita.[52] Troops in Bosnia and Kosovo were vital to stopping the ongoing conflicts there in the 1990s, but they have been less helpful in accomplishing the goals of occupation and nation building. Instead, the occupations of Bosnia and Kosovo have largely stagnated with hardened ethnic divisions remaining in place.

Second, advocates of this argument like to point to the occupations of Germany and Japan with their massive numbers of troops as evidence of the importance of troop strength to occupation success, but this is correlation without causation. Insurgencies failed to emerge in western Germany and

Japan because the threat environment removed the incentive for an insurgency to break out, not because of the large number of troops present. To be clear, large numbers of troops are often necessary for implementing a successful strategy of coercion in unfavorable threat environments. Further, in cases of successful occupation, military force may deter resistance and may be essential for protecting an occupied territory from an external threat, but troops alone, in the absence of an external threat or an effective strategy of coercion, are unlikely to solve the political problems, especially nationalism, that are at the heart of opposition to occupation.[53] Certainly, the latent threat of coercive violence loomed in the background in both Germany and Japan, but the military presence alone did not allow for the building of political, economic, and social institutions. To the extent that coercive violence was a significant factor in these occupations, it was primarily during the war itself, prior to the occupation, that violence set the stage for a successful occupation by leaving Japan and Germany vulnerable to an external threat.

Future policymakers would be wise to reject the deceptively easy solutions of more planning and more resources, and think instead about the threat environment that is likely to shape the outcome of the occupations they undertake. Understanding how better to conduct an occupation is important, but perhaps more important is asking the question of whether occupation is a wise strategy at all. Based on the threat environment, policymakers should be able to anticipate which occupations are most likely to meet resistance, and these predictions should factor into the decision to carry out the invasion and occupation of another country.

Future Research Questions

This book is a first attempt at explaining occupation success and failure, but it certainly is not the definitive word. Much research remains to be done. For example, this book has introduced some basic logics and performed some preliminary tests of those logics, but considerably more testing is required to evaluate conclusively the validity of my arguments. Future research should include more case studies of occupations as well as efforts to collect more data on which statistical analysis might be performed.

The research in this book could also potentially be broadened by future researchers. In the previous chapter, I probed whether or not the same logic suggested in this book applies to cases of UN occupation. Future research might press further to see how well the argument holds up in other UN cases or, alternatively, whether the basic logic introduced here can also be applied to similar, but different, phenomena such as empire and colonialism. More broadly, the logic of this argument might be applied to the entire class of events called "nation build-ing" that has received so much attention in recent years.

Finally, future research should look at how effective coercion strategies can be implemented in occupied territories. As I have argued, coercion is necessary for success in occupied territories with unfavorable threat environments. Future research might examine the prospects for successful coercion, and the challenges of implementing such a strategy.

The Future of Military Occupation

Military occupation is among the most difficult tasks that a state can under-take. To secure their interests, occupying powers often attempt to impose new political, economic, and social institutions on a state that it has just defeated in war. Occupied populations are likely to resist this imposition, and unsurprisingly, the track record of occupation is not encouraging.

Occupying a foreign country should be an option of last resort for political leaders. Successful occupation requires extensive time and resources that are only likely to be available under relatively rare conditions. Sometimes occupation, such as the occupations of Japan and Germany after World War II, will be necessary. In those cases, occupying powers should do their best to maximize their likelihood of success by either capitalizing on a favorable threat environment or implement-ing coercive strategies that can overcome an unfavorable threat environment. Military occupation under less propitious conditions should be avoided. Military occupations in regions of lesser geopolitical concern are less likely to succeed. Neither the occupied population nor the occupying power is likely to perceive the external threat in these conditions that is critical to occupation success.

With the continuing problem posed by failing and failed states, military occupation is likely to continue to be an attractive policy option in states on the periphery of the international system.[54] By occupying these weak or failing states, and imposing new institutions on them, powerful states such as the United States may be able to eliminate the threat these states pose. History suggests, however, that such occupations are likely to be fraught with danger.

This is not to suggest that great powers must completely reject such interven-tions and occupations in the future. All policy choices involve weighing the risks and the rewards of the policy. If the threat posed by the failed state is sufficient, then the costs and risks of occupation may be acceptable. In such cases, however, occupying powers would be wise to embark on such operations with the sobriety that the history of military occupation teaches rather than the hubris that has been so common.

CASE SELECTION

In order to identify cases of occupation, I began by examining the aftermath of every international war since 1815.[1] The year 1815 marked the end of the Napoleonic Wars and the beginning of the modern era of nation-states. Occupation most often, but not always, follows in the aftermath of war. Therefore, in addition to examining the aftermath of war, I conducted a survey of international history since 1815 to determine if there had been any other occupations that had not followed a major war. This survey uncovered cases such as the U.S. occupations of Haiti and the Dominican Republic in the early twentieth century that did not follow a war.

In constructing the data set, I excluded three types of occupation. First, wartime occupations, such as the German occupation of France during World War II, are excluded from the data set.[2] In cases of wartime occupation, it can be difficult to determine whether the occupying power intends to permanently conquer the occupied territory or restore sovereignty at some point in the future. Thus, while the German occupation of France ended up being temporary, it is unclear whether Germany intended to restore full French sovereignty had it won World War II.

Second, I exclude occupations carried out under the auspices of the United Nations.[3] This includes two different types of operations. "Caretaker" occupations are designed simply to hold a territory until a long-term settlement of the status of the territory is devised by the United Nations or another international body. In these cases, an international organization such as the United Nations grants temporary occupation rights to a great power. Cases of caretaker occupations include the British occupations of Cyrenaica, Tripolitania, Eritrea, and Somalia in the wake of World War II. In these cases, Britain was simply holding these territories until the United Nations could decide their postwar fate.[4] The goals of caretaker occupations are so trivial that they seem an odd fit with other cases in the data set.

The other type of UN occupation excluded from the data set are more ambitious operations as in East Timor and Kosovo. I exclude these cases so as to focus on occupation as an instrument of foreign policy available to individual states. Part of the challenge of occupation is that it most often follows in the wake of military intervention and the forcible removal of a government. The United Nations does not defeat other territories and seize temporary sovereignty over those territories as individual states (or groups of allied states) have done. In chapter 4, I discuss the cases of East Timor and Kosovo in order to examine the possible benefits of multilateralism to occupation and the possibility of extending the argument of this book to UN operations.

Third, this book does not examine a relatively rare category of occupation, collateral occupation. Collateral occupations hold foreign territory until some indemnity is repaid. For example, following the Franco-Prussian War in 1870–71, fifty thousand German troops occupied six departments of France until the French paid 1.5 billion francs in war reparations. When the French finished paying on September 16, 1873, the German troops withdrew.[5] Again, the logic and motivation of a collateral occupation are different than those in the other occupations in the data set. The simple quid pro quo logic of collateral occupation does not pose the same political challenges that are typically encountered in other types of occupation.

As with any exercise like this, there are certain borderline cases that could arguably be included or excluded from this data set. The most challenging borderline cases are the cases of Soviet control in Eastern and Central Europe after World War II. The rationale for excluding these cases is discussed in the introduction. Among the other important borderline cases I exclude are:

> *United States in Veracruz, Mexico (1914):* Qualifies as a military intervention without an occupation. The United States intervened in Veracruz in order to restore order, but it stopped short of seizing meaningful sovereignty. In addition, the operation only lasted for six months.[6]
>
> *France in Syria and Lebanon (interwar period mandates):* Although France and Great Britain both acquired their territories through the League of Nations mandate system, French intentions to evacuate Syria and Lebanon were much less clear than British intentions in Iraq and Palestine. As David Fromkin writes, "But France, in particular, regarded the pledge of independence [in the League of Nations mandate] as window-dressing, and approached Syria and Lebanon in an annexationist spirit."[7]

United States in Nicaragua (1927–34): Qualifies as a military intervention without an occupation. United States forces operated in Nicaragua without seizing sovereign control over the country.[8]

Soviet Union in Afghanistan (1979–89): Though Soviet goals in Afghanistan remain somewhat debated, most agree that Moscow intended to undertake a limited intervention that would support its client regime in Kabul without occupying the country. According to former Soviet foreign minister Eduard Shevardnadze, "The people who made the decision about intervening with armed force did not plan to stay in Afghanistan for any length of time, or to create the sixteenth or seventeenth Soviet republic."[9] The Soviets subsequently found it impossible to extricate themselves from Afghanistan for a full decade. I consider this case an intervention without an occupation, but even if it is considered an occupation, the Soviet difficulties during their intervention in Afghanistan would only support the argument in this book.[10]

On the other hand, I include certain borderline cases like the British occupation of Egypt, the U.S. occupation of the Philippines, and the Israeli occupation of the West Bank and Gaza. The first two of these cases could be excluded on the grounds that they constituted colonialism. The third case is borderline since Israeli intentions with regard to those territories at the conclusion of the 1967 war were unclear. If my argument for including these cases is ultimately unpersuasive, then I would maintain that the remaining cases yield robust conclusions nonetheless:

The British Occupation of Egypt (1882–1954): Prime Minister William Gladstone reluctantly took on the occupation of Egypt and explicitly rejected the idea of creating an Egyptian colony. Gladstone stated that "an indefinite occupation would be absolutely at variance with all the principles and views of Her Majesty's Government and the pledge they have given to Europe."[11] As I discussed in chapter 3, the occupation of Egypt eventually grew into a colonial mission, but this was not how the British originally represented their intentions in Egypt.

The U.S. Occupation of the Philippines (1898–1954): Although many in the United States argued for the annexation of the Philippines, anti-imperialist groups pushed against the transformation of the United States into a colonial power. After the anti-American insurgency in the Philippines shortly following the onset of the occupation, the movement to withdraw from the Philippines gained strength.[12] As early as 1907, President Theodore Roosevelt lamented, "The Philippines form our heel of Achilles. They are all that makes the present situation with Japan dangerous." Yet the United States could not withdraw until nearly four decades later, after World War II.[13]

The Israeli Occupation of the West Bank and Gaza (1967–present): Israel acquired these territories as a result of the 1967 war. At the time, Israel's intentions with regard to the territories were much debated. On the one hand, some saw the territories as potential bargaining chips in an eventual peace settlement with Israel's Arab neighbors. Defense Minister Moshe Dayan is quoted as saying that he was "waiting for a telephone call from King Hussein," presumably with the purpose of negotiating a peace treaty.[14] Others envisioned a division of the West Bank that would provide strategic depth to Israel while returning some of the territory to Arab control. Yet others were committed to retaining the territory as a part of Israel.[15] Israel's intentions with regard to the occupied territories were thus divided. As with the U.S. occupation of the Philippines where U.S. intentions were also much debated, I opt to include the case of the Israeli occupation of the West Bank and Gaza.

Appendix 2

MILITARY OCCUPATIONS, 1815–2007

This appendix reviews the thirty cases of military occupation since 1815—twenty-six completed and four incomplete occupations. For a discussion of case selection criteria, see appendix 1. For each occupation, I provide a judgment about the outcome of the occupation, an explanation of how that judgment was reached, and an analysis of the threat environment in each case. As an indicator of direct cost, I also provide a representative estimate of the number of troops involved in the occupation.[1] Absolute force size is, however, an admittedly crude indicator of occupation costs. A complete account of the costs of an occupation would include indirect costs, which are harder to quantify.

Multilateral (United Kingdom, Russia, Prussia, Austria) Occupation of France, 1815–18

Force Size: 150,000
Outcome: Success

Explanation: The multilateral occupation of France after the Napoleonic Wars sought to remove Bonapartists from power and restore the Bourbon rule. With this more limited, restorative goal, the occupying powers were able to avoid offending French nationalism as an attempt to install an entirely new government might have. The French population, however, was not content with the occupation and resisted the presence of thousands of their erstwhile enemies in their territory. The French government under occupation worked continuously for an early end to the occupation. After a relatively short, multilateral occupation, a stable monarchical government under Louis XVIII was restored to France.

Threat Environment: Unusually, this occupation succeeded without the presence of a commonly perceived external threat. France was a defeated power with no particular adversary after the war that it shared in common with the occupying powers. The limited, restorative nature of the occupation explains this unusual success.[2]

French Occupation of Mexico, 1861–67

Force Size: 30,000
Outcome: Failure

Explanation: France, initially supported by Great Britain and Spain, intervened in Mexico after Mexico's president, Benito Juárez, announced that Mexico was going to suspend repayment of its European debt. Eventually, France's ambitions grew to include replacing the Mexican government with a monarchical government under Maximilian that would support French interests in the Western Hemisphere. Emergent Mexican nationalism led Mexican liberals to violently resist the French effort to install a foreign sponsored government. As a consequence, France had to resort to efforts to coerce the Mexican population into accepting Maximilian as monarch. When coercion failed and the U.S. threatened to intervene, Paris opted to end the occupation rather than invest further resources into it.

Threat Environment: While France perceived a threat to its interests in the Western Hemisphere, Mexican leaders did not welcome any protection offered by France against an external threat.[3]

Russian Occupation of Ili Region (China), 1871–81

Force Size: 2,000
Outcome: Mixed

Explanation: The Russian occupation of the Chinese region of Ili aimed to stabilize the region and its border with China until China could demonstrate its ability to govern the Xinjiang province of which Ili was a part. Available information on the occupation of Ili is limited, but the result of the occupation appears to have been mixed from the Russian perspective. On the one hand, the occupation was not particularly costly to the Russians, whose control of Ili was relatively passive. On the other hand, the occupation does not appear to have accomplished very much for Russia. The Russians were surprised when the Chinese succeeded in restoring order to the province, and they consequently returned sovereignty to China in the 1881 Treaty of St. Petersburg.

Threat Environment: The local population in Ili did not welcome strong centralized control by either Russia or China, nor did they perceive protections from either Russia or China as necessary. Based on the limited data available, there appears to have been little resistance to the occupation, mostly because the Russians pursued a relatively passive approach to controlling Ili.[4]

British Occupation of Egypt, 1882–1954

Force Size: Initially 30,000; reduced to less than 10,000
Outcome: Failure

Explanation: The British entered Egypt with little desire for a prolonged occupation. Instead, London hoped to restore stability, find a reliable local government, and withdraw as soon as possible. In the end, the British maintained a presence in Egypt for seventy-two years until finally completely withdrawing in 1954. The cost to the British, especially relative to the initial goal of a short-term occupation, was large, and the long-term accomplishments were limited. On the positive side, the British maintained access to the strategically vital Suez Canal, though it is unclear that an extended occupation of Egypt was necessary for achieving this goal.

Threat Environment: The British feared that an unfriendly power would gain control over the Suez Canal, but the Egyptian population did not share this perception of an external threat and grew weary of British occupation. London was reluctant to end the occupation until a stable pro-British government was established in Egypt.[5]

U.S. Occupation of Cuba, 1898–1902

Force Size: 45,000
Outcome: Failure

Explanation: The United States occupied Cuba in the wake of the Spanish-American War. Given its geographic proximity and potentially lucrative sugar industry, Cuba was seen as important to American national interests. The United States hoped to install a stable government that would allow it to maximize investment possibilities in Cuba. By 1902, increasing pressure to withdraw from both Cubans and at home in the United States led the United States to move toward withdrawal under the terms of the Platt Amendment. Ultimately, however, the United States withdrew from Cuba too soon, and it was compelled to reintervene in Cuba in 1906 and again in 1912. The inability to foster stability in Cuba renders the first occupation of Cuba a failure.

Threat Environment: While U.S. leaders had some fear of a potential German threat to stability in the Western Hemisphere, the Cuban population did not perceive an external threat from which they wanted U.S. protection.[6]

U.S. Occupation of the Philippines, 1898–1945

Force Size: 70,000–125,000
. Outcome: Mixed

Explanation: In addition to Cuba, the United States occupied the Philippines in the aftermath of the Spanish-American War. The geographic distance between the United States and the Philippines raised questions about the desirability of controlling the Philippines, but the United States ultimately sent a large force to occupy the archipelago and establish a U.S. presence in Asia. Shortly after the occupation began, an insurgency erupted, leading some to question the wisdom of continuing the mission. The result of the long-term occupation of the Philippines is mixed. On the positive side, the occupation did provide the United States with a beachhead in an area of the world of increasing importance to it. In addition, by the end of the occupation, the Philippines had a democratic form of government, albeit a weak democracy. On the negative side, the U.S. presence in the Philippines lasted nearly fifty years, and the strategic benefits of that presence are debatable. In addition, as a potential indirect cost, the U.S. presence in East Asia arguably contributed to animosity between the United States and Japan in the years before World War II.

Threat Environment: No commonly perceived external threat facilitated occupation success in the Philippines. The most dangerous threat to the survival of the Philippines emerged from rival ethnic and political groups within the archipelago.[7]

U.S. Occupation of Cuba, 1906–9

Force Size: 9,000
Outcome: Failure

Explanation: When instability reemerged in Cuba in 1906, the United States was compelled to reintervene by its commitments under the Platt Amendment (which committed the United States to intervene in Cuba in the event of any political instability). In fact, disgruntled Cubans precipitated instability in Cuba precisely to force the United States to send military forces back to the island. Once again, however, the United States faced pressure, especially domestically, to withdraw its forces from Cuba. In 1909, the second occupation of Cuba came to a close having accomplished little more than the first occupation. The United States was forced to reintervene once again in 1912. For these reasons, this occupation must be considered a failure.

Threat Environment: As in the first occupation of Cuba, no external threat was perceived by the Cuban population that motivated them to accept U.S. occupation. If anything, the primary threat to the survival of the Cuban state was violent disagreement among different political parties within Cuba.[8]

U.S. Occupation of Haiti, 1915–34

Force Size: 2,000
Outcome: Failure

Explanation: The United States intervened in Haiti in order to restore political order, protect U.S. economic interests in the island, and ensure that Germany was unable to gain control over access to the strategically significant Panama Canal. Within a few years of the beginning of the occupation, the United States was finding it difficult to create a stable and reliable government, yet the increasing American financial commitment to Haiti made withdrawal infeasible. The United States faced an unfavorable threat environment in Haiti, especially once Germany had been defeated in World War I. As a consequence, it had to rely unsuccessfully on coercion to control Haiti. In the end, the United States remained in Haiti for nearly twenty years and left that country having accomplished little.

Threat Environment: Though the United States initially perceived a German threat to the Panama Canal, the Haitian population never shared this threat perception. In fact, the Haitian population had a more established favorable relationship with European countries than with the United States.[9]

U.S. Occupation of the Dominican Republic, 1916–24

Force Size: 3,000
Outcome: Failure

Explanation: The U.S. occupation of the Dominican Republic was in many ways a twin occupation of the simultaneous occupation of Haiti. As in Haiti, the United States sought to foster political stability, protect and expand economic interests, and prevent European encroachments into the Western Hemisphere. Also as in Haiti, however, the United States was unable to accomplish any of its goals other than preventing Germany from controlling the Panama Canal (and it is unclear that Germany ever had that ambition). Though shorter than the occupation of Haiti, the occupation of the Dominican Republic offered little long-term benefit to either the United States or the Dominican Republic.

Threat Environment: The United States intervention in the Dominican Republic was motivated, in part, by a perceived German threat. Like the Haitians, though, the Dominicans did not share this threat perception with the United States.[10]

Multilateral (United Kingdom, France, Italy) Occupation of Istanbul (Turkey), 1918–23

Force Size: 30,000 British; 18,000 France; 2,000 Italian
Outcome: Failure

Explanation: The occupation of Istanbul after World War I was not as ambitious as some other occupations. The participating countries did not aim to install a specific government in Istanbul, but rather they aimed to create a temporary international administration of Istanbul that would allow for safe passage through the vital Dardanelles. Ultimately, the occupation foundered in the face of strident opposition from the population of Istanbul who rejected the plan to transform Istanbul into an international city. Ultimately, it is questionable whether occupying Istanbul was necessary to ensure passage through the Dardanelles, and the occupying powers had accomplished little when the occupation ended in 1923.

Threat Environment: Emerging from World War I, the population of Istanbul perceived no external threat from which the multilateral coalition could protect it. Instead, the population sensed that the European powers had intervened primarily to secure their own interests, not those of the people of Istanbul.[11]

Multilateral (France, United Kingdom, United States) Occupation of the Rhineland (Germany), 1918–30

Force Size: 150,000

Outcome: Failure

Explanation: The multilateral occupation of the Rhineland region of Germany after World War I was intended to preserve order and stability until a legitimate postwar German government could be established and questions about German reparations were resolved. The Rhineland was an important industrial center for Germany, and the occupation prevented German exploitation of the region. The occupation had relatively modest ambitions in that it did not try to install any particular government in the Rhineland or in Germany, more generally. Inasmuch as the goal of the occupation was to foster long-term stability in the center of Europe, the occupation must be considered a failure. By the early 1930s, Germany was again asserting itself in threatening ways. Clearly, the occupation cannot be held solely responsible for the sequence of events leading to World War II, but neither did the occupation cement a peaceful order in Central Europe.

Threat Environment: The absence of an external threat perceived either by all of the occupying powers or by the occupied population undermined the occupation. Ultimately, the occupation disintegrated as the occupying powers either lost interest in the occupation or became convinced that France, not Germany, was a greater obstacle to stability in Central Europe.[12]

British Occupation of Iraq, 1918–32

Force Size: Initially 25,000 British troops; British troops eventually reduced and replaced by Indian troops and air power

Outcome: Failure

Explanation: The British occupation of Iraq was conducted under a League of Nations mandate to guide Iraq toward independence with a stable indigenous government. Shortly after the occupation began, however, Britain encountered significant resistance from the Iraqi population, and the British strategy of occupying Iraq essentially from the air was ineffective at maintaining control over Iraq. Ultimately, Britain installed a monarchy in Iraq that lacked popular support and legitimacy and left Iraq unstable. The occupation failed to create a stable, reliable, and popular government within Iraq. This was a less severe and expensive failure than in some other occupations since the cost to Britain was consciously kept to a minimum in the wake of the expenses of World War I.

Threat Environment: The primary threat to the survival of the artificially constructed country of Iraq was internal. Multiple emergent nationalisms within Iraq sought self-determination and resented British occupation.[13]

British Occupation of Palestine, 1919–48

Force Size: Initial intervention force of approximately 90,000; Quickly
    reduced to under 10,000
Outcome: Mixed

Explanation: Like the occupation of Iraq, the British occupation of Palestine was carried out under the auspices of a League of Nations mandate. As a mandatory power, Britain was obligated to guide Palestine to independence. The British also had strategic interests in the region, mostly related to the vital Suez Canal. During the occupation period, the British maintained a relatively low profile in Palestine while simmering tensions among various ethnic and religious groups plagued the territory. Arab riots in 1936 reflected growing unhappiness with perceived British favoritism toward the Jewish population in Palestine. After the 1939 MacDonald White Paper limited Jewish immigration and land purchases, Zionist groups as well became increasingly dissatisfied with the occupation. In 1947, Britain abandoned the mandate, leaving the United Nations to resolve remaining difficulties. A verdict of mixed success is appropriate in this case. On the one hand, the British occupation contributed to the founding of the state of Israel to which the British had maintained a lukewarm commitment. On the other hand, the region has obviously been plagued with violence ever since.

Threat Environment: The primary threat to the security of Palestine was from internal divisions among the population of the territory. No commonly perceived external threat facilitated occupation success.[14]

French Occupation of Saar (Germany), 1920–35

Force Size: 7,000
Outcome: Mixed

Explanation: France occupied the Saar region of Germany with two goals: (1) maintain order until a League of Nations mandated plebiscite could be held in 1935 and (2) extract valuable coal from the Saar in the interim. France did not seek to install a particular government in the Saar, but rather was willing to wait and allow the population to choose between France and Germany in the plebiscite. The presence of the League of Nations in the Saar also prevented France from pursuing any more aggressive annexationist goals. The occupation is coded as a mixed success. France succeeded in mining valuable coal from the region, but the population ultimately elected to rejoin Germany rather than become a part of France. A more successful occupation might have prevented the Saar from rejoining Germany and allowed France to capture the Saar's economic potential.

Threat Environment: While France hoped to ensure that German would not regain the valuable territory of the Saar, the population did not share this same perceived external threat. If anything, this population viewed France as a greater threat.[15]

Multilateral (United Kingdom, United States) Occupation of Italy, 1943–48

Force Size: Several hundred thousand from 1943 until 1945; force dramatically reduced after 1945 and replaced with civilian advisors

Outcome: Success

Explanation: The United States and United Kingdom occupied Italy following its defeat in World War II. The occupation began in the southern part of the country and proceeded north as the defeat of Italy was concluded. The British and the Americans aimed primarily to ensure that Germany did not recapture Italy as the larger war continued. Once Germany was defeated, attention turned to creating a stable, sustainable government that would be friendly to Western powers. The occupation succeeded in helping to rebuild Italy and incorporate it into the emerging Western democratic bloc of countries. Even so, the chaotic Italian political system remained vulnerable to Soviet-inspired communism after the occupation concluded.

Threat Environment: The occupation of Italy benefited from two successive commonly perceived external threats. First the Germans and then Soviet-inspired communism served as external threats that allowed the occupation to succeed.[16]

Soviet Occupation of Eastern Austria, 1945–55

Force Size: 200,000
Outcome: Failure

Explanation: The Soviet Union occupied eastern Austria at the conclusion of World War II with the goal of incorporating it into the emerging communist bloc in Central and Eastern Europe. The division of Austria, agreed to at the end of the war, made it more difficult for the Soviet Union to achieve its goals in Austria as opposed to some other countries in Central and Eastern Europe where the Soviets enjoyed exclusive control. Unlike elsewhere in Central and Eastern Europe where the Soviet pursued a prolonged empire, the Soviets sought to withdraw from Austria, leaving behind a friendly communist state. Ultimately, the Austrian population voted to reject communism and incorporation into the Soviet sphere. The Soviets were forced to accept the Austrian State Treaty of 1955, which officially created a neutral Austria. The failure to incorporate Austria into the Soviet sphere renders this occupation a failure.

Threat Environment: While the Soviet Union sought to secure a buffer in Central and Eastern Europe, the Austrian population rejected the Soviet-inspired communism. The potential threat posed by the Western powers was not perceived by the Austrian population.[17]

Multilateral (United Kingdom, United States, France) Occupation of Western Austria, 1945–55

Force Size: 20,000–100,000
Outcome: Success

Explanation: The American, British, and French occupation authorities in western Austria sought primarily to prevent Austria from becoming a part of the Soviet bloc. In order to do this, the occupying powers advocated the creation of a Western, liberal democracy with an open economy. Though Austria was rendered neutral by the 1955 treaty, the western allies were more successful than the Soviet Union in Austria. While Austrians did not necessarily welcome the Western occupying powers, they did prefer them to the prospect of living in a Soviet-controlled state. In the end, Austria did not become a communist state or part of the Soviet bloc, and Austria did become a democratic state with a relatively open economy, even if it did not become a member of the North Atlantic Treaty Organization (NATO) or other Western institutions.

Threat Environment: Both the Western, occupying powers and the western Austrian population perceived a threat from Soviet-inspired communism. The population tolerated occupation as long as this threat was present, and the Western powers maintained the occupation until the neutrality treaty was consummated.[18]

Multilateral (United Kingdom, United States, France) Occupation of Western Germany, 1945–52

Force Size: 400,000
Outcome: Success

Explanation: In the waning months of World War II, the allied powers agreed to divide postwar Germany into four zones to be controlled by the United States, Great Britain, France, and the Soviet Union. Eventually, as cold war tension rose, Germany was divided into two primary occupation zones, one in the west and the other in the east. Within a decade, the Western powers succeeded in creating a democratic political system in Germany with a thriving industrial economy. As predicted, a commonly perceived external threat motivated the United States and its allies to continue the occupation and led the western German population to accept the occupation. Therefore, the multilateral occupation of western Germany must be considered a success.

Threat Environment: The Western powers were welcome to remain in West Germany in order to protect the country from the threat posed by the Soviet Union. At the same time, the occupying powers viewed the security of western Germany as critical in the emerging cold war with the Soviet Union.[19]

U.S. Occupation of Japan, 1945–52

Force Size: Initially 450,000; gradually reduced
Outcome: Success

Explanation: The United States occupation of Japan was a remarkable success. It transformed Japan from a wartime enemy to a productive, democratic, and peaceful member of the international system, and the United States accomplished this goal after having dropped two atomic weapons on Japan and firebombed Japan's largest cities. By the end of the occupation, the United States was able to withdraw with a secure and reliable Japanese government in place and with Japan enmeshed in a variety of treaties that maintained its security but prevented it from threatening others. Under perhaps the most challenging circumstances, then, the occupation succeeded.

Threat Environment: The presence of a commonly perceived external threat in the form of Soviet-inspired communism sustained U.S. interest in the occupation and led the Japanese population and leadership to embrace the occupation.[20]

U.S. Occupation of the Ryukyus, 1945–72

Force Size: 20,000
Outcome: Success

Explanation: Separate from the occupation of the main Japanese islands, the United States also occupied the Ryukyu islands, including Okinawa. The Ryukyus held particular geostrategic value for the United States in the emerging cold war with the Soviet Union, which is why the United States continued to occupy the islands after the occupation of the rest of Japan had come to a close. Citizens of the Ryukyus grew weary of the extended, large, and sometimes overbearing American presence, but their resistance to the occupation was mostly passive. While the occupation was relatively costly for the United States, the value was equally high because of the location of the islands.

Threat Environment: Like the more general occupation of Japan, the occupation of the Ryukyus enjoyed a propitious threat environment in the form of the threat posed by the Soviet Union.[21]

Soviet Occupation of Northern Korea, 1945–48

Force Size: 40,000; gradually reduced to under 10,000
Outcome: Success

Explanation: The United States and the Soviet Union agreed in August 1945 to divide Korea, with the Soviet Union occupying the northern part of the peninsula and the United States occupying the southern part. The Soviet Union had more success in the north by combining a coercive apparatus that could control any opposition that emerged with a strategy that effectively accommodated Korean nationalism. The Soviet occupation succeeded as it provided the Soviet Union with a mostly reliable communist ally in northeast Asia at relatively low cost.

Threat Environment: Most Koreans did not welcome occupation after three decades of colonialism, and they initially did not share the Soviet perception of a threat from the United States. Eventually, though, the threat environment improved as the Soviets and their chosen northern Korean government eliminated opposition through coercion, leaving behind a leadership and population that was mostly supportive of the new government.[22]

U.S. Occupation of Southern Korea, 1945–48

Force Size: 45,000
Outcome: Mixed

Explanation: The U.S. occupation of southern Korea was less successful than the Soviet occupation of northern Korea. The U.S. decision to impose a pro–U.S., anticommunist government met with substantial opposition among the southern Korean population, which would have independently chosen a more socialist government. Coercion proved difficult for the United States and the right-wing regime it supported in Korea. Eventually, significant insurgencies erupted in various parts of the country in reaction to the ineffectiveness of the Rhee government, especially with regard to issues of land reform. The United States did gain a foothold in Northeast Asia through the occupation of southern Korea, but Syngman Rhee would remain an unwieldy ally and the costs of the occupation were not insignificant. The contemporary strong alliance between the United States and South Korea was a product of the Korean War more than of the initial U.S. occupation of the country.

Threat Environment: The initial threat environment in Korea was unfavorable. The Korean population desired independence more than occupation, and the geopolitical value of southern Korea was questioned in Washington. Unlike the Soviets in northern Korea, the United States was unable to pursue strategies that improved that threat environment.[23]

Israeli Occupation of West Bank/Gaza, 1967–

Force Size: Varying
Outcome: Failure

Explanation: Israel occupied the West Bank and Gaza Strip after its victory in the 1967 war. The fate of these territories was a matter of some dispute within

Israel, with some arguing that Israel should annex these territories to Israel while others looked for a strategy that would allow Israel to withdraw from the territories. Israel did not seek to create new governmental institutions in either the West Bank or Gaza Strip. Instead, it simply sought to ensure that the populations within these territories did not pose a threat to Israel. The occupation deserves some credit for having prevented the emergence of a more coherent Palestinian threat to Israel. At the same time, however, the occupation did little to quell opposition in the West Bank, Gaza, and the wider Arab world to Israel.

Threat Environment: The greatest threat perceived by the populations of the West Bank and Gaza Strip has been Israel. Israel, meanwhile, has seen the population of the West Bank and Gaza as a threat to its security. This type of threat environment, in which the occupying power is viewed as the greatest threat to the occupied population, is least conducive to occupation success.[24]

Vietnamese Occupation of Cambodia, 1979–89

Force Size: 180,000
Outcome: Failure

Explanation: Vietnam occupied Cambodia in an effort to forestall further border incursions that threatened to destabilize Vietnam. The Vietnamese hoped to achieve this goal by occupying Cambodia and installing a friendly communist government. The effort to install a government from abroad was ultimately successful, but met with violent resistance. The occupation was a losing venture for both Vietnam and Cambodia. The occupation took longer and cost more than Vietnam had anticipated or wanted. Cambodia continued to be the site of conflict, which was only finally resolved with the aid of a UN peacekeeping force. In short, the Vietnamese effort to stabilize Cambodia through occupation was a failure.

Threat Environment: No commonly perceived external threat existed. In fact, many Cambodians viewed Vietnam as posing the greatest threat to their security.[25]

Israeli Occupation of Southern Lebanon, 1982–2000

Force Size: Initial force of 76,000 reduced to a substantially smaller security force of varying size
Outcome: Failure

Explanation: Israel occupied southern Lebanon in an effort to control the Palestine Liberation Organization, which posed a threat to Israeli security. The occupation did not have any state-building ambitions; instead, it merely sought to defeat these threats and create a buffer between any threats that survived and Israel. In the end, Israel was unable to defeat the groups that posed a threat to it and was forced to withdraw when it recognized that its goals were unlikely to be realized through the continuing occupation of southern Lebanon. Though the counterfactual of what would have happened without the occupation is difficult to evaluate, it is clear that the Israeli occupation did not achieve its ambitions.

Threat Environment: The primary threat to Lebanon's security was posed by internally divisive groups supported by foreign allies. To the extent that Lebanese desired protection from an external threat, however, it was protection from Israel, not protection by Israel.[26]

Syrian Occupation of Lebanon, 1976–2005

Force Size: 15,000–40,000
Outcome: Failure

Explanation: Syria viewed the occupation of Lebanon as a way of enhancing Syrian security. Instability in Lebanon that attended the Lebanese civil war threatened to destabilize Syria. Not only did Syria intervene in Lebanon with thousands of troops, but it also actively supported Lebanese political groups that served as proxies for Syrian interests. Lebanon, however, remained a source of instability for almost all of the period of Syrian occupation, and the Lebanese people eventually rejected the occupation and the overbearing Syrian influence in Lebanese politics. The division of Lebanon into a variety of different nationalist groups meant that the Syrian presence was welcomed by some groups but vehemently opposed by other groups. In 2005, Syria was forced to withdraw its troops from Lebanon. While the occupation may indeed have protected Syria from some instability in Lebanon, the occupation also ended with a Syrian disgrace and with most Lebanese rejecting any residual Syrian influence in Lebanese politics.

Threat Environment: Internal threats to Lebanese security made occupation success difficult. While some groups shared a common sense of threat with Syria, other significant groups did not.[27]

NATO/EU Occupation of Bosnia, 1995–

Force Size: 12,000–60,000
Outcome: Uncertain

Explanation: The NATO occupation of Bosnia followed years of civil war in the former Yugoslavia that culminated in an attempt at "ethnic cleansing" in the former Yugoslav province of Bosnia. NATO intervened both to prevent future conflict and to establish, with the assistance of the United Nations, a stable and representative government that would respect the rights of all citizens of Bosnia. Whether or not Bosnia will ever be stable enough for NATO or the EU to withdraw remains an open question, so it remains too early to pass final judgment on the occupation of Bosnia. The occupation has not faced widespread violence largely because the Bosnian state has been constituted in such a way that Bosnian Serb, Croat, and Muslim nationalisms have been accommodated by a power-sharing arrangement. On the one hand, this occupation has ensured that widespread conflict does not again engulf Bosnia, but on the other hand, the occupying powers are now tied down to Bosnia, unable to leave for fear of a resurgence of violence.

Threat Environment: The occupation of Bosnia faces an unfavorable threat environment dominated by internal threats posed by the three major groups constituting its population.[28]

NATO Occupation of Kosovo, 1999–

Force Size: 60,000
Outcome: Uncertain

Explanation: Like the occupation of Bosnia, the occupation of the former Yugoslav province of Kosovo is a UN and NATO enterprise. The NATO military force (KFOR) and UN political presence (UNMIK) were charged with creating an autonomous region of Kosovo that would yet remain a part of Serbia. Continuing ethnic tension between the majority Albanians and the minority Serbs in Kosovo have made it difficult for this occupation to achieve its goals. Kosovar Albanians have grown impatient with the continuous delays in granting them complete control over Kosovo, and the small remaining Serb population fears for its safety. Kosovo is eventually expected to gain greater independence, but it remains uncertain how soon the international presence in Kosovo will be able to withdraw.

Threat Environment: The occupation of Kosovo has been plagued by the unfavorable threat environment in Kosovo. While the Albanian Kosovar population perceives a threat from Serbia, Kosovo faces significant internal divisions between the Serb and Albanian populations. In the face of these internal divisions, the interest of NATO powers in sustaining the occupation has waned.[29]

NATO Occupation of Afghanistan, 2001–

Force Size: 13,000–20,000 U.S.; 10,000 Other NATO countries
Outcome: Uncertain

Explanation: The United States led an invasion of Afghanistan following the terrorist attacks of September 11, 2001. Together with its NATO allies, the United States proceeded to take control of the capital of Kabul while eschewing a more comprehensive occupation of the entire country. Since the initial invasion, NATO has fostered and supported the creation of a democratically elected central government while regional warlords and their militias continue to exert considerable control in the outer Afghan provinces. The eventual fate of the occupation and Afghanistan remains uncertain. On the one hand, the establishment of any type of responsible central government is a positive step. On the other hand, the central government and army remain weak. Without the ability to exert control in the outer provinces, the Afghan central government is unlikely to be able to control potential dangers in more remote parts of the country.

Threat Environment: Afghanistan faces numerous internal divisions that threaten its coherence as a country. These groups as well as the NATO occupiers do not agree on any commonly perceived external threat. The lack of a commonly perceived external threat would likely have made comprehensive occupation of the country more difficult, but the more limited occupation effort has introduced other difficulties in rebuilding a coherent Afghanistan.[30]

Multilateral (Primarily United States and United Kingdom) Occupation of Iraq, 2003–

Force Size: 150,000
Outcome: Uncertain

Explanation: A multilateral coalition made up largely of American and British forces invaded Iraq in the spring of 2003 in an effort to remove Saddam Hussein's regime from power and ensure that Iraq did not have either weapons of mass destruction or the capabilities to produce them. While the initial invasion went smoothly, the coalition encountered an antioccupation insurgency within months of the invasion. This insurgency was comprised of both Iraqi nationalists and foreign terrorist fighters. Eventually, this antioccupation insurgency began to transform into an intra-Iraqi fight among the major ethnic groups within Iraq. The United States and its coalition partners have had to rely heavily on coercion, and efforts at accommodation and inducement have been unsuccessful in the face of continuing violence. The prospects for a peaceful solution in Iraq that advances U.S. and British interests appears unlikely at this point, but given the ongoing nature of the occupation, it is also premature to pass final judgment on the occupation at this point.

Threat Environment: Consistent with other cases, the occupation of Iraq has been undone by the absence of a commonly perceived external threat. Instead, Iraq is divided internally among different national groups, and the interest of the United States has waned as sectarian violence has increased.[31]

Notes

INTRODUCTION

1. General Douglas A. MacArthur, letter to U.S. Congress, "In Support of Appropriations for Occupation Purposes," February 20, 1947, Government Section, Supreme Commander for the Allied Powers, *Political Reorientation of Japan, September 1945–September 1948* (Washington, D.C.: U.S. Government Printing Office, 1949), 2:764.

2. On these comments, both made in San Antonio, Texas, see Eric Schmitt, "2 U.S. Officials Liken Guerrillas to Renegade Postwar Nazi Units," *New York Times,* August 26, 2003. For a criticism of the analogy, see Daniel Benjamin, "Condi's Phony History," *Slate,* August 29, 2003, www.slate.com. On the werewolves, whose accomplishments were actually quite minimal, see H. R. Trevor-Roper, *The Last Days of Hitler* (New York: Macmillan, 1947), 44–48.

3. On state failure, see Robert I. Rotberg, *State Failure and State Weakness in a Time of Terror* (Washington, D.C.: Brookings Institution Press, 2003).

4. On attempts to impose democracy by force, see Karin von Hippel, *Democracy by Force: U.S. Military Intervention in the Post–Cold War World* (New York: Cambridge University Press, 2000).

5. On the distinction between balancing and bandwagoning, see Stephen M. Walt, *The Origins of Alliances* (Ithaca, N.Y.: Cornell University Press, 1987).

6. International legal scholar Eyal Benvinisti defines occupation as "the effective control of a power (be it one or more states or an international organization, such as the United Nations) over a territory to which that power has no sovereign title, without the volition of the sovereign of that territory." Eyal Benvenisti, *The International Law of Occupation* (Princeton, N.J.: Princeton University Press, 1993), 4.

7. An occupying power need not occupy an entire country. Certain occupations, such as the allied occupation of Istanbul after World War I, have only involved the occupation of a city or region.

8. Though not always true, colonial ventures are also often more focused on resource extraction than military occupations.

9. I require a duration of at least one year for an incursion to qualify as an occupation.

10. On the consolidation of the Soviet Empire in Eastern Europe, see Vojtech Mastny, *The Cold War and Soviet Insecurity: The Stalin Years* (New York: Oxford University Press, 1996); and Vladislav Zubok and Constantine Pleshakov, *Inside the Kremlin's Cold War: From Stalin to Khrushchev* (Cambridge, Mass.: Harvard University Press, 1996).

11. In the initial aftermath of World War II, the inclination was to limit the industrial power of both Japan and Germany. Once the cold war had begun, the United States reversed its position and encouraged industrialization. On the cold war impetus to rebuild the Japanese economy, see John W. Dower, *Embracing Defeat: Japan in the Wake of World War II* (New York: W. W. Norton, 1999), 525–46. The initial punitive Morgenthau Plan for the treatment of postwar Germany was quickly abandoned in favor of a policy that would rebuild Germany and guarantee its place in the Western bloc. On American policy toward postwar Germany, see Carolyn Eisenberg, *Drawing the Line: The American Decision to Divide Germany, 1944–1949* (New York: Cambridge University Press, 1996); and Marc

Trachtenberg, *A Constructed Peace: The Making of the European Settlement, 1945–1963* (Princeton, N.J.: Princeton University Press, 1999). Melvyn Leffler argues, "Europe could not be defended without German troops and German industry. Yet West Germans had little incentive to align with the West unless they were assured that their border would be protected, their economy liberated from controls, and their sovereignty fully restored." Melvyn Leffler, *A Preponderance of Power: National Security, the Truman Administration, and the Cold War* (Stanford, Calif.: Stanford University Press, 1992), 385–86. On the rebuilding of German industry, see Volker R. Berghahn, "West German Reconstruction and American Industrial Culture, 1945–1960," in *The American Impact on Postwar Germany*, ed. Reiner Pommerin (Providence, R.I.: Berghahn Books, 1995), 65–82.

12. Ernst Fraenkel, *Military Occupation and the Rule of Law: Occupation Government in the Rhineland, 1918–1923* (New York: Oxford University Press, 1944); Walter A. McDougall, *France's Rhineland Diplomacy, 1914–1924: The Last Bid for a Balance of Power in Europe* (Princeton, N.J.: Princeton University Press, 1978), 58; Keith L. Nelson, *Victors Divided: America and the Allies in Germany, 1918–1923* (Berkeley, Calif.: University of California Press, 1975), 23; and U.S. Army, *American Military Government of Occupied Germany, 1918–1920* (Washington, D.C.: U.S. Government Printing Office, 1943), which specifically compares the limited goals of the Rhineland occupation to the more ambitious goals of the Cuban and Filipino occupations (268).

13. For a discussion of the difficulty of assessing the success or failure of any particular policy, see David A. Baldwin, *Economic Statecraft* (Princeton, N.J.: Princeton University Press, 1985), 115–34. See also Daniel Byman and Matthew Waxman, *The Dynamics of Coercion: American Foreign Policy and the Limits of Military Might* (New York: Cambridge University Press, 2002), 33–37.

14. In both of these occupations, a primary concern was preventing Germany and Japan from reemerging as threats to their regions. On Germany, see John Gimbel, *The American Occupation of Germany, 1945–1949* (Stanford, Calif.: Stanford University Press, 1968), 150–51. On Japan, see Eiji Takemae, *Inside GHQ: The Allied Occupation of Japan and Its Legacy* (New York: Continuum, 2002), 203. Ultimately, the Japanese constitution included the famous Article 9, which strictly limits the purposes for which Japan can have a military.

15. On the initial role of the Philippines in the emerging Japanese-American rivalry leading up to World War II, see Walter LaFeber, *The Clash: A History of U.S.–Japan Relations* (New York: W. W. Norton, 1997), 60–62. Japan initially supported U.S., as opposed to German, annexation of the Philippines, but by the 1930s, Tokyo had its own desire to acquire the Philippines.

16. Mixed successes are cases where the occupying power accomplished short-term goals but not long-term goals, or where certain benefits were achieved but at high costs. In short, cases where a simple declaration of success or failure is unjustified.

17. Ernest Gellner, *Nations and Nationalism* (Ithaca, N.Y.: Cornell University Press, 1983), 1.

18. Ibid., 2.

19. See especially James D. Fearon and David D. Laitin, "Ethnicity, Insurgency, and Civil War," *American Political Science Review* 97, no. 3 (February 2003): 75–90. See also Paul Collier and Anke Hoeffler, "Greed and Grievance in Civil War," *Oxford Economic Papers* 56, no. 4 (October 2004): 563–95; and Stathis Kalyvas, "'New' and 'Old' Civil War: A Valid Distinction?" *World Politics* 54, no. 1 (October 2001): 99–118.

20. Michael Hechter, *Containing Nationalism* (New York: Oxford University Press, 2000), 31.

21. The phrase "demand for sovereignty" comes from Michael Hechter. See Hechter, *Containing Nationalism*, 113–33. On the evolution of the international norm of self-determination,

see Michael Hechter and Elizabeth Borland, "National Self-Determination: The Emergence of an International Norm," in *Social Norms*, eds. Michael Hechter and Karl-Dieter Opp (New York: Russell Sage Foundation, 2001), 186–233.

22. The capability to wage the insurgency is an obvious, but essential, permissive condition for an insurgency in the face of occupation.

23. The theory offered here is a macrolevel account of nationalist resistance to military occupation. At the expense of some parsimony, one might add explanatory power by incorporating other microlevel accounts of resistance. See Stathis Kalyvas, *The Logic of Violence in Civil Wars* (New York: Cambridge University Press, 2006); and Kalyvas, "The Ontology of 'Political Violence': Action and Identity in Civil Wars," *Perspective on Politics* 1, no. 3 (September 2003): 475–94.

24. For one exception that includes wartime occupation, see Eric Carlton, *Occupation: The Policies and Practices of Military Conquerors* (New York: Routledge, 1992). On a related theme, see Peter Liberman, *Does Conquest Pay? The Exploitation of Occupied Industrial Societies* (Princeton, N.J.: Princeton University Press, 1996).

25. On nation building or state building, see James Dobbins et al., *America's Role in Nation-Building: From Germany to Iraq* (Santa Monica, Calif.: RAND, 2003); James Dobbins et al., *The UN's Role in Nation-Building: From the Congo to Iraq* (Santa Monica, Calif.: RAND, 2005); James Dobbins et al., *The Beginner's Guide to Nation-Building* (Santa Monica, Calif.: RAND, 2007); Francis Fukuyama, *State-Building: Governance and World Order in the 21st Century* (Ithaca, N.Y.: Cornell University Press, 2004); Minxin Pei and Sara Kasper, *Lessons from the Past: The American Record of Nation Building* (Washington, D.C.: Carnegie Endowment for International Peace, 2003).

26. Dobbins et al., *America's Role in Nation-Building.*

27. On drawing wrong lessons from the occupation of Germany after World War II, see Douglas Porch, "Occupational Hazards," *The National Interest*, no. 72 (summer 2003): 35–47.

28. See Nisuke Ando, *Surrender, Occupation, and Private Property in International Law: An Evaluation of U.S. Practice in Japan* (Oxford: Clarendon Press, 1991); Benvenisti, *International Law of Occupation;* Doris Appel Graber, *The Development of the Law of Belligerent Occupation, 1863–1914* (New York: Columbia University Press, 1949); David B. Rivkin Jr. and Darin R. Bartram, "Military Occupation: Legally Ensuring a Lasting Peace," *Washington Quarterly* 26, no. 3 (summer 2003): 87–103; Gerhard von Glahn, *The Occupation of Enemy Territory: A Commentary on the Law and Practice of Belligerent Occupation* (Minneapolis: University of Minnesota Press, 1957).

29. On counterinsurgency, see Ivan Arreguin-Toft, "How the Weak Win Wars: A Theory of Asymmetric Conflict," *International Security* 26, no. 1 (summer 2001): 93–128; Douglas Blaufarb, *The Counterinsurgency Era: U.S. Doctrine and Performance* (New York: Free Press, 1977); Harry Eckstein, ed., *Internal War: Problems and Approaches* (New York: Free Press, 1964); David Galula, *Counterinsurgency Warfare: Theory and Practice* (New York: Praeger, 1964); Nathan Leites and Charles Wolf Jr., *Rebellion and Authority: An Analytic Essay on Insurgent Conflicts* (Chicago: Markham, 1970); Gil Merom, *How Democracies Lose Small Wars: State, Society, and the Failures of France in Algeria, Israel in Lebanon, and the United States in Vietnam* (New York: Cambridge University Press, 2003); John A. Nagl, *Learning to Eat Soup with a Knife: Counterinsurgency Lessons from Malaya and Vietnam* (Chicago: University of Chicago Press, 2005); William Odom, *On Internal War: American and Soviet Approaches to Third World Clients and Insurgents* (Durham, N.C.: Duke University Press, 1992); D. Michael Shafer, *Deadly Paradigms: The Failure of U.S. Counterinsurgency Policy* (Princeton, N.J.: Princeton University Press, 1988); and George K. Tanham and Dennis J. Duncanson, "Some Dilemmas of Counterinsurgency," *Foreign Affairs* 48 (January 1970): 113–22.

30. Dobbins et al., *America's Role in Nation-Building* and Dobbins et al., *UN's Role in Nation-Building.*

31. For example, this claim is an implication of the argument in Martha Finnemore, *The Purpose of Intervention: Changing Beliefs about the Use of Force* (Ithaca, N.Y.: Cornell University Press, 2003).

32. On "typological theorizing," see Alexander L. George and Andrew Bennett, *Case Studies and Theory Development in the Social Sciences* (Cambridge, Mass.: MIT Press, 2005). See also Colin Elman, "Explanatory Typologies in Qualitative Studies of International Politics," *International Organization* 59, no. 2 (spring 2005): 293–326.

33. Eiji Takemae, perhaps the leading Japanese historian of the U.S. occupation of Japan, suggests the value in comparing the occupations of Japan and southern Korea. See Takemae, *Inside GHQ,* 564–65.

1. WHEN TO OCCUPY

1. See Michael Hechter, *Containing Nationalism* (New York: Oxford University Press, 2000), 116.

2. In rare instances, internal threats can serve the same purpose as external threats. If the group that is trying to dismantle the occupied territory is sufficiently small and other groups aim to keep the country unified, then the occupying power can still succeed by protecting the occupied territory from the separatist minority.

3. On the occupation of post-Napoleonic France, see Thomas Dwight Veve, *The Duke of Wellington and the British Army of Occupation in France, 1815–1818* (Westport, Conn.: Greenwood, 1992).

4. On the food crisis within Germany, see John H. Backer, *Priming the German Economy: American Occupational Policies, 1945–1948* (Durham, N.C.: Duke University Press, 1971), 31–59.

5. On initial tension between the French occupying force and the German population, see F. Roy Willis, *The French in Germany, 1945–1949* (Stanford, Calif.: Stanford University Press, 1962), 71.

6. See Richard L. Merritt, *Democracy Imposed: U.S. Occupation Policy and the German Public, 1945–1949* (New Haven, Conn.: Yale University Press, 1995), 259.

7. On Yalta, see Russell D. Buhite, *Decisions at Yalta: An Appraisal of Summit Diplomacy* (Wilmington, Del.: Scholarly Resources, 1986); Diane Shaver Clemens, *Yalta* (New York: Oxford University Press, 1970); Robert Dallek, *Franklin D. Roosevelt and American Foreign Policy* (New York: Oxford University Press, 1995), 506–25; Richard F. Fenno, *The Yalta Conference* (Boston: Heath, 1955); Jonathan L. Snell, ed., *The Meaning of Yalta: Big Three Diplomacy and the New Balance of Power* (Baton Rouge: Louisiana State University Press, 1956); Edward R. Stettinius, *Roosevelt and the Russians: The Yalta Conference* (Garden City, N.Y.: Doubleday, 1949); Athan Theoharis, "Roosevelt and Truman on Yalta: The Origins of the Cold War," *Political Science Quarterly* 87, no. 2 (June 1972): 210–41; and Athan G. Theoharis, *The Yalta Myths: An Issue in U.S. Politics, 1945–1955* (Columbia: University of Missouri Press, 1970).

8. Kenneth O. McCreedy, "Planning the Peace: Operation Eclipse and the Occupation of Germany," *Journal of Military History* 65 (2001): 713–40.

9. On the negotiations to divide Germany into zones, see Tony Sharp, *The Wartime Alliance and the Zonal Division of Germany* (Oxford: Clarendon, 1975).

10. On the Reparations Commission, see Backer, *Priming the German Economy,* 67–69.

11. On the Morgenthau Plan, see Henry Morgenthau Jr., *Germany is Our Problem* (New York: Harper and Brothers, 1945).

12. Quoted in Patricia Meehan, *A Strange Enemy People: Germans under the British, 1945–1950* (London: Peter Owen, 2001), 43.

13. For the text of JCS 1067, see *Germany, 1947–1949: The Story in Documents* (Washington, D.C.: U.S. Government Printing Office, 1950), 21–33.

14. On the reparations agreement at Potsdam, see Carolyn Woods Eisenberg, *Drawing the Line: The American Decision to Divide Germany, 1944–1949* (New York: Cambridge University Press, 1996), 113–20.

15. On the Potsdam conference, see Herbert Feis, *Between War and Peace: The Potsdam Conference* (Princeton, N.J.: Princeton University Press, 1960); James L. Gormly, *From Potsdam to the Cold War: Big Three Diplomacy, 1945–1947* (Wilmington, Del.: Scholarly Resources, 1990), 29–70; and Charles L. Mee, *Meeting at Potsdam* (New York: M. Evans, 1975).

16. See Thomas Grosser, "The Integration of Deportees into the Society of the Federal Republic of Germany," *Journal of Communist Studies and Transition Politics* 16, no. 1–2 (March–June 2000): 125–147.

17. See Marc Trachtenberg, *A Constructed Peace: The Making of the European Settlement, 1945–1963* (Princeton, N.J.: Princeton University Press, 1999), 44–46.

18. Note that this was not the first time that the demilitarization of Germany had been proposed. The idea had first been raised by Senator Arthur Vandenburg of Michigan in January 1945. At Yalta and throughout 1945, the idea periodically resurfaced but never was seriously considered. On the treaty proposal, see Foreign Relations of the United States (hereafter FRUS), 1946, vol. 2, *Council of Foreign Ministers,* 146, 166–73.

19. See Anne Deighton, *The Impossible Peace: Britain, the Division of Germany, and the Origins of the Cold War* (New York: Oxford University Press, 1990). On the British occupation zone, also see Noel Annan, *Changing Enemies: The Defeat and Regeneration of Germany* (London: Harper Collins, 1995).

20. On the "French thesis" that precluded support for zonal unification, see Willis, *French in Germany, 1945–1949,* 29–44.

21. For the text of Byrnes's speech, see *Germany, 1947–1949,* 3–8.

22. On the geopolitical significance of Byrnes's speech, see Melvyn Leffler, *A Preponderance of Power: National Security, the Truman Administration, and the Cold War* (Stanford, Calif.: Stanford University Press, 1993), 120; and Trachtenberg, *Constructed Peace,* 50.

23. For the text of JCS 1779, see *Germany, 1947–1949,* 41.

24. Willis, *French in Germany, 1945–1949,* 113–14.

25. Backer, *Priming the German Economy,* 187.

26. On the London agreements, see John Gimbel, *The American Occupation of Germany, 1945–1949* (Stanford, Calif.: Stanford University Press, 1968), 194–230.

27. "Text of Occupation Statute promulgated on 12th May 1949 by the Military Governors and Commanders in Chief of the Western Zones," *Official Gazette of the Allied High Commission for Germany,* September 23, 1949, no. 1, 13–15.

28. On the end of denazification and the lack of American objections, see Norbert Frei, *Adenauer's Germany and the Nazi Past: The Politics of Amnesty and Integration,* trans. Joel Golb (New York: Columbia University Press, 2002).

29. On the evolving place of Germany in western defense strategy, see Trachtenberg, *Constructed Peace.*

30. On the Pleven Plan to create a European army as part of the EDC, see William Hitchcock, *France Restored: Cold War Diplomacy and the Quest for Leadership in Europe, 1944–1954* (Chapel Hill, N.C.: University of North Carolina Press, 1998), 144. On the failed effort to create a European Defense Community, see Trachtenberg, *Constructed Peace,* 120–25.

31. On the negotiations leading to the repeal of the Occupation Statute, see Thomas Allen Schwartz, *America's Germany: John J. McCloy and the Federal Republic of Germany* (Cambridge, Mass.: Harvard University Press, 1991), 269–78.

32. On the direct occupation costs paid by Germans through their taxes, see Willis, *French in Germany, 1945–1949,* 117–25.

33. In the first four years of Marshall Plan assistance, the United States provided $1.4 billion in aid to Germany.

34. Jane Perry Clark Carey reports, "The memory of their expulsion and of the Communists in the East has served to keep them thus far bitterly anti-Communist." Jane Perry Clark Carey, "Political Organization of the Refugees and Expellees in West Germany," *Political Science Quarterly* 66, no. 2 (June 1951): 191–215. See also Grosser, "The Integration of Deportees into the Society of the Federal Republic of Germany." On abuses in the Soviet occupation zone, see Norman N. Naimark, *The Russians in Germany: A History of the Soviet Zone of Occupation* (Cambridge, Mass.: Harvard University Press, 1995).

35. John Lewis Gaddis, *We Now Know: Rethinking Cold War History* (New York: Clarendon Press, 1997), 287.

36. Naimark, *Russians in Germany,* 250.

37. The forces of the western occupying powers also committed crimes against the German people, though the extent of such behavior was generally less than in the Soviet zone. See Giles MacDonough, *After the Reich: The Brutal History of the Allied Occupation* (New York: Basic Books, 2007).

38. Participants in the surveys were chosen at random based on ration-card numbers assigned to each citizen within the occupied zone. In order to conduct the surveys, the field staff would visit the homes or offices of the respondents and ask them prepared questionnaires. Like any public opinion polling, there are limitations on the reliability of these surveys. The surveys were mostly conducted by Americans within the American zone of occupation. It would be understandable if the population feared retribution for giving answers that were seen as critical of the United States. The Opinion Survey Section was aware of this possible bias. To test for its effect, they conducted one survey in which half of the interviewers were said to be representatives of the Military Government and half of the interviewers were said to be from a "German public opinion institute." In general, this experiment revealed that the problems introduced by Americans conducting the polling were minimal. For the most part, these effects were limited to questions regarding American prestige and National Socialism. Leo P. Caspri, chief of the Opinion Survey Section, surmised, "The conclusion seems fair that on the scope of sponsorship MG polling is an entirely workable method of inquiry in occupied Germany." Quoted in Richard L. Merritt, *Democracy Imposed: U.S. Occupation Policy and the German Public, 1945–1949* (New Haven, Conn.: Yale University Press, 1995), 79–80.

39. OMGUS Survey Report No. 67 (October 10, 1947), "German Attitudes Toward International Leadership." Summarized in Anna J. Merritt and Richard L. Merritt, eds., *Public Opinion in Occupied Germany: The OMGUS Surveys, 1945–1949* (Urbana: University of Illinois Press, 1970), 170.

40. OMGUS Survey Report No. 76 (October 29, 1947), "German Attitudes toward the Four Occupying Powers." Summarized ibid., 180–81.

41. OMGUS Survey Report No. 113 (April 15, 1948), "AMZON Attitudes and Information about Russia." Summarized ibid., 228–29.

42. OMGUS Survey Report No. 130 (July 23, 1948), "Berlin Reactions to the Air Lift and the Western Powers." Summarized ibid., 248–49.

43. Konrad Adenauer, *Memoirs: 1945–1953,* trans. Beate Ruhm von Oppen (London: Weidenfeld and Nicolson, 1965), 78–79.

44. See Hans-Peter Schwarz, *Konrad Adenauer: A German Politician and Statesman in a Period of War, Revolution, and Reconstruction,* vol. 1, *From the German Empire to the Federal Republic, 1876–1952,* trans. Louise Willmot (Providence, R.I.: Berghahn, 1995), 308. On Adenauer's views of the Soviet threat, see 318–19.

45. On American impressions of Schumacher, see Schwartz, *America's Germany: John J. McCloy and the Federal Republic of Germany,* 54–56.

46. John J. McCloy, "From Military Government to Self-Government," in *Americans as Proconsuls: United States Military Government in Germany and Japan, 1944–1952,* ed. Robert Wolfe (Carbondale: Southern Illinois University Press, 1984), 114–23. Quote on 122.

47. For a discussion, see Eugene Davidson, *The Death and Life of Germany: An Account of the American Occupation* (Columbia: University of Missouri Press, 1999), 47–69; and John Gimbel, *A German Community under American Occupation: Marburg, 1945–1952* (Stanford, Calif.: Stanford University Press, 1961), 15–30.

48. The only significant accomplishment of the werewolves was the assassination of the American-appointed mayor of the mid-sized German city of Aachen. On the werewolves, see H. R. Trevor-Roper, *The Last Days of Hitler* (New York: Macmillan, 1947), 44–48.

49. Quoted in Douglas Botting, *From the Ruins of the Reich: Germany, 1945–1949* (New York: Crown, 1985), 121.

50. Ibid., 123–24.

51. Clay to Eisenhower, May 26, 1946, in *The Papers of General Lucius D. Clay: Germany, 1945–1949,* ed. Jean Edward Smith (Bloomington: Indiana University Press, 1974), 1:184.

52. While much of the civilian infrastructure had been annihilated, the majority of German industry managed to survive the massive bombing of World War II. Only 15–20 percent of German industry had been destroyed by the war, including only 10 percent of the steel and mining industry. See Botting, *From the Ruins of the Reich,* 125.

53. FRUS, 1945, *The Conferences at Malta and Yalta,* 617.

54. On the role of the Soviet threat in motivating the American population and Congress, see Trachtenberg, *A Constructed Peace,* 50–51.

55. See Hans Schmidt, *The United States Occupation of Haiti, 1915–1934* (New Brunswick, N.J.: Rutgers University Press, 1995), 67.

56. Ivan Musicant, *The Banana Wars: A History of United States Military Intervention in Latin America from the Spanish-American War to the Invasion of Panama* (New York: Macmillan, 1990), 171.

57. Schmidt, *United States Occupation of Haiti,* 41.

58. On the geopolitics of Haiti in the early nineteenth century, see Brenda Gayle Plummer, *Haiti and the Great Powers, 1902–1915* (Baton Rouge: Louisiana State University Press, 1988).

59. Lansing to McCormick. Reprinted as appendix B of the report of the Inquiry into Occupation and Administration of Haiti and the Dominican Republic, Senate Report No. 794, 67th Congress, 2nd Session, April 20, 1922.

60. Dana G. Munro, *Intervention and Dollar Diplomacy in the Caribbean, 1900–1921* (Princeton, N.J.: Princeton University Press, 1964), 331.

61. On the initial Haitian reaction to the U.S. occupation, see David Healy, *Gunboat Diplomacy in the Wilson Era: The U.S. Navy in Haiti, 1915–1916* (Madison: University of Wisconsin Press, 1976), 62–81; and Mary A. Renda, *Taking Haiti: Military Occupation and the Culture of U.S. Imperialism, 1915–1940* (Chapel Hill: University of North Carolina Press, 2001).

62. For Rear Admiral W. B. Caperton's firsthand account of the intervention in Haiti, see the excerpt from "History of Flag Career Rear Admiral W. B. Caperton, U.S. Navy," http://www.history.navy.mil/library/online/haiti_cap.htm.

63. On the formation of the Haitian Garde, see James H. McCrocklin, *Garde D'Haiti: Twenty Years of Organization and Training by the United States Marine Corps* (Annapolis, Md.: United States Naval Institute, 1956).

64. Schmidt, *United States Occupation of Haiti*, 97.

65. Munro, *Intervention and Dollar Diplomacy in the Caribbean*, 370.

66. Quoted in Schmidt, *United States Occupation of Haiti*, 95.

67. Robert Debs Heinl Jr., *Written in Blood: The Story of the Haitian People, 1492–1995* (Lanham, Md.: University Press of America, 1996), 430.

68. Ibid., 430–31.

69. Official Marine statistics cited in Schmidt, *United States Occupation of Haiti*, 102.

70. A series of articles in the *Nation* by James Weldon Johnson brought the situation in Haiti to the attention of the American people. The articles, all titled "Self-Determining Haiti," included: "I. The American Occupation" (August 28, 1920), "II. What the United States Has Accomplished" (September 4, 1920), "III. Government of, by, and for the National City Bank" (September 11, 1920), and "IV. The Haitian People" (September 25, 1920).

71. On the role of Haiti in the 1920 U.S. presidential election, see Heinl, *Written in Blood*, 446–47; Schmidt, *United States Occupation of Haiti*, 118–19.

72. Schmidt, *United States Occupation of Haiti*, 108.

73. Heinl, *Written in Blood*, 447.

74. As Hans Schmidt summarizes, "The period from the 1922 financial and administrative reorganization to the 1929 strikes and riots was a time of peace, political stability, and relatively economic prosperity." Schmidt, *United States Occupation of Haiti*, 135.

75. For a review of occupation policies, see Paul H. Douglas, "The American Occupation of Haiti I," *Political Science Quarterly* 42, no. 2 (June 1927): 228–58; and Douglas, "The American Occupation of Haiti II," *Political Science Quarterly* 42, no. 3 (September 1927): 368–96.

76. On the student strikes, see Heinl, *Written in Blood*, 462–64; and Schmidt, *United States Occupation of Haiti*, 189–206.

77. For details of the Cayes massacre, see Heinl, *Written in Blood*, 464–65; Schmidt, *United States Occupation of Haiti*, 199–205.

78. Hoover's Annual Message to Congress, December 3, 1929. On Hoover's comments, see Schmidt, *United States Occupation of Haiti*, 200–01.

79. For details on foreign criticism of the U.S. occupation, see ibid., 204.

80. On the effort to withdraw from Haiti, see Dana G. Munro, "The American Withdrawal from Haiti, 1929–1934," *Hispanic American Historical Review* 49, no. 1 (February 1969): 1–26.

81. The report of the Forbes Commission is reprinted in FRUS, 1930, 3:217–37.

82. Schmidt, *United States Occupation of Haiti*, 220–23.

83. For a convincing argument that U.S. concerns about German ambitions in the Caribbean were unwarranted, see Nancy Mitchell, *The Danger of Dreams: German and American Imperialism in Latin America* (Chapel Hill: University of North Carolina Press, 1999). See also Plummer, *Haiti and the Great Powers;* and Alfred Vagts, "Hopes and Fears of an American-German War, 1870–1915, I," *Political Science Quarterly* 54, no. 4 (December 1939): 514–35.

84. For a postscript on the U.S. occupation of Haiti, see Schmidt, *United States Occupation of Haiti*, 231–37.

85. According to the United States Marine Corps History and Museum Divisions, the number of U.S. marines killed in action during the entire occupation was only ten while twenty-six were wounded. See http://hqinet001.hqmc.usmc.mil/HD/Historical/Frequently_Requested/Casualties.htm.

86. Quoted in Mitchell, *Danger of Dreams*, 1.

87. L. Ton Evans, Testimony before the U.S. Senate Inquiry in Occupation of Haiti and Santo Domingo, *Inquiry into Occupation of Haiti and Santo Domingo* (Washington: U.S. Government Printing Office, 1922), 199.

88. Heinl, *Written in Blood*, 407.

89. Ibid., 475–76.

90. Byrnes to Patterson, June 11, 1946, FRUS, 1946, 2:486–88.

2. HOW TO OCCUPY

1. On the importance of creating social ties with both the population and local elites, see Paul K. MacDonald, "Occupation or Empire? Explaining America's Failure in Iraq," Unpublished manuscript, October 2006.

2. On the emperor's role, see Eiji Takemae, *Inside GHQ: The Allied Occupation of Japan and its Legacy* (New York: Continuum, 2002), 281–84; and John W. Dower, *Embracing Defeat: Japan in the Wake of World War II* (New York: W. W. Norton, 1999), 387–90.

3. See the discussion of shifting U.S. occupation policy toward Germany in chapter 2.

4. James Dobbins et al., *America's Role in Nation-Building: From Germany to Iraq* (Santa Monica, Calif.: RAND, 2003), 158.

5. Similar analysis has been performed for the number of troops per capita that are necessary to ensure security during stability operations. In general, 20 troops per 1000 inhabitants has been viewed as a guideline for success, but again, this number has been arrived at inductively without any allowance for how geography, for example, might affect that number. See James T. Quinlivan, "Force Requirements in Stability Operations," *Parameters* (winter 1995), 59–69. For a governmental report accepting this guidance, see Defense Science Board, "Transition to and from Hostilities" (Washington, DC: Office of the Under Secretary of Defense for Acquisition, Technology, and Linguistics, December 2004), 42.

6. Thomas Schelling, *Arms and Influence* (New Haven, Conn.: Yale University Press, 1966), 31.

7. On coercion, see Daniel Byman and Matthew Waxman, *The Dynamics of Coercion: American Foreign Policy and the Limits of Military Might* (New York: Cambridge University Press, 2002).

8. See Ivan Arreguin-Toft, "How the Weak Win Wars: A Theory of Asymmetric Conflict," *International Security* 26, no. 1 (summer 2001): 93–128; Gil Merom, *How Democracies Lose Small Wars: State, Society, and the Failures of France in Algeria, Israel in Lebanon, and the United States in Vietnam* (New York: Cambridge University Press, 2003); and John A. Nagl, *Learning to Eat Soup with a Knife: Counterinsurgency Lessons from Malaya and Vietnam* (Chicago: University of Chicago Press, 2005).

9. On Soviet strategies in Central and Eastern Europe, see Norman N. Naimark, *The Russians in Germany: A History of the Soviet Zone of Occupation* (Cambridge, Mass.: Harvard University Press, 1995); and Sergiu Verona, *Military Occupation and Diplomacy: Soviet Troops in Romania, 1944–1958* (Durham, N.C.: Duke University Press, 1992).

10. Vladislav Zubok and Constantine Pleshakov, *Inside the Kremlin's Cold War: From Stalin to Khrushchev* (Cambridge, Mass.: Harvard University Press, 1996), 147.

11. The issue of just how expensive it was for the Soviet Union to maintain its empire remains a matter of dispute. See Nick Bisley, *The End of the Cold War and Causes of Soviet Collapse* (New York: Palgrave, 2004); Keith Crane, *The Soviet Economic Dilemma of Eastern Europe* (Santa Monica, Calif.: RAND, 1986); and Alex Nove, *Studies in Economics and Russia* (New York: St. Martin's Press, 1990).

12. See Robert Jervis, *System Effects: Complexity in Political and Social Life* (Princeton, N.J.: Princeton University Press, 1997), 125–31.

13. Anna Louise Strong, *Inside North Korea: An Eyewitness Report* (Montrose, Calif.: 1950), 3.

14. On the evolution of Korean nationalism, see Bruce Cumings, *The Origins of the Korean War*, vol. 2, *The Roaring of the Cataract, 1947–1950* (Princeton, N.J.: Princeton

University Press, 1990); Tae-yol Ku, *Korea under Colonialism: The March First Movement and Anglo-Japanese Relations* (Seoul: Seoul Computer Press, 1985).

15. See Ku, *Korea under Colonialism;* Erik Van Ree, *Socialism in One Zone: Stalin's Policy in Korea, 1945–1947* (New York: Berg, 1989), 18–19.

16. William Stueck, *Rethinking the Korean War: A New Diplomatic and Strategic History* (Princeton, N.J.: Princeton University Press, 2002), 20.

17. Foreign Relations of the United States (hereafter FRUS) 1944, vol. 5, *The Near East, South Asia, Africa, The Far East,* 1240.

18. For the Cairo Declaration, see FRUS, *The Conferences at Cairo and Tehran,* 1943, 448–49. Emphasis added.

19. For more on U.S. planning for the postwar management of Korea, see "Memorandum Prepared by the Inter-Divisional Area Committee on the Far East," May 4, 1944, FRUS, 1944, 5:1239–42.

20. Bruce Cumings, *The Origins of the Korean War,* vol. 1, *Liberation and the Emergence of Separate Regimes, 1945–1947* (Princeton, N.J.: Princeton University Press, 1981), 106.

21. Quoted in William Stueck, "The Coming of the Cold War to Korea," in *Korea under the American Military Government, 1945–1948,* ed. Bonnie B. C. Oh (Westport, Conn.: Praeger, 2002), 42.

22. Cumings, *Origins of the Korean War,* 1:113.

23. Ibid., 1:118.

24. President Truman was more skeptical of Soviet intentions than Roosevelt had been. Truman did not share FDR's faith that a cooperative postwar arrangement could be established, but trusteeship and the division of Korea at the 38th parallel was a useful compromise. See Michael C. Sandusky, *America's Parallel* (Alexandria, Va.: Old Dominion Press, 1983), 311.

25. An interesting historical question is why Stalin accepted this proposal. Militarily, the Soviets appeared to be in position to conquer the entire peninsula if they so desired. William Stueck argues that Stalin realized that his position in Korea was quite vulnerable and that the United States might cut a deal with the Japanese before the Soviet Union could establish its control over northern Korea. See Stueck, "Coming of the Cold War to Korea," 50–51. Bruce Cumings speculates that Stalin accepted the partition of the peninsula for two reasons. First, control over the north was sufficient to give him the influence he desired over East Asia. Second, by agreeing to the U.S. proposal, he left open the possibility of further cooperation with the United States. See Cumings, *Origins of the Korean War,* 1:121. Erik Van Ree agrees with Cumings first argument, claiming that Stalin's primary interest in Korea was in access to warm-water ports, which he could acquire in the north. Further, Van Ree argues that the Soviet Union simply did not have the military resources in Korea to conquer the rest of the peninsula. Van Ree, *Socialism in One Zone,* 42–44, 50–51, 63.

26. James I. Matray, *The Reluctant Crusade: American Foreign Policy in Korea, 1941–1950* (Honolulu: University of Hawaii Press, 1985), 26–27.

27. FRUS, 1945, vol. 6, *The British Commonwealth, The Far East,* 1074.

28. As Jeon Sang Sook succinctly states, "The US Military Government's sole concern in Korea was to prevent the peninsula from coming under the influence of the Soviet Union, with which it shared a border." Jeon Sang Sook, "U.S. Korea Policy and the Moderates during the U.S. Military Government Era," in *Korea under the American Military Government, 1945–1948,* ed. Bonnie B. C. Oh (Westport, Conn.: Praeger, 2002), 82. See "Memorandum Prepared by the Inter-Divisional Area Committee on the Far East," 1224–28.

29. Stueck, *Rethinking the Korean War,* 20.

30. James I. Matray, "Hodge Podge: American Occupation Policy in Korea, 1945–1948," *Korean Studies* 19 (1995): 20.

31. E. Grant Meade, *American Military Government in Korea* (New York: King's Crown, 1951), 50–51.

32. Matray, *Reluctant Crusade,* 50.

33. Chan-Pyo Park, "The American Military Government and Framework for Democracy in South Korea," in *Korea under the American Military Government, 1945–1948,* ed. Bonnie B. C. Oh (Westport, Conn.: Praeger, 2002), 126. See also Cumings, *Origins of the Korean War,* 1:128.

34. Peter Lowe, *The Origins of the Korean War,* 2d ed. (New York: Longman, 1997), 25.

35. On resistance to Japanese colonial rule within Korea, see Cumings, *Origins of the Korean War,* 1:3–67. On the formation of the KPG after the 1919 revolts, see Matray, *Reluctant Crusade,* 7.

36. Hodge to MacArthur, FRUS, 1945, 6:1133–34.

37. Matray, "Hodge Podge," 25.

38. Benninghoff to Secretary of State, FRUS, 1945, 6:1049–53.

39. SWNCC 101/4, FRUS, 1945, 6:1096–1103.

40. For the section of the Moscow Agreement addressing Korea, see FRUS, 1945, vol. 2, *General: Political and Economic Matters,* 820–21.

41. "Koreans See Trusteeship as Long Delay," *Pacific Stars and Stripes,* December 31, 1945, 1. Quoted in Sandusky, *America's Parallel,* 36.

42. Cumings, *Origins of the Korean War,* 1:213.

43. MacArthur to Joint Chiefs of Staff, December 16, 1945, FRUS, 1945, 6:1144–48.

44. Matray, *Reluctant Crusade,* 56–57. See SWNCC 176/8, "Basic Initial Directive to the Commander in Chief, U.S. Army Forces, Pacific, for the Administration of Civil Affairs in Those Areas of Korea Occupatied by U.S. Forces," October 17, 1945, FRUS, 1945, 6:1073–91, especially paragraph 9(g) on 1081. See also Frank Lockhart, Acting Director, Office of Far Eastern Affairs, to Rhee, June 5, 1945, FRUS, 1945, 6:1029–30; Acheson to Hurley, September 21, 1945, FRUS, 1945, 6:1053–54.

45. According to Cumings, this was a "tempestuous marriage of convenience." Bruce Cumings, *Korea's Place in the Sun: A Modern History* (New York: W. W. Norton, 1997), 216. See Vincent to Acheson, November 16, 1945, FRUS, 1945, 6:1127–28.

46. On the shift in the Korean Communist Party and the Soviet role in orchestrating this shift, see Van Ree, *Socialism in One Zone,* 143–44.

47. See MacArthur (on behalf of Hodge) to Byrnes, February 24, 1946, FRUS, 1946, vol. 8, *The Far East,* 640–42.

48. For example, see Rhee to Truman, May 15, 1945, FRUS, 1945, 6:1028–29; Rhee to Lockhart, Acting Chief of the Office of Far Eastern Affairs, FRUS, 1945, 6:1032–36; Ben C. Limb, Acting Chairman of the Korean Commission to John Carter Vincent, Director of the Office of Far Eastern Affairs, FRUS, 1945, 6:1115–16.

49. Truman to Pauley, July 16, 1946, FRUS, 1946, 8:713–14. See discussion in Stueck, *Rethinking the Korean War,* 37–38.

50. Bonnie B. C. Oh, "Kim Kyu-sik and the Coalition Effort," in *Korea under the American Military Government, 1945–1948,* ed. Bonnie B. C. Oh (Westport, Conn.: Praeger, 2002), 103–22.

51. See Memorandum of Conversation Held in the Division of Japanese Affairs, July 16, 1946, FRUS, 1946, 8:715–16.

52. Cumings, *Origins of the Korean War,* 1:259–62; Matray, *Reluctant Crusade,* 95–98.

53. On the Autumn Harvest Uprisings, see Cumings, *Origins of the Korean War,* 1:351–81; Matray, "Hodge Podge," 27; Park, "American Military Government," 135.

54. Cumings, *Origins of the Korean War,* 1:252.

55. MacArthur to Eisenhower, October 28, 1946, FRUS, 1946, 8:750–51.

56. Cumings, *Origins of the Korean War,* 1:378.

57. For a survey of the various options before the United States in early 1947, see "Draft Report of the Special Interdepartmental Committee on Korea," February 25, 1947, FRUS, 1947, vol. 6, *The Far East,* 610–18.

58. Hodge to Byrnes, December 31, 1946, FRUS, 1946, 8:785–86.

59. On this debate, see Cumings, *Origins of the Korean War,* 2:45–48. See also Matray, *Reluctant Crusade,* 98.

60. Matray, *Reluctant Crusade,* 100–01.

61. Ibid., 115–16.

62. Quoted in Cumings, *Origins of the Korean War,* 2:46.

63. Ibid., 2:59.

64. Lowe, *Origins of the Korean War,* 43.

65. Patterson to the Acting Secretary of State, April 4, 1947, FRUS, 1947, 6:625–28.

66. See JCS 1769/1, "United States Assistance to Other Countries from the Standpoint of National Security," April 29, 1947. Reprinted in Thomas H. Etzold and John Lewis Gaddis, eds., *Containment: Documents on American Policy and Strategy* (New York: Columbia University Press, 1978), 71–83. Emphasis added.

67. Forrestal to Secretary of State, September 26, 1947, FRUS, 1947, 6:817–18.

68. Kennan to Butterworth, September 24, 1947, FRUS, 1947, 6:814.

69. William Stueck, *The Wedemeyer Mission: American Politics and Foreign Policy during the Cold War* (Athens: University of Georgia Press, 1984), 25–27.

70. Report to the President on China-Korea, September 1947, Submitted by Lieutenant General A. C. Wedemeyer, September 19, 1947, FRUS, 1947, 6:796–803. Quote on 803.

71. MacArthur to the Secretary of State, July 2, 1947, FRUS, 1947, 6:682–84.

72. Jacobs to Secretary of State, September 8, 1947, FRUS, 1947, 6:783.

73. Matray, *Reluctant Crusade,* 125, 130–31.

74. See Soviet Minister for Foreign Affairs Molotov to the Secretary of State, October 9, 1947, FRUS, 1947, 6:827–28.

75. Cumings, *Origins of the Korean War,* 2:70.

76. Hodge to the Department of the Army for the Joint Chiefs of Staff, November 3, 1947, FRUS, 1947, 6:852–53.

77. NSC 8, "Report by the National Security Council on the Position of the United States with Respect to Korea," April 2, 1948, FRUS, 1948, vol. 6, *The Far East and Australasia,* 1164–69.

78. Marshall to the Secretary of the Army (Kenneth Royall), June 23, 1948, FRUS, 1948, 6:1224–25.

79. NSC 8/2, March 22, 1949, in FRUS, 1949, vol. 7, *The Far East and Australasia, Part 2,* 969–78.

80. On the Cheju rebellion, see John Merrill, "The Cheju Rebellion," *Journal of Korean Studies* 2 (1980): 139–98. The Yosu Rebellion started when elements of the South Korean Army refused to accept their assigned counterinsurgency task on Cheju Island. See Cumings, *Origins of the Korean War,* 2:259–67.

81. Merrill, "The Cheju Rebellion," 194–95.

82. On repression, see Cumings, *Origins of the Korean War,* 2:213. Also see the table ibid., 273.

83. Matray, *Reluctant Crusade,* 228.

84. On the possibility that the United States left Korea prematurely, see Matray, *Reluctant Crusade,* 180; and Stueck, "Coming of the Cold War to Korea," 54.

85. Matray, "Hodge Podge," 21.

86. Meade, *American Military Government in Korea,* 236.

87. Merrill, "Cheju Rebellion."

88. Cumings, *Origins of the Korean War*, 1:299. By the end of January 1946, only 60 Japanese remained of the 70,000 who had held government positions when the occupation began in the fall of 1945. The occupation administration did, however, continue to rely heavily on Koreans who had collaborated with the Japanese. George M. McCune, "Korea: The First Year of Liberation," *Pacific Affairs* 20, no. 1 (March 1947): 8.

89. Bonnie B. C. Oh, "Introduction," in *Korea under the American Military Government, 1945–1948*, ed. Bonnie B. C. Oh (Westport, Conn.: Praeger, 2002), 1–11.

90. G-2 "Weekly Reports," Nos. 23 and 24, February 10–17 and February 17–24, 1946. Quoted in Cumings, *Origins of the Korean War*, 1:234.

91. Cumings, *Origins of the Korean War*, 1:433.

92. See ibid., 2:250–95; Matray, *Reluctant Crusade*, 141.

93. Park, "American Military Government," 135.

94. Jacobs to the Secretary of State, September 19, 1947, FRUS, 1947, 6:803–7. Quote on 806.

95. Public opinion numbers suggest that Koreans were relatively moderate in their political positions. A survey conducted by the U.S. Military Government in August 1946 found 70% support for socialism compared to only 7% support for communism and 14% support for capitalism. Cited in Jeon Sang Sook, "U.S. Korean Policy and the Moderates during the U.S. Military Government Era," in *Korea under the American Military Government, 1945–1948*, ed. Bonnie B. C. Oh (Westport, Conn.: Praeger, 2002), 94.

96. Cumings, *Origins of the Korean War*, 2:52.

97. Andrei Lankov, *From Stalin to Kim Il Sung: The Formation of North Korea, 1945–1960* (New Brunswick, N.J.: Rutgers University Press, 2002), 5.

98. See Charles K. Armstrong, *The North Korean Revolution, 1945–1950* (Ithaca, N.Y.: Cornell University Press, 2003), 43–45; Lankov, *From Stalin to Kim Il Sung*, 6. Armstrong maintains, however, that, "by comparison [with eastern Europe and Manchuria], the period of widespread assaults on Korean women in the Soviet zone of occupation were relatively short-lived."

99. Sydney A. Seiler, *Kim Il-Sung, 1941–1948* (Lanham, Md.: University Press of America, 1994), 48.

100. Van Ree, *Socialism in One Zone*, 50.

101. For a discussion of the limited Soviet goals in northern Korea, see Cumings, *Origins of the Korean War*, 2:330–31. Cumings describes the Soviet strategy as "low-risk/high-gain." See also Kathryn Weathersby, "Soviet Aims in Korea and the Origins of the Korean War, 1945–1950: New Evidence from the Russian Archives," Cold War International History Project Working Paper (1993), 25.

102. Zhukov and Zabrodin, "Korea, Short Report," June 29, 1945, AVP RF, Fond 0430, Opis 2, Delo 18, Papka 5, 1.18–30. See summary and discussion in Weathersby, "Soviet Aims in Korea," 10–11.

103. "Order of Ivan Chistiakov, Commanding General of the Soviet Army of Occupation in North Korea, 25th Army," reprinted in Armstrong, *North Korean Revolution*, 250–51. Emphasis added.

104. Armstrong, *North Korean Revolution*, 54.

105. Van Ree, *Socialism in One Zone*, 154.

106. Armstrong, *North Korean Revolution*, 62.

107. For a description of the structure of the Soviet occupation authority, see In Ho Lee, "The Soviet Military Government in Korea," *Korea Observer* 23, no. 4 (1992): 534–37.

108. Bradley K. Martin, *Under the Loving Care of the Fatherly Leader: North Korea and the Kim Dynasty* (New York: St. Martin's, 2004), 52.

109. Dae-Sook Suh, *Kim Il Sung: The North Korean Leader* (New York: Columbia University Press, 1988), 67.

110. Lankov, *From Stalin to Kim Il Sung,* 10.

111. For a detailed summary of Kim's activities during World War II, see Armstrong, *North Korean Revolution,* 26–37.

112. Many Koreans were unconvinced that this was the "real" Kim Il-Sung because of his youthful appearance. See Seiler, *Kim Il-Sung,* 56.

113. Cumings, *Origins of the Korean War,* 1:401.

114. For a description of the Sinuiju incident, see Armstrong, *North Korean Revolution,* 63; and Martin, *Under the Loving Care of the Fatherly Leader,* 54.

115. Armstrong, *North Korean Revolution,* 64.

116. See Cumings, *Origins of the Korean War,* 1:403–04.

117. Armstrong, *North Korean Revolution,* 69.

118. Ibid., 113.

119. On the ruthless repression of opposition to Kim's regime, see ibid., 2:316.

120. Martin, *Under the Loving Care of the Fatherly Leader,* 57. The number is perhaps as high as 1.8 million people or 17% of the North Korean population. See Gregory Henderson, "The Politics of Korea," in *Two Koreas—One Future?* ed. John Sullivan and Roberta Foss (Lanham, Md.: University Press of America, 1987), 100.

121. Cumings, *Origins of the Korean War,* 1:425–26. While far more refugees moved from north to south in the first years of the occupation, there were a number of leftist intellectuals who immigrated from southern to northern Korea. These numbers were, however, a relatively modest 25,000 people. Armstrong, *North Korean Revolution,* 167.

122. See Robert A. Scalapino and Chong-Sik Lee, *Communism in Korea,* part 1, *The Movement* (Berkeley: University of California Press, 1972), 380. Initially, emigration from North Korea was motivated by a simple desire for people to return to their home villages. After land reform began in the spring of 1946, more Koreans fled North Korea to escape Soviet policies there. See Armstrong, *North Korean Revolution,* 46–47.

123. Martin, *Under the Loving Care of the Fatherly Leader,* 57.

124. Armstrong, *North Korean Revolution,* 152.

125. Lankov, *From Stalin to Kim Il Sung,* 24.

126. U.S. Department of State, *North Korea: A Case Study in the Techniques of Takeover* (Washington, D.C.: U.S. Government Printing Office, 1961), 56.

127. Ibid., 57. For the effects of land reform, see also Cumings, *Origins of the Korean War,* 1:416–17; Lankov, *From Stalin to Kim Il Sung,* 33.

128. Cited in Armstrong, *North Korean Revolution,* 85.

129. Ibid., 87.

130. Ibid., 93.

131. See Cumings, *Origins of the Korean War,* 2:344; U.S. Department of State, *North Korea: A Case Study in the Techniques of Takeover,* 101.

132. George M. McCune, *Korea Today* (Cambridge, Mass.: Harvard University Press, 1950), 214. For the original Pauley report, see "Report on Japanese Assets in Soviet-Occupied Korea to the President of the United States" (Washington, D.C.: U.S. Government Printing Office, June 1946).

133. Armstrong, *North Korean Revolution,* 159.

134. Ibid., 45.

135. Van Ree, *Socialism in One Zone: Stalin's Policy in Korea, 1945–1947,* 50, 200. See also Weathersby, "Soviet Aims in Korea," 25.

136. On relations between Stalin and Kim on this point, see Weathersby, "Soviet Aims in Korea."

137. There is a continuing debate among historians over whether Kim started the Korean War on his own or whether he sought Soviet approval first. As usual, the truth is probably somewhere in between. For a compelling account based on newly available

sources from the former Soviet archives, see ibid. More generally, historians continue to debate how independent Kim Il-Sung was throughout the occupation. Charles Armstrong's central thesis revolves around how Kim's success can be attributed to his nationalism. Robert Scalapino and Chong-Sik Lee argue, on the other hand, that, "Kim was a puppet of a foreign power to an extent unmatched by any other individual's relationship to a foreign power during this period." Given the relatively small Soviet presence in northern Korea even at the height of the occupation, Scalapino and Lee's argument seems somewhat implausible. See Scalapino and Lee, *Communism in Korea,* 1:381.

138. U.S. Department of State, *North Korea: A Case Study in the Techniques of Takeover,* 12.

139. Sergiu Verona, *Military Occupation and Diplomacy: Soviet Troops in Romania, 1944–1958* (Durham, N.C.: Duke University Press, 1992), 49. The Soviets also had 65,000 troops in Austria, 55,000 in Hungary, 126,000 in Bulgaria, more than 100,000 in Poland, and more than 300,000 in eastern Germany at the same time.

140. Armstrong, *North Korean Revolution,* 153. It is difficult to do a simple exchange to determine how expensive this actually was to the Soviets, but the Pauley Commission concluded that the Soviets were "devoting considerable effort to rejuvenate economic activity in Northern Korea." See also Van Ree, *Socialism in One Zone,* 178.

141. Van Ree, *Socialism in One Zone,* 182.

142. Armstrong, *North Korean Revolution,* 164.

143. U.S. Department of State, *North Korea: A Case Study in the Techniques of Takeover,* 5.

144. Cumings, *Origins of the Korean War,* 2:303.

145. Philip Deane, *I Was a Captive in Korea* (New York: W. W. Norton, 1953), 68–69.

146. Armstrong, *North Korean Revolution,* 68.

147. See the Korean views of communism, the Soviet Union, and Kim's regime as summarized in William C. Bradbury, *Mass Behavior in Battle and Captivity: The Communist Soldier in the Korean War* (Chicago, Ill.: University of Chicago Press, 1968), 226. This report was based on polling done of Korean soldiers during the Korean War.

148. "Aims of the Soviet Delegation; Statement by Col. Gen. T. F. Shtikov, Head of the Soviet Delegation, Joint American-Soviet Commission," March 20, 1946, reprinted in McCune, *Korea Today,* 279–81. Emphasis added.

149. Cumings, *Origins of the Korean War,* 1:426.

150. Ibid., 2:327.

151. Armstrong, *North Korean Revolution,* 107.

152. Lankov, *From Stalin to Kim Il Sung,* 40.

153. Quoted in Armstrong, *North Korean Revolution,* 232.

154. On the relative effectiveness of the North Korean regime, see Lankov, *From Stalin to Kim Il Sung,* 26–27.

155. Van Ree, *Socialism in One Zone,* 112.

156. Wayne Patterson and Hilary Conroy, "Duality and Dominance: A Century of Korean-American Relations," in *One Hundred Years of Korean-American Relations, 1882–1982,* ed. Yur-Bok Lee and Wayne Patterson (Tuscaloosa: University of Alabama Press, 1986), 7.

3. WHEN TO LEAVE

1. John W. Dower, *Embracing Defeat: Japan in the Wake of World War II* (New York: W. W. Norton, 1999), 525. According to Marlene J. Mayo, "All of the Japan hands thought that the occupation should be short in time and small in scale." Marlene J. Mayo, "American Wartime Planning for Occupied Japan: The Role of the Experts," in *Americans as Proconsuls: United States Military Government in Germany and Japan, 1944–1952,* ed. Robert Wolfe (Carbondale, Ill.: Southern Illinois University Press, 1984), 3–51.

2. See Hans Schmidt, *The United States Occupation of Haiti, 1915–1934* (New Brunswick, N.J.: Rutgers University Press, 1995), 133, 164.

3. *London Chronicle,* December 7, 1898. Cited in David F. Healy, *The United States in Cuba, 1898–1902: Generals, Politicians, and the Search for Policy* (Madison, Wis.: University of Wisconsin Press, 1963), 51.

4. Quoted in Philip S. Foner, *The Spanish-Cuban-American War and the Birth of American Imperialism, 1895–1902* (New York: Monthly Review Press, 1972), 2:395.

5. Louis A. Pérez Jr., *Cuba and the United States: Ties of Singular Intimacy,* 3d ed. (Athens: University of Georgia Press, 2003), 107.

6. Jules Robert Benjamin, *The United States and Cuba: Hegemony and Dependent Development, 1880–1934* (Pittsburgh, Pa.: University of Pittsburgh Press, 1977), 4.

7. A Planter in Cuba, "The Argument for Autonomy," *Outlook,* no. 58 (April 23, 1898), 1012.

8. Olney to Dupuy de Lôme, April 14, 1896, Foreign Relations of the United States (hereafter FRUS), 1897, 543–44.

9. Pérez, *Cuba and the United States,* 86–88.

10. Calixto García to Editor, December 18, 1897, *New York Journal,* January 5, 1898. Quoted in Pérez, *Cuba and the United States,* 90.

11. William R. Day to Stewart Woodford, March 27, 1898, FRUS, 1898, 711–12.

12. Quoted in Pérez, *Cuba and the United States,* 93.

13. Healy, *United States in Cuba, 1898–1902,* 22.

14. Cited in Pérez, *Cuba and the United States,* 95.

15. McKinley, Annual Message to Congress, December 6, 1897. James D. Richardson, *A Compilation of the Messages and Papers of the Presidents* (Washington, D.C.: U.S. Government Printing Office, 1899), 10:127–36.

16. While the Teller Amendment passed Congress, another amendment that would have required recognition of a provisional Cuban government was withdrawn when McKinley made it clear that he would veto such a resolution. McKinley was concerned about endorsing any particular Cuban government.

17. For the text of the Teller Amendment, see *Congressional Record,* 55th Congress, 2nd Session (1898), 31:3988.

18. Cited in Healy, *The United States in Cuba,* 34.

19. Hugh Thomas, *Cuba: The Pursuit of Freedom* (London: Picador, 2001), 246.

20. Quoted in Pérez, *Cuba and the United States,* 118.

21. James H. Hitchman, "The American Touch in Imperial Administration: Leonard Wood in Cuba, 1898–1902," *The Americas* 24, no. 4 (April 1968): 397.

22. Quoted in Walter Millis, *The Martial Spirit: A Study of Our War with Spain* (Cambridge, Mass.: Riverside Press, 1931), 362.

23. Quoted in George Kennan, "Cuban Character," *Outlook,* no. 63 (December 23, 1899): 1021–22.

24. Foner, *Spanish-Cuban-American War,* 2:413; Healy, *United States in Cuba,* 40–41.

25. General Order 101, Leonard Wood, *Civil Report of Brigadier General Leonard Wood, Military Governor of Cuba, for the Period from December 20, 1899, to December 31, 1900* (Washington, D.C.: U.S. Government Printing Office, 1901), 1:1–5.

26. *Congressional Record,* 55th Congress, 3d Session (1898), 32:2807–11. Foner, *The Spanish-Cuban-American War,* 2:469

27. McKinley to Brooke, December 28, 1898. For the entire message see C. S. Olcott, *Life of William McKinley* (Boston: Houghton Mifflin, 1918), 2:196–202.

28. Message of the President, December 5, 1898. FRUS, 1898, lxvii.

29. *Civil Report of Major-General John R. Brooke, Military Governor, Island of Cuba* (Washington, D.C.: U.S. Government Printing Office, 1900), 7.

30. As David Healy notes about the occupation in general, "In default of a declared official policy for Cuba, everyone felt free to work out policies of his own." Healy, *United States in Cuba,* 97.

31. James Harrison Wilson, *Under the Old Flag* (New York: Appleton, 1912), 2:479–80.

32. José M. Hernández, *Cuba and the United States: Intervention and Militarism, 1868–1933* (Austin: University of Texas Press, 1993), 74.

33. Cited ibid., 76.

34. Quoted in Healy, *The United States in Cuba,* 54.

35. Cited in Louis A. Pérez Jr., *Cuba between Empires, 1878–1902* (Pittsburgh, Pa.: University of Pittsburgh Press, 1983), 263. See also *New York Journal Magazine,* February 26, 1899.

36. "Gómez's Farewell Advice," *New York Times,* June 7, 1899.

37. Foner, *Spanish-Cuban-American War,* 2:522.

38. Cited in Healy, *The United States in Cuba,* 101.

39. Ibid., 101.

40. Quoted in Thomas, *Cuba: The Pursuit of Freedom,* 258.

41. Hermann Hagedorn, *Leonard Wood* (New York: Harper and Brothers, 1931), 1:371.

42. Pérez, *Cuba between Empires,* 304–5. For another view that Cuba must inevitably be annexed by the United States for its own benefit, see Herbert Pelham Williams, "The Outlook in Cuba," *Atlantic Monthly* 83, no. 500 (June 1899), 827–36.

43. Quoted in Pérez, *Cuba between Empires,* 279.

44. James H. Hitchman, *Leonard Wood and Cuban Independence, 1898–1902* (The Hague: Martinus Nijhoff, 1971), 31.

45. Quoted in Healy, *United States in Cuba,* 132.

46. Wood to Root, February 23, 1900. Cited in Pérez, *Cuba between Empires,* 306–7.

47. Jules R. Benjamin, *The United States and the Origins of the Cuban Revolution: An Empire of Liberty in an Age of National Liberation* (Princeton, N.J.: Princeton University Press, 1990), 67; Pérez, *Cuba between Empires,* 184; Louis A. Pérez Jr., *Cuba Under the Platt Amendment, 1902–1934* (Pittsburgh, Pa.: University of Pittsburgh Press, 1986), 37.

48. Pérez, *Cuba between Empires,* 300–01.

49. Wood to Root, December 30, 1899. Cited in Pérez, *Cuba between Empires,* 301.

50. For the text, see *Civil Report of General Leonard Wood,* 1:36.

51. Pérez, *Cuba under the Platt Amendment,* 37.

52. On the postal scandal, see Healy, *United States in Cuba,* 139–40.

53. Foner, *Spanish-Cuban-American War,* 2:541.

54. Healy, *United States in Cuba,* 146.

55. "Report of the Secretary of War, 1901," 57th Congress, 1st Session, *House Documents* (Washington, D.C.: U.S. Government Printing Office), 2:49. Cited in *Spanish-Cuban-American War,* 2:557.

56. On the influence of events in the Philippines on thinking about the occupation of Cuba, see Healy, *United States in Cuba,* 72.

57. Wood to Root, February 8, 1901. Cited in Thomas, *Cuba: The Pursuit of Freedom,* 262.

58. Cited in Healy, *United States in Cuba,* 156–57.

59. Named for Senator Orville H. Platt of Connecticut. For Platt's views, see Orville H. Platt, "The Pacification of Cuba," *Independent,* no. 53 (June 27, 1901), 1464–68.

60. *Congressional Record,* 56th Congress, 2nd Session (1901), 34:2954.

61. On concerns about European interference, see Healy, *United States in Cuba,* 212.

62. Philip C. Jessup, *Elihu Root* (New York: Dodd, Mead, and Company, 1938), 1:314.

63. Foner, *Spanish-Cuban-American War,* 2:583–92.

64. For a discussion of the formal Cuban constitutional convention response to the Platt Amendment, see ibid., 603–12.

65. Salvador Cisneros Betancourt, *Appeal to the American People on Behalf of Cuba* (New York: Evening Post Printing House, 1900), 13.

66. Root to Wood, March 2, 1901. Cited in Pérez, *Cuba between Empires,* 325. Jessup, *Elihu Root,* 1:316.

67. Healy, *United States in Cuba,* 174.

68. Wood to Root, April 2, 1901. Cited in Hitchman, *Leonard Wood and Cuban Independence,* 142.

69. These leaders may have secretly desired U.S. annexation of Cuba and saw the Platt Amendment as a step in that direction. Healy, *United States in Cuba,* 175.

70. Quoted ibid., 178.

71. Leonard Wood, "The Military Government of Cuba," *Annals of the American Academy of Political and Social Science,* no. 21 (March 1903), 30.

72. James D. Richardson, ed., *Messages and Papers of the Presidents* (Washington, D.C.: U.S. Government Printing Office, 1909), 15:6923.

73. Quoted in Thomas, *Cuba: The Pursuit of Freedom,* 276.

74. Ibid., 278.

75. Roosevelt to White, September 13, 1906. Cited in Perez, *Cuba Under the Platt Amendment,* 97.

76. Roosevelt to Foraker, September 28, 1906. Cited ibid., 105.

77. On fears that a reintervention in Cuba would resemble the war in the Philippines, see Allan Reed Millett, *The Politics of Intervention: The Military Occupation of Cuba, 1906–1909* (Columbus: Ohio State University Press, 1968), 67.

78. Cited in Pérez, *Cuba Under the Platt Amendment,* 98.

79. Cited in Pérez, *Cuba and the United States,* 154.

80. Roosevelt to Estrada Palma, September 25, 1902. Quoted in Thomas, *Cuba: The Pursuit of Freedom,* 281.

81. Quoted in Ivan Musicant, *The Banana Wars: A History of United States Military Intervention in Latin America from the Spanish-American War to the Invasion of Panama* (New York: Macmillan, 1990), 67.

82. Quoted in Foner, *Spanish-Cuban-American War,* 2:435.

83. Lieutenant J. W. Heard to Adjutant General, August 21, 1898, United States Department of War, *Annual Report of the War Department: Report of the Major-General Commanding the Army, 1898,* United States Congress, House of Representatives, 55th Congress, 3d Session, House Document No. 2, Ser. 3745 (Washington, D.C., 1898), 375–76. Cited in Louis A. Pérez Jr., "Supervision of a Protectorate: The United States and the Cuban Army, 1898–1908," *Hispanic American Historical Review* 52, no. 2 (May 1972): 252.

84. Hernández, *Cuba and the United States,* 87. "Gómez's Farewell Advice," *New York Times,* June 7, 1899.

85. Quoted in Louis A. Pérez Jr., "Incurring a Debt of Gratitude: 1898 and the Moral Sources of United States Hegemony in Cuba," *American Historical Review* 104, no. 2 (April 1999): 363.

86. Ibid., 363.

87. Cited in Foner, *Spanish-Cuban-American War,* 2:527.

88. Elihu Root's biographer writes that Washington was "worried by the bugaboo of German aggression." Jessup, *Elihu Root,* 1:314.

89. Hitchman, *Leonard Wood and Cuban Independence,* 89. For Alfred Thayer Mahan's thinking on the strategic importance of Cuba, see excerpts from his writing in Robert F. Smith, *What Happened in Cuba? A Documentary History* (New York: Twayne, 1963), 97–102. See also Jessup, *Elihu Root,* 1:315.

90. In February 1899, Henry Adams wrote, "The thought of another Manila at Havana sobers even an army contractor." Adams to Cameron, February 26, 1899, in *Letters of Henry Adams,* ed. Worthington Chauncy Ford (Boston: Houghton Mifflin, 1930–1938), 2:20. Cited in Louis A. Pérez Jr., *Lords of the Mountain: Social Banditry and Peasant Protest in Cuba, 1878–1918* (Pittsburgh, Pa.: University of Pittsburgh Press, 1989), 121. On pressure from the conflict in the Philippines, see Pérez, *Cuba between Empires, 1878–1902,* 336–38.

91. Root to Wood, January 9, 1901. Cited in Healy, *United States in Cuba,* 153.

92. Wood to Root, January 31, 1901. Cited in Hitchman, *Leonard Wood and Cuban Independence,* 113.

93. Pérez, *Cuba and the United States,* 104.

94. Taft to Elihu Root, September 14, 1906. Quoted in Pérez, *Cuba between Empires,* 382.

95. On the poor state of the Cuban army after the war against Spain, see Hernández, *Cuba and the United States,* 69–70.

96. Pérez, *Cuba between Empires,* 343–44; Pérez, *Lords of the Mountain,* 124–25; Thomas, *Cuba: The Pursuit of Freedom,* 282.

97. On the weakness of the Cuban rural guard, see Hernández, *Cuba and the United States,* 111–15.

98. *Congressional Record,* 56th Congress, 2nd Session (1901), 34:3151.

99. Pérez, *Cuba between Empires,* 383.

100. Afaf Lufti Al-Sayyid, *Egypt and Cromer: A Study in Anglo-Egyptian Relations* (New York: Praeger, 1968), xi. Counting differently, Hopkins identifies sixty-six declarations of intent to withdraw between 1882 and 1922. See A. G. Hopkins, "The Victorians and Africa: A Reconsideration of the Occupation of Egypt, 1882," *Journal of African History* 27, no. 2 (1986): 388.

101. The phrase "rescue and retire" appears to have first been used by Sir Wilfrid Lawson in the course of a debate over whether to censure Gladstone's government for the missteps in Sudan. See *Hansard's* 274, 3rd Series, February 14, 1884, 901. While Lawson initially used the phrase to describe only policy in Sudan, Gladstone extends the description to all of Britain's Egypt policy later in the debate. See ibid., 912–13. See Hopkins, "The Victorians and Africa," 367.

102. On Gladstone's objections, see D. A. Farnie, *East and West of Suez: The Suez Canal in History, 1854–1956* (Oxford: Clarendon Press, 1969), 282.

103. As John Marlowe relates, the Egyptian nationalists had at least six different general grievances that they hoped to redress through their movement. First, Colonel Urabi's group demanded more native Egyptian officers in the Egyptian army, replacing the high number of Circassians. Second, the nationalists were disgruntled by the growing influence of the west in Egypt brought about by Egyptian indebtedness. Third, many Egyptians were unhappy to see the special privileges that Europeans received in Egypt. Through the so-called Capitulations, Europeans in Egypt were exempt from Egyptian taxation and courts. Fifth, many wealthier Egyptians were unhappy with an increase in the land taxes that they were asked to pay. Sixth and finally, numerous European officials had received high-paying jobs in the Egyptian government even though they were hardly qualified. John Marlowe, *Cromer in Egypt* (New York: Praeger, 1970), 56–58. See also Donald Malcolm Reid, "The Urabi Revolution and the British Conquest, 1879–1882," in *The Cambridge History of Egypt,* vol. 2: *Modern Egypt from 1517 to the End of the Twentieth Century,* ed. W. M. Daly (New York: Cambridge University Press, 1998), 217–51.

104. Quoted in Robert T. Harrison, *Gladstone's Imperialism in Egypt: Techniques of Domination* (Westport, Conn.: Greenwood, 1995), 74.

105. The Earl of Cromer, *Modern Egypt* (New York: Macmillan, 1908), 1:203.

106. For the entire text of the joint note, see John Marlowe, *Anglo-Egyptian Relations, 1800–1953* (London: Cresset, 1954), 118.

107. Cited in Al-Sayyid, *Egypt and Cromer,* 16.

108. For a detailed account of the riots and the argument that Tawfiq himself may actually have been behind the riots, see M. E. Chamberlain, "The Alexandria Massacre of 11 June 1882 and the British Occupation of Egypt," *Middle Eastern Studies* 13, no. 1 (January 1977): 14–39.

109. Harrison, *Gladstone's Imperialism in Egypt,* 99.

110. At this point, the French backed out, withdrawing their fleet from the area. The French premier Charles de Freycinet recognized that he was unlikely to get approval from the French parliament for a military intervention in Egypt so he chose instead to withdraw, leaving the British alone to deal with the nationalist revolt. Al-Sayyid, *Egypt and Cromer,* 24; and John S. Galbraith and Afaf Lufti al-Sayyid-Marsot, "The British Occupation of Egypt: Another View," *International Journal of Middle East Studies* 9, no. 4 (November 1978): 485.

111. Peter Mansfield, *The British in Egypt* (New York: Holt, Rinehard, and Winston, 1972), 67.

112. On the final defeat of Urabi's forces, see Hermann Vogt, *The Egyptian War of 1882* (Nashville, Tenn.: Battery Press, 1883); and Donald Featherstone, *Tel el-Kebir 1882: Wolseley's Conquest of Egypt* (New York: Praeger, 2005).

113. Making the argument for the "bondholders' war" is Alexander Scholch, "The 'Men on the Spot' and the English Occupation of Egypt in 1882," *The Historical Journal* 19, no. 3 (September 1976): 773–85. See also Hopkins, "The Victorians and Africa."

114. The strategic priorities argument is made by Ronald Robinson and John Gallagher, *Africa and the Victorians: The Climax of Imperialism in the Dark Continent* (New York: St. Martin's, 1961).

115. Al-Sayyid, *Egypt and Cromer,* 2.

116. For a critical view of the canal justification for intervention, see Galbraith and al-Sayyid-Marsot, "The British Occupation of Egypt," 472; Hopkins, "The Victorians and Africa," 373–74.

117. *Hansard's* 272, 3rd series, July 25, 1882, 1720.

118. On Gladstone, see Paul Knaplund, *Gladstone's Foreign Policy* (London: Archon, 1970); and H. C. G. Matthew, *Gladstone, 1875–1898* (Clarendon: Oxford, 1995).

119. William E. Gladstone, "Aggression on Egypt and Freedom in the East," *Nineteenth Century* 2, no. 6 (August 1877): 159.

120. Ibid., 161.

121. Ibid., 155–56.

122. Gladstone himself was a bondholder of two Egyptian Tribute Loans, which accounted for a high 37% of his portfolio. It remains unclear how significant a role his personal investments played in his choice of policies in Egypt. See Matthew, *Gladstone, 1875–1898,* 135–37.

123. Gladstone to Granville. Quoted in Knaplund, *Gladstone's Foreign Policy,* 171.

124. Quoted in Harrison, *Gladstone's Imperialism in Egypt,* 156.

125. Quoted in Mansfield, *The British in Egypt,* 56.

126. Harrison, *Gladstone's Imperialism in Egypt,* 6.

127. Quoted in David Steele, "Britain and Egypt 1882–1914: The Containment of Islamic Nationalism," in *Imperialism and Nationalism in the Middle East,* ed. Keith M. Wilson (London: Mansell, 1983), 7.

128. Galbraith and al-Sayyid-Marsot, "The British Occupation of Egypt: Another View," 476.

129. Marlowe, *Cromer in Egypt,* 67.

130. *Hansard's* 172, 3rd Series, July 24, 1882, 1590.

131. The Earl of Dufferin to Lord Granville, February 6, 1883 in *British Sessional Papers*, 83:40–95.

132. Al-Sayyid, *Egypt and Cromer*, 34.

133. On Baring, later Lord Cromer, see Roger Owen, *Lord Cromer: Victorian Imperialist, Edwardian Proconsul* (New York: Oxford, 2004).

134. Marlowe, *Cromer in Egypt*, 81. As Owen writes, "The underlying imperative ... was to ensure that the military occupation would be as short as possible." Owen, *Lord Cromer*, 186.

135. Quoted in Robert L. Tignor, "Lord Cromer: Practitioner and Philosopher of Imperialism," *Journal of British Studies* 2, no. 2 (May 1963): 144–45.

136. See Owen, *Lord Cromer*, 187–89.

137. Marlowe, *Cromer in Egypt*, 96.

138. Quoted ibid., 96.

139. C. J. Lowe, *The Reluctant Imperialists: British Foreign Policy, 1878–1902* (London: Routledge and Kegan Paul, 1967), 1:58. Robinson and Gallagher, *Africa and the Victorians*, 139–40.

140. On the London Conference, see Robert L. Tignor, *Modernization and British Colonial Rule in Egypt, 1882–1914* (Princeton, N.J.: Princeton University Press, 1966), 77–78.

141. Sir Evelyn Baring to Archibald Philip Primrose, fifth earl of Rosebery, February 15, 1886. Quoted in R. C. Mowat, "From Liberalism to Imperialism: The Case of Egypt, 1875–1887," *The Historical Journal* 16, no. 1 (March 1973): 120.

142. On the evolution of Baring's views on the possibility of ending the occupation, see Tignor, "Lord Cromer."

143. Cromer, *Modern Egypt*, 1:333. Also see Baring to Granville, October 9, 1883. Reprinted in Cromer, *Modern Egypt*, 2:362–65.

144. Lord Milner, *England in Egypt* (London: Edward Arnold, 1903), 83.

145. Quoted in Steele, "Britain and Egypt," 11.

146. Quoted in Tignor, *Modernization and British Colonial Rule in Egypt*, 84.

147. Owen, *Lord Cromer*, 218–19.

148. Quoted in Al-Sayyid, *Egypt and Cromer*, 46.

149. For discussion, see Marlowe, *Cromer in Egypt*, 117.

150. Quoted ibid., 118.

151. Al-Sayyid, *Egypt and Cromer*, 50–51.

152. Salisbury to Henry Wolff, February 23, 1887. Reprinted in Lady Gwendolen Cecil, *Life Of Robert, Marquis of Salisbury* (London: Hodder and Stoughton, 1971 [1932]), 4:41–43.

153. Salisbury to Cairns, February 20, 1885, Reprinted in Lady Gwendolen Cecil, *Life Of Robert, Marquis of Salisbury* (London: Hodder and Stoughton, 1971 [1931]), 3:126.

154. Quoted in Robinson and Gallagher, *Africa and the Victorians*, 270.

155. On the popular, but controversial, elimination of the corvée, see Owen, *Lord Cromer*, 227–30.

156. Quoted in Mowat, "From Liberalism to Imperialism," 120.

157. Quoted in Robinson and Gallagher, *Africa and the Victorians*, 279.

158. Quoted in Marlowe, *Cromer in Egypt*, 141.

159. Mansfield, *British in Egypt*, 175–76.

160. Milner, *England in Egypt*, 28.

161. Quoted in Al-Sayyid, *Egypt and Cromer*, 65. On Baring's transformation from favoring a speedy withdrawal to his efforts to extend the occupation, see Owen, *Lord Cromer*, 246.

162. Milner, *England in Egypt*, 76–78.

163. Tignor, *Modernization and British Colonial Rule in Egypt*, 241.

164. Marlowe, *Cromer in Egypt*, 133–34.

165. For a description of the salon meetings, see Al-Sayyid, *Egypt and Cromer*, 95.

166. For an excellent discussion of the variation in Egyptian nationalism, see Tignor, *Modernization and British Colonial Rule in Egypt*, 148–54. On Cromer's simultaneous concern and dismissal of the nationalist recrudescence in Egypt, see Steele, "Britain and Egypt," 14.

167. Al-Sayyid, *Egypt and Cromer*, 101–2.

168. Quoted in Marlowe, *Cromer in Egypt*, 161–62.

169. Quoted ibid., 169.

170. Quoted in Philip Magnus, *Gladstone: A Biography* (London: John Murray, 1954), 408.

171. On the challenge posed to Cromer by the return to power of Gladstone, see Owen, *Lord Cromer*, 265.

172. Marlowe, *Cromer in Egypt*, 170.

173. Al-Sayyid, *Egypt and Cromer*, 117–18.

174. See Tignor, *Modernization and British Colonial Rule in Egypt*, 320, and G. John Ikenberry and Charles A. Kupchan, "Socialization and Hegemonic Power," *International Organization* 44, no. 3 (summer 1990): 311–13.

175. Quoted in Marlowe, *Cromer in Egypt*, 173.

176. Quoted in Al-Sayyid, *Egypt and Cromer*, 122.

177. The earl of Cromer, *Abbas II* (London: Macmillan, 1915), 58.

178. Al-Sayyid, *Egypt and Cromer*, 123–24; Owen, *Lord Cromer*, 271–73.

179. Quoted in Al-Sayyid, *Egypt and Cromer*, 118.

180. Ibid., 123.

181. Quoted in Marlowe, *Cromer in Egypt*, 172.

182. Tignor, *Modernization and British Colonial Rule in Egypt*, 271.

183. Marlowe, *Cromer in Egypt*, 264–65; Owen, *Lord Cromer*, 334–35.

184. Tignor, *Modernization and British Colonial Rule in Egypt*, 281.

185. Al-Sayyid, *Egypt and Cromer*, 147–48.

186. Marlowe, *Cromer in Egypt*, 266–67.

187. Tignor, *Modernization and British Colonial Rule in Egypt*, 293.

188. On the divided contemporary conclusions about Cromer's time in Egypt, see Owen, *Lord Cromer*, 347–48.

189. For a summary of the flaws in the Gorst administration, see Tignor, *Modernization and British Colonial Rule in Egypt*, 314.

190. Prior to 1919, the nationalist movement in Egypt had been mostly peaceful, although an increase in crime indicated the possibility of more violence. See ibid., 307.

191. Baring to Childers, February 26, 1884. Quoted in Robinson and Gallagher, *Africa and the Victorians*, 137.

192. Robinson and Gallagher, *Africa and the Victorians*, 281.

193. Marlowe, *Cromer in Egypt*, 296.

194. For Ferguson's argument, see Niall Ferguson, *Colossus: The Price of America's Empire* (New York: Penguin, 2004), 217–25; Niall Ferguson, "True Lies: Lessons from the British Empire," *The New Republic*, June 2, 2003, 16–19.

195. See Mansfield, *The British in Egypt*, 162; Marlowe, *Cromer in Egypt*, 284; Owen, *Lord Cromer*, 286; Tignor, *Modernization and British Colonial Rule in Egypt*, 102; William M. Welch Jr., *No Country for a Gentleman: British Rule in Egypt, 1883–1907* (New York: Greenwood, 1988), 57, 60.

196. On the economic effects of the occupation, see Marlowe, *Cromer in Egypt*, 286–87. For a more positive assessment of the economic impact of the occupation, see Ferguson, *Colossus*, 222.

197. *The Diary of Edward Goschen, 1900–1914*, ed. Christopher H. D. Howard, Camden Fourth Series, vol. 25 (London: Office of the Royal Historical Society, 1980), 165.

198. See Tignor, *Modernization and British Colonial Rule in Egypt*, 105–6.

199. Michael W. Doyle, *Empires* (Ithaca, N.Y.: Cornell University Press, 1986), 218.

200. Cromer, *Modern Egypt*, vol. 2, 359.

201. On the nationalist reaction to Cromer's efforts to tighten control over Egypt, see Owen, *Lord Cromer*, 332–33.

202. Why the Egyptian opposition did not turn violent earlier is somewhat of a puzzle. John Marlowe offers two explanations. First, much of the Egyptian peasant population had not yet been incorporated into the nationalist movement, so mass violence was unlikely. Second, divisions within the nationalist movement prevented any concerted uprising against the occupation. Marlowe, *Cromer in Egypt*, 261.

203. Al-Sayyid, *Egypt and Cromer*, 202.

204. Quoted in Robinson and Gallagher, *Africa and the Victorians*, 124.

205. Quoted in Marlowe, *Cromer in Egypt*, 243.

206. Hopkins, "The Victorians and Africa," 388.

207. Quoted in Kenneth Bourne, *The Foreign Policy of Victorian England, 1830–1902* (Oxford: Clarendon, 1970), 448.

208. Quoted in Mowat, "From Liberalism to Imperialism," 122.

209. The Soviet Union was not yet a participant in the war in the Pacific, so they were not a signatory to the Potsdam Declaration on Japan. Reprinted in Supreme Commander for the Allied Powers (SCAP) Government Section, *Political Reorientation of Japan, September 1945–September 1948* (Washington, D.C.: U.S. Government Printing Office, 1949), 2:413.

210. Ibid., 423–26.

211. Ibid., 427.

212. Ibid., 428–39.

213. Quoted in Richard B. Finn, *Winners in Peace: MacArthur, Yoshida, and Postwar Japan* (Berkeley, Calif.: University of California Press, 1992), 16.

214. Douglas MacArthur, *Reminiscences* (New York: McGraw-Hill, 1964) 282–84.

215. SCAP Government Section, *Political Reorientation of Japan, September 1945–September 1948*, 2:442–51.

216. MacArthur, Statement on the Demobilization of Japanese Armed Forces, October 15, 1945. Ibid., 742.

217. Ibid., 460.

218. Ibid., 565–66.

219. Ibid., 467–69.

220. Finn, *Winners in Peace*, 40.

221. On the divide in the U.S. government over the fate of the emperor, see Ray A. Moore and Donald L. Robinson, *Partners for Democracy: Crafting the New Japanese State under MacArthur* (New York: Oxford University Press, 2002), 6. See also John W. Dower, *Embracing Defeat: Japan in the Wake of World War II* (New York: W. W. Norton, 1999), 217–24.

222. For discussion, see Dower, *Embracing Defeat*, 308–17. For MacArthur's response to the rescript, see SCAP Government Section, *Political Reorientation of Japan, September 1945–September 1948*, 2:746.

223. SCAP Government Section, *Political Reorientation of Japan, September 1945–September 1948*, 2:471.

224. The draft was written by the Government Section of the occupation administration, but for the purposes of public and allied consumption, it was carefully presented as a Japanese product. On the process of drafting the constitution, see Moore and Robinson, *Partners for Democracy,* 13.

225. Dower, *Embracing Defeat,* 360.

226. The draft presented to the Japanese cabinet is available in SCAP Government Section, *Political Reorientation of Japan, September 1945–September 1948,* 2:631–36.

227. On the debate over the new constitution, see Dower, *Embracing Defeat,* 374–404.

228. Rescript available in SCAP Government Section, *Political Reorientation of Japan, September 1945–September 1948,* 2:670.

229. Theodore Cohen, *Remaking Japan: The American Occupation as New Deal* (New York: The Free Press, 1987), 42.

230. John W. Dower, *Japan in War and Peace* (New York: New Press, 1993), 169–79.

231. Ibid., 179.

232. Dower, *Embracing Defeat,* 69. Emphasis added.

233. Michael Schaller, *The American Occupation of Japan: The Origins of the Cold War in Asia* (New York: Oxford, 1995), 77.

234. Quoted ibid., 90.

235. See Edwin Martin to John Hilldring, March 12, 1947, in FRUS, 1947, vol. 6, *The Far East,* 184–86.

236. See Memorandum by the Joint Chiefs of Staff to the State-War-Navy Coordinating Committee, May 12, 1947, in FRUS, 1947, vol. 1, *General: The United Nations,* 734–50, quote at 745.

237. See Schaller, *The American Occupation of Japan,* 91.

238. For MacArthur's views of Japanese neutrality, see ibid., 65–66. See also Frederick S. Dunn, *Peace-Making and the Settlement with Japan* (Princeton, N.J.: Princeton University Press, 1963), 55. Dunn describes MacArthur's vision of Japan as "the Switzerland of the Pacific."

239. See MacArthur's interview with press correspondents in SCAP Government Section, *Political Reorientation of Japan, September 1945–September 1948,* 2:765–66.

240. On George Kennan's opposition to an early peace treaty with Japan, see Walter LaFeber, *The Clash: A History of U.S.–Japan Relations* (New York: W. W. Norton, 1997), 273.

241. For the text of NSC 13/2, see FRUS, 1948, vol. 6, *The Far East and Australasia,* 857–62.

242. See Hans H. Baerwald, "The Purge in Occupied Japan," in *Americans as Proconsuls: United States Military Government in Germany and Japan, 1944–1952,* ed. Robert Wolfe (Carbondale, Ill.: Southern Illinois University Press, 1984), 188–97.

243. Finn, *Winners in Peace,* 204–5.

244. On Dodge, see Dower, *Embracing Defeat,* 540; Schaller, *The American Occupation of Japan,* 145; Eiji Takemae, *Inside GHQ: The Allied Occupation of Japan and its Legacy* (New York: Continuum, 2002), 173.

245. Finn, *Winners in Peace,* 199.

246. Schaller, *The American Occupation of Japan,* 110.

247. Dower, *Embracing Defeat,* 453–54.

248. Ibid., 474.

249. Cited in Takemae, *Inside GHQ,* 482.

250. On the significance of NSC 48, see Dower, *Japan in War and Peace,* 183–84. For the text of NSC 48/1 and NSC 48/2, see Thomas H. Etzold and John Lewis Gaddis, eds., *Containment: Documents on American Policy and Strategy, 1945–1950* (New York: Columbia University Press, 1978), 252–76.

251. On the critical role of Japan in reinvigorating the economies of Southeast Asia, see LaFeber, *The Clash*, 281.

252. On concerns about an independent Japan, see Dower, *Japan in War and Peace*, 161; and Schaller, *The American Occupation of Japan*, 276.

253. Finn, *Winners in Peace*, 256.

254. Letter cited ibid., 263.

255. Dower, *Japan in War and Peace*, 182.

256. Schaller, *American Occupation of Japan*, 257.

257. Dean Acheson, *Present at the Creation: My Years in the State Department* (New York: W.W. Norton, 1967), 257.

258. It is worth noting that the Soviet Union did not attend the San Francisco conference and was not a party to the peace treaty.

259. For an argument that U.S. occupation policies contributed little directly to the reemergence of the Japanese economy, see Yoshiro Miwa and J. Mark Ramseyer, "The Good Occupation," Harvard University, John M. Olin Center for Law, Economic, and Business, Discussion Paper no. 514, May 2005.

260. Cited in LaFeber, *The Clash*, 275.

261. For anecdotal indications of Japanese popular support, see Sodei Rinjiro, *Dear General MacArthur: Letters from the Japanese during the American Occupation* (Lanham, Md.: Rowman and Littlefield, 2001). In particular, see 230–240.

262. Cohen, *Remaking Japan*, 61; and Dower, *Embracing Defeat*, 205.

263. Dower, *Embracing Defeat*, 227.

264. Schaller, *American Occupation of Japan*, 48–49.

265. Takemae, *Inside GHQ*, 509.

266. As the war in Japan approached its close, Prince Konoe Fumimaro and future prime minister Yoshida Shigeru warned of the danger of a Soviet victory in World War II or a communist revolution that would overthrow the imperial order of Japanese society. See Schaller, *American Occupation of Japan*, 6.

267. Yoshida Shigeru, *The Yoshida Memoirs: The Story of Japan in Crisis*, trans. Yoshida Kenichi (London: Heinemann, 1961), 52–53.

268. See Cohen, *Remaking Japan*; Dower, *Embracing Defeat*, 45–46; and Finn, *Winners in Peace*, 11–12.

269. On the food crisis in postwar Japan, see Takemae, *Inside GHQ*, 76–79.

270. Schaller, *American Occupation of Japan*, 52–53.

271. Dower, *Japan in War and Peace*, 176.

272. From early in the planning stages of the occupation of Japan, U.S. leaders recognized that there were two threats they would be facing in Japan: communism and a resurgent nationalism. See Mayo, "American Wartime Planning for Occupied Japan," 41.

273. Cohen, *Remaking Japan*, 455. It is worth noting that the Japanese, themselves, paid twice as much in occupation costs. See Finn, *Winners in Peace*, 37.

274. Dower, *Embracing Defeat*, 299.

275. See MacArthur to the Chief of Staff, United States Army, Dwight D. Eisenhower, January 25, 1946 in FRUS, 1946, vol. 7, *The Near East and Africa*, 395–97. For discussion, see Moore and Robinson, *Partners for Democracy*, 48–49.

276. Dower, *Embracing Defeat*, 278.

277. Ibid., 525. Statement Issued by the Supreme Commander, Allied Forces in Japan, September 17, 1945 in FRUS, 1945, vol. 6, *The British Commonwealth, The Far East*, 715–16.

278. Quoted in Cohen, *Remaking Japan*, 401.

279. Roger Buckley, *Occupation Diplomacy: Britain, the United States, and Japan, 1945–1952* (New York: Cambridge University Press, 1982), 132. Theodore Cohen makes a similar assertion. Cohen, *Remaking Japan*, xiv.

280. Buckley, *Occupation Diplomacy*, 252, fn. 42; and Schaller, *American Occupation of Japan*, 82.

281. Secretary of State Dean Acheson to Certain Diplomatic Offices in FRUS, 1949, vol. 7, *The Far East and Australasia, Part 2*, 736–37.

282. Quoted in Robert B. Textor, *Failure in Japan* (New York: John Day, 1951), 340.

283. Moore and Robinson, *Partners for Democracy*, 172.

4. WHO OCCUPIES

1. See especially Martha Finnemore, *The Purpose of Intervention: Changing Beliefs about the Use of Force* (Ithaca, N.Y.: Cornell University Press, 2003). Finnemore's argument is specifically applied to humanitarian intervention, but following the logic of her argument, the need to generate legitimacy should be even higher in military occupations.

2. John W. Dower, "A Warning from History: Don't Expect Democracy in Iraq," *Boston Review* 28, no. 1 (February–March 2003), bostonreview.mit.edu/BR28.1/dower.html.

3. Note that Kosovo is included in the data set of occupation as an ongoing contemporary occupation. There, though, I am referring to the NATO dimension of the Kosovo mission. Kosovo is an odd occupation in that regard since it is a joint UN-NATO mission.

4. For a summary of Habibie's "second option," see Ian Martin, *Self-Determination in East Timor: The United Nations, the Ballot, and International Intervention* (Boulder, Colo.: Lynne Rienner, 2001), 20–24.

5. Press Statement by Gusmão, April 5, 1999. Quoted ibid., 30.

6. Statement by Secretary General Kofi Annan, September 10, 1999. Quoted ibid., 109–10.

7. Available at http://daccessdds.un.org/doc/UNDOC/GEN/N99/264/81/PDF/N992 6481.pdf?OpenElement.

8. Available at http://daccessdds.un.org/doc/UNDOC/GEN/N99/312/77/PDF/N993 1277.pdf?OpenElement.

9. On the need for UNMISET, see Paulo Gorjao, "The Legacy and Lessons of the United Nations Transitional Administration in East Timor," *Contemporary Southeast Asia* 24, no. 2 (August 2002): 323. On UNMISET in general, see Katsumi Ishizuka, "Peacekeeping in East Timor: The Experience of UNMISET," *International Peacekeeping* 10, no. 3 (autumn 2003): 44–59. On the continuing security threats facing East Timor, including potential internal divisions, see Anthony L. Smith, "Timor Leste: Strong Government, Weak State," *Southeast Asian Affairs* (2004): 279–94. On tension between Christians and Muslims in East Timor, see Rajiv Chandrasekaran, "In East Timor, A Crucible of Tolerance," *Washington Post*, June 8, 2000.

10. On the population's general acceptance of the UN mandate in East Timor, see Ian Martin and Alexander Mayer-Rieckh, "The United Nations and East Timor: From Self-Determination to State-Building," *International Peacekeeping* 12, no. 1 (spring 2005): 136.

11. On the welcome afforded to the United Nations in East Timor, see Jarat Chopra, "The UN's Kingdom of East Timor," *Survival* 42, no. 3 (autumn 2000): 28.

12. Rajiv Chandrasekaran, "Saved from Ruin: The Reincarnation of East Timor," *Washington Post*, May 19, 2002.

13. Patrick Candio and Roland Bleiker, "Peacebuilding in East Timor," *The Pacific Review* 14, no. 1 (March 2001): 64.

14. On the challenges of reconstruction in East Timor, see Seth Mydans, "Ruined East Timor Awaits a Miracle," *New York Times*, April 22, 2000.

15. On the importance of a clear end goal, see Simon Chesterman, *You, the People: The United Nations, Transitional Administration, and State-Building* (New York: Oxford University Press, 2004), 135.

16. Anthony Goldstone, "UNTAET with Hindsight: The Peculiarities of Politics in an Incomplete State," *Global Governance* 10, no. 1 (January–March 2004), 84.

17. Jarat Chopra, who served as head of the Office of District Administration for UNTAET, offers a critical appraisal of the UN's effort to devolve responsibility to the Timorese. Chopra and Hohe advocate for "participatory intervention," which would better incorporate local decision makers into the administration of an international occupation. See Jarat Chopra, "Building State Failure in East Timor," *Development and Change* 33, no. 5 (November 2002): 989, 994–95; and Jarat Chopra and Tanja Hohe, "Participatory Intervention," *Global Governance* 10, no. 3 (July–September 2004): 289–306. For another critique of the UN performance incorporating East Timorese into governance, see Goldstone, "UNTAET with Hindsight." Goldstone maintains that UNTAET was more concerned with achieving short-term humanitarian goals than with achieving long-term stability and capacity. See also Anthony L. Smith, "Timor Leste, Timor Timur, East Timor, Timor Lorosa'e: What's in a Name?" *Southeast Asian Affairs* (2002): 55; Astri Suhrke, "Peacekeepers as Nation-builders: Dilemmas of the UN in East Timor," *International Peacekeeping* 8, no. 4 (winter 2001): 13.

18. Chopra, "UN's Kingdom of East Timor," 34.

19. Briefing by Ian Martin, Sergio Vieira de Mello, and Xanana Gusmão, November 11, 1999, www.un.org/peace/etimor/DR/br191199.htm. For more on Timorization, see James Dunn, *East Timor: A Rough Passage to Independence* (New South Wales: Longueville, 2003), 372.

20. For details, see Chesterman, *You, the People,* 137.

21. Chopra, "UN's Kingdom of East Timor," 33.

22. John Aglionby, "Bungled UN Aid Operation Slows East Timor's Recovery," *Guardian,* August 30, 2000.

23. Speech by Vieira de Mello, June 2, 2000. Quoted in Suhrke, "Peacekeepers as Nation-builders," 16.

24. Quoted in Chesterman, *You, the People,* 140.

25. Gorjao, "Legacy and Lessons," 320.

26. Ibid., 321.

27. For Gusmão's speech, see http://www.pcug.org.au/~wildwood/JanNewYear.htm

28. In reality, even the East Timorese leaders recognized that they would need considerable assistance during their transition to independence. See James Cotton, "'Peacekeeping' in East Timor: An Australian Policy Departure," *Australian Journal of International Affairs* 53, no. 3 (November 1999): 245–46.

29. Rajiv Chandrasekaran, "East Timorese Wave Their Flag as Independence Is Proclaimed," *Washington Post,* May 20, 2002.

30. See Martin and Mayer-Rieckh, "United Nations and East Timor," 136.

31. Chesterman, *You, the People,* 1.

32. On the legitimacy conveyed by UN approval, see James Cotton, "The Emergence of an Independent East Timor: National and Regional Challenges," *Contemporary Southeast Asia* 22, no. 1 (April 2000): 237–46.

33. Even in East Timor, though, the local population questioned the undemocratic nature of the foreign presence and its reluctance to grant power to indigenous forces. See Gorjao, "Legacy and Lessons," 330.

34. See Anthony L. Smith, "The Role of the United Nations in East Timor's Path to Independence," *Asian Journal of Political Science* 9, no. 2 (December 2001): 43.

35. Anthony Goldstone concludes that UNTAET was a "necessary disease" in East Timor. Goldstone, "UNTAET with Hindsight," 96.

36. Quoted in Jonathan Steele, "Nation Building in East Timor," *World Policy Journal* 19, no. 2 (summer 2002): 79.

37. Rajiv Chandrasekaran, "Saved from Ruin: The Reincarnation of East Timor," *Washington Post,* May 19, 2002.

38. On lessons from the UN presence in East Timor, see Sergio Vieira de Mello, "UNTAET: Lessons to Learn for Future UN Peace Operations," Presented to the Oxford University European Affairs Society, October 26, 2001. I thank Richard Caplan for providing me with Vieira de Mello's remarks.

39. Anthony Deutsch, "East Timor: U.N.-Led Police Force Needed," Associated Press, June 8, 2006.

40. "East Timor Commanding World's Attention," Associated Press, June 8, 2006, and Jane Perlez, "A Nation-Building Project Comes Apart in East Timor," *New York Times,* July 14, 2006.

41. See Timothy Garton Ash, "Anarchy and Madness," *New York Review of Books,* February 10, 2000, 48.

42. For a discussion of the composition of UNMIK, see William G. O'Neill, *Kosovo: An Unfinished Peace* (Boulder, Colo.: Lynne Rienner, 2002).

43. UNMIK Regulation 1999/1 (July 25, 1999), On the Authority of the Interim Administration in Kosovo, http://www.unmikonline.org/regulations/1999/reg01–99.htm.

44. Richard Caplan, *International Governance of War-Torn Territories: Rules and Reconstruction* (New York: Oxford University Press, 2005), 99.

45. The creation of the Joint Interim Administrative Structure co-opted many Albanian leaders into the UN-led reconstruction project. See Alexandros Yannis, "Kosovo under International Administration," *Survival* 43, no. 2 (summer 2001): 39.

46. For Steiner's review of his time in Kosovo, see Michael Steiner, "Seven Principles for Building Peace," *World Policy Journal* 20, no. 2 (summer 2003): 87–93.

47. For a discussion of "standards before status," see Caplan, *International Governance of War-Torn Territories,* 216–17.

48. For more on the riots, see International Crisis Group, "Collapse in Kosovo," ICG Europe Report no. 155, April 2004.

49. James Traub, "Making Sense of the Mission, *New York Times Magazine,* April 11, 2004, 32.

50. Quoted in Jonathan Steele, "If Kosovo Is Left in Limbo, It Will Be a Victory for Milosevic," *Guardian,* April 22, 2005, 26.

51. Kosovar Albanian leaders have now signaled a willingness to move forward toward independence on their own if UNMIK does not accelerate the process of independence. As moderate Kosovar Albanian leader Bajram Rexhepi has indicated, "We don't want to undertake unilateral decisions . . . but we shall be forced to do that and have moral justification for this move if the international community hesitates." Quoted in International Crisis Group, *Collapse in Kosovo,* 5. Ibrahim Rugova, Kosovo's first president, has similarly said, "We are drafting our own constitution, as is our right, and in due time it will be presented to the parliament, which will either vote on it or send it for a referendum." Quoted in Eric Jansson, "Kosovo's Draft Constitution Widens Serbia Gulf," *Financial Times,* May 16, 2005, 2.

52. For a critical appraisal of the international mission in Kosovo, see Iain King and Whit Mason, *Peace at Any Price: How the World Failed Kosovo* (Ithaca, N.Y.: Cornell University Press, 2006).

53. Chesterman, *You, the People,* 226.

54. Further, the possibility exists of conflict between Kosovar Albanians and UNMIK. See Alexandros Yannis, "The UN as Government in Kosovo," *Global Governance* 10, no. 1 (January–March 2004), 77.

55. In fact, Albanians tend to see KFOR as a liberating force, while Serbs see it as an occupying force. See Yannis, "Kosovo under International Administration," 36.

56. Kim Sengupta, "Albanians Rejoice in Their March to Freedom," *Independent* (London), October 30, 2000.

57. Joshua Kucera, "UN Welcome Wearing Thin," *Pittsburgh Post-Gazette,* September 22, 2002. See also, Helena Smith, "Angry Kosovars Call on 'Colonial' UN Occupying Force to Leave," *Observer,* October 19, 2003.

58. Quoted in Michael J. Jordan, "Even in Eager Kosovo, Nation-Building Stalls," *Christian Science Monitor,* September 22, 2004.

59. On the inability of KFOR to effectively control the Kosovo Liberation Army, see Chesterman, *You, the People,* 64.

60. Of the level of financial support, RAND analysts have written, "International assistance for Kosovo's reconstruction proved more generous than for any earlier postconflict response or any since." James Dobbins et al., *America's Role in Nation-Building: From Germany to Iraq* (Santa Monica, Calif.: RAND, 2003), 125.

61. Caplan, *International Governance of War-Torn Territories,* 39.

62. Scott Taylor, "'The Most Dangerous Place on Earth,'" *Ottawa Citizen,* June 22, 2002.

63. In 2004, UNMIK had a favorable rating from less than a quarter of the Kosovar population. For public opinion data, see International Crisis Group, "Kosovo: Toward Final Status," ICG Europe Report no. 161, January 2005, 4.

64. The lack of progress toward self-governance may also be delaying investment in Kosovo. See Caplan, *International Governance of War-Torn Territories,* 151.

65. Kai Eide, "Report on the Situation in Kosovo," November 30, 2004, S/2004/932.

66. A further problem is that the elites with which UNMIK has been working do not necessarily have sufficient control over the population. See International Crisis Group, "Collapse in Kosovo," 34.

67. On Kosovar impatience, see Caplan, *International Governance of War-Torn Territories,* 22.

68. Even the latest UNMIK chief Søren Jessen-Petersen, has recognized, "I think there's a limit to how long you can keep a place in limbo." Press conference in Pristina, August 17, 2004. Available at http://www.unmikonline.org/press/2004/trans/tr170804.pdf

69. As the International Crisis Group has written, "Rather than orienting on state-building, UNMIK is mainly working toward its own escape strategy." International Crisis Group, "Kosovo after Haradinaj," ICG Europe Report no. 163, May 2005, 28. Meanwhile, Kosovar Albanians appear to be biding their time until UNMIK withdraws.

70. For a critical, yet ultimately more optimistic, analysis of the UN and NATO effort in Kosovo, see Elizabeth Pond, *Endgame in the Balkans: Regime Change, European Style* (Washington, D.C.: Brookings Institution Press, 2006), 98–120.

71. On dissatisfaction with UNMIK, see Yaroslav Trofimov, "Uneasy Peace: UN's Long Stay, Power in Kosovo Stir Resentment," *Wall Street Journal,* January 3, 2003.

72. Kai Eide, "Report on the Situation in Kosovo," November 30, 2004, S/2004/932

73. For the public opinion data, see UNDP Kosovo, "Fast Facts on Kosovo, Early Warning Report #14," December 2006, Availableathttp://www.kosovo.undp.org/repository/docs/FactsEWS_14.pdf

74. John Aglionby, "Bungled UN Aid Operation Slows East Timor's Recovery," *Guardian,* August 30, 2000.

75. Chesterman, *You, the People,* 135.

76. See John G. Cockell, "Civil-Military Responses to Security Challenges in Peace Operations: Ten Lessons from Kosovo," *Global Governance* 8, no. 4 (October–December 2002): 484; Yannis, "Kosovo under International Administration," 32.

77. Yannis, "Kosovo under International Administration," 35.

78. See F. Roy Willis, *The French in Germany, 1945–1949* (Stanford, Calif.: Stanford University Press, 1962).

79. On allied involvement in the occupation, see Richard B. Finn, *Winners in Peace: MacArthur, Yoshida, and Postwar Japan* (Berkeley: University of California Press, 1992), 154–55.

80. On U.S. efforts to exclude the Soviet Union from the occupation, see Michael Schaller, *The American Occupation of Japan: The Origins of the Cold War in Asia* (New York: Oxford University Press, 1985), 57–58.

81. On the role of the British, see Roger Buckley, *Occupation Diplomacy: Britain, the United States, and Japan, 1945–1952* (New York: Cambridge University Press, 1982); and Peter Bates, *Japan and the British Commonwealth Occupation Force, 1946–1952* (New York: Brassey's, 1993). See also Schaller, *American Occupation of Japan*, 100, 135–36.

82. On the Far Eastern Commission, see Dale M. Hellegers, *We the Japanese People: World War II and the Origins of the Japanese Constitution* (Stanford, Calif.: Stanford University Press, 2001), 507–9. On MacArthur's efforts to write the Japanese constitution without allied input, see Ray A. Moore and Donald L. Robinson, *Partners for Democracy: Crafting the New Japanese State under MacArthur* (New York: Oxford University Press, 2002), 81–110.

83. On MacArthur's attempt to completely dominate the occupation, see Eiji Takemae, *Inside GHQ: The Allied Occupation of Japan and its Legacy* (New York: Continuum, 2002), 97.

84. John Dower notes that Japan's Asian neighbors were disquieted when the United States began to encourage Japanese rearmament. See John W. Dower, *Japan in War and Peace* (New York: New Press, 1993), 160.

CONCLUSION

1. Norman Lewis, *Naples '44: A World War II Diary of Occupied Italy* (New York: Carroll and Graf, 1978), 169.

2. On U.S. goals in Afghanistan, see Larry Goodson, "Afghanistan's Long Road to Reconstruction," *Journal of Democracy* 14, no. 1 (January 2003): 85.

3. On historical background leading up to the invasion, see Amalendu Misra, *Afghanistan: The Labyrinth of Violence* (Malden, Mass.: Polity Press, 2004).

4. Thomas J. Barfield, "Problems in Establishing Legitimacy in Afghanistan," *Iranian Studies* 37, no. 2 (June 2004): 290.

5. For UNSC 1383, see http://daccessdds.un.org/doc/UNDOC/GEN/N01/681/09/PDF/N0168109.pdf?OpenElement. For UNSC 1386, see http://daccessdds.un.org/doc/UNDOC/GEN/N01/708/55/PDF/N0170855.pdf?OpenElement.

6. On the UN role in Afghanistan, see Simon Chesterman, "Walking Softly in Afghanistan: the Future of UN State-Building," *Survival* 44, no. 3 (autumn 2002): 37–46.

7. Previously, there had been great reluctance to moving ISAF operations beyond the area of Kabul. See Goodson, "Afghanistan's Long Road to Reconstruction," 95. On the provincial reconstruction teams, see Michael J. Dziedzic and Michael K. Seidl, "Provincial Reconstruction Teams and Military Relations with International and Nongovernmental Organizations in Afghanistan" (Washington, D.C.: United States Institute of Peace, 2005).

8. Larry Goodson, "Afghanistan in 2003: The Taliban Resurface and a New Constitution is Born," *Asian Survey* 44, no. 1 (January/February 2004): 15.

9. On the constitution, see Barnett R. Rubin, "Crafting a Constitution for Afghanistan," *Journal of Democracy* 15, no. 3 (July 2004): 5–20.

10. Larry Goodson, "Afghanistan in 2004: Electoral Progress and an Opium Bloom," *Asian Survey* 45, no. 1 (January/February 2005): 90.

11. For a review of the different nationalisms within Afghanistan, see Anthony Hyman, "Nationalism in Afghanistan," *International Journal of Middle East Studies* 34, no. 2 (May 2002): 299–315.

12. External support to the Taliban from Pakistan has only hindered efforts to stabilize Afghanistan. See Seth G. Jones, "Pakistan's Dangerous Game," *Survival* 49, no. 1 (spring 2007): 15–32.

13. Jonathan Goodhand, "From War Economy to Peace Economy? Reconstruction and State Building in Afghanistan," *International Affairs* 58, no. 1 (fall 2004): 163.

14. On the development of the army, see Ali A. Jalali, "Rebuilding Afghanistan's National Army," *Parameters* 32, no. 2 (fall 2002): 72–87; and Kathy Gannon, "Afghanistan Unbound," *Foreign Affairs* 83, no. 3 (May–June 2004), 35–46.

15. See Ali A. Jalali, "Afghanistan in 2002: The Struggle to Win the Peace," *Asian Survey* 43, no. 1 (January–February 2003): 181–82. On the low level of aid to Afghanistan relative to other postconflict operations, see Gannon, "Afghanistan Unbound," 41.

16. James Dobbins, "Ending Afghanistan's Civil War," testimony before the U.S. House of Representatives Armed Services Committee, January 30, 2007.

17. On the dangers of relying on warlords in Afghanistan, see Gannon, "Afghanistan Unbound"; Astri Suhrke, Kristian Berg Harpviken, and Arne Strand, "After Bonn: Conflictual Peace Building," in *Reconstructing War-Torn Societies: Afghanistan,* ed. Sultan Barakat (New York: Palgrave Macmillan, 2004), 75–92.

18. For lessons learned from Afghanistan from the perspective of the first postwar U.S. ambassador to Afghanistan, see Zalmay Khalilzad, "How to Nation-Build: Ten Lessons from Afghanistan," *National Interest* no. 80 (summer 2005): 19–27.

19. On the importance of building regional institutions, see Alexander Thier and Jarat Chopra, "The Road Ahead: Political and Institutional Reconstruction in Afghanistan," in *Reconstructing War-Torn Societies: Afghanistan,* ed. Sultan Barakat (New York: Palgrave Macmillan, 2004), 96.

20. "Afghan Public Opinion amongst Rising Violence," Report of the Program on International Policy Attitudes, December 14, 2006, http://www.worldpublicopinion.org/pipa/pdf/dec06/Afghanistan_Dec06_rpt.pdf.

21. Generally, on the effort to rebuild Afghanistan in comparative perspective, see Kimberly Zisk Marten, *Enforcing the Peace: Learning from the Imperial Past* (New York: Columbia University Press, 2004).

22. Vice President Richard Cheney on the television show *Meet the Press,* March 16, 2003.

23. In addition to media reports, this case study is drawn largely from the following sources: Ali A. Allawi, *The Occupation of Iraq: Winning the War, Losing the Peace* (New Haven, Conn.: Yale University Press, 2007); Rajiv Chandrasekaran, *Imperial Life in the Emerald City: Inside Iraq's Green Zone* (New York: Knopf, 2006); Patrick Cockburn, *The Occupation: War and Resistance in Iraq* (New York: Verso, 2006); Larry Diamond, *Squandered Victory: The American Occupation and the Bungled Effort to Bring Democracy to Iraq* (New York: Times Books, 2005); Mark Etherington, *Revolt on the Tigris: The Al-Sadr Uprising and the Governing of Iraq* (Ithaca, N.Y.: Cornell University Press, 2005); Ahmed S. Hashim, *Insurgency and Counter-Insurgency in Iraq* (Ithaca, N.Y.: Cornell University Press, 2006); Eric Herring and Glen Ranwala, *Iraq in Fragments: The Occupation and Its Legacy* (Ithaca, N.Y.: Cornell University Press, 2006); George Packer, *The Assassins' Gate: America in Iraq* (New York: Farrar, Straus and Giroux, 2005); Thomas E. Ricks, *Fiasco: The American Military Adventure in Iraq* (New York: Penguin, 2006); Anthony Shadid, *Night Draws Near: Iraq's People in the Shadow of America's War* (New York: Henry Holt, 2005); and Rory Stewart, *The Prince of the Marshes: And Other Occupational Hazards of a Year in Iraq* (New York: Harcourt, 2006).

24. For early commentary on what was expected in Iraq, see Conrad C. Crane and Andrew W. Terrill, *Reconstructing Iraq: Insights, Challenges, and Missions for Military Forces in a Post-Conflict Scenario* (Carlisle, Pa.: Strategic Studies Institute, U.S. Army War

College, 2003); and Julie Kosterlitz, "Occupational Hazards," *National Journal*, 35, no. 12 (March 2003): 910–15.

25. On Bremer's arrival in Iraq, see Diamond, *Squandered Victory*, 37.

26. On the changing objectives in Iraq, see Rajiv Chandrasekaran, "Attacks Force Retreat from Wide-Ranging Plans for Iraq," *Washington Post*, December 28, 2003.

27. On the insurgency in Iraq, see Bruce Hoffman, "Insurgency and Counterinsurgency in Iraq," RAND, June 2004.

28. For UNSC 1546, see http://daccessdds.un.org/doc/UNDOC/GEN/N04/381/16/PDF/N0438116.pdf?OpenElement.

29. Diamond, *Squandered Victory*, 38.

30. L. Paul Bremer III, *My Year in Iraq: The Struggle to Build a Future of Hope* (New York: Simon and Schuster, 2006), 37.

31. On the concern of some moderate Shiites about the influence of Iran, see Diamond, *Squandered Victory*, 122–23.

32. In June 2007, the United States launched an effort to cooperate with moderate Sunni groups within Iraq in fighting against more extreme Sunni elements, including al-Qaeda. In a classic illustration of the threat environment logic, U.S. Major General Rick Lynch observed, "[The Sunni moderates] say, 'We hate you because you are occupiers, but we hate Al Qaeda even worse, and we hate the Persians even more.'" John F. Burns and Alissa J. Rubin, "U.S. Arming Sunnis in Iraq to Battle Old Qaeda Allies," *New York Times*, June 11, 2007.

33. The population of Iraq is roughly 60% Shiite, 25% Sunni Arab, and 15% Kurdish.

34. U.S. Department of State, Office of Research, "Iraqis Say Coalition Troops are Vital Now, but Prefer Handoff to Own Security Forces," January 6, 2004, 3.

35. Oxford Research International, "National Survey of Iraq," November 2005, http://news.bbc.co.uk/1/shared/bsp/hi/pdfs/12_12_05_iraq_data.pdf.

36. Based on weekly ABC News–Washington Post public opinion surveys, see http://www.washingtonpost.com/wp-srv/politics/includes/postpoll_iraqwar_030606.htm

37. Packer, *The Assassins' Gate*, 243.

38. On the spending allocations, see Amy Belasco, "The Cost of Iraq, Afghanistan, and Enhanced Base Security Since 9/11," Congressional Research Service Report, October 7, 2005, and Nina Serafino, Curt Tarnoff, and Dick K. Nanto, "U.S. Occupation Assistance: Iraq, Germany and Japan Compared," Congressional Research Service, March 23, 2006.

39. Hearing of the U.S. Senate Armed Services Committee, February 25, 2003.

40. Rumsfeld quote from media availability with Afghan President Hamid Karzai on February 27, 2003. Wolfowitz quote from Hearing of the U.S. House of Representatives Budget Committee, February 27, 2003, www.defenselink.mil.

41. See James Fallows, "Blind into Baghdad," *Atlantic Monthly*, 293, no. 1 (January–February 2004): 52–74.

42. Rumsfeld and General Richard Myers Press Briefing, April 11, 2003, http://www.defenselink.mil/transcripts/2003/tr20030411-secdef0090.html.

43. On the decision to disband the army, see Diamond, *Squandered Victory*, 294.

44. On the promotion of democracy, see Thomas Carothers, *Aiding Democracy Abroad: The Learning Curve* (Washington, D.C.: Carnegie Endowment for International Peace, 1999).

45. Karin von Hippel, *Democracy by Force: U.S. Military Intervention in the Post-Cold War World* (New York: Cambridge University Press, 2000).

46. On the hubris of states, see James C. Scott, *Seeing Like a State: How Certain Schemes to Improve the Human Condition Have Failed* (New Haven, Conn.: Yale University Press, 1998).

47. "Defining Missions, Setting Deadlines: Meeting New Security Challenges in the Post-Cold War World," remarks at George Washington University, March 6, 1996. Quoted in Karin von Hippel, *Democracy by Force: U.S. Military Intervention in the Post–Cold War World* (New York: Cambridge University Press, 2000), 1.

48. Roger Owen, *Lord Cromer: Victorian Imperialist, Edwardian Proconsul* (New York: Oxford University Press, 2004), 332.

49. On the lack of preparation for the occupation of Iraq, see Diamond, *Squandered Victory*, 34; Anthony Shadid, *Night Draws Near*, 132.

50. Robert L. Tignor, *Modernization and British Colonial Rule in Egypt, 1882–1914* (Princeton, N.J.: Princeton University Press, 1966), 190.

51. Hugh Borton, "Preparation for the Occupation of Japan," *Journal of Asian Studies* 25, no. 2 (February 1966): 203–12; Eiji Takemae, *Inside GHQ: The Allied Occupation of Japan and Its Legacy* (New York: Continuum, 2002), 156–59; and Earl F. Ziemke, "Improvising Stability and Change in Postwar Germany," in *Americans As Proconsuls: United States Military Government in Germany and Japan, 1944–1952,* ed. Robert Wolfe (Carbondale, Ill.: Southern Illinois University Press, 1984), 52–66.

52. James Dobbins et al., *America's Role in Nation-Building: From Germany to Iraq* (Santa Monica, Calif.: RAND Corporation, 2003), 151.

53. A 1999 war game of a potential invasion of Iraq known as "Desert Crossing" expected significant postwar challenges even if the invasion included 400,000 troops. Documents related to this war game have been posted electronically by the nongovernmental National Security Archive at http://www.gwu.edu/~nsarchiv/NSAEBB/NSAEBB207/index.htm#documents.

54. For an alternative strategy for addressing failed states, see James D. Fearon and David D. Laitin, "Neotrusteeship and the Problem of Weak States," *International Security* 28, no. 4 (spring 2004): 5–43.

APPENDIX 1

1. To do this, I used the Correlates of War data set, which is available online at http://cow2.la.psu.edu.

2. On wartime occupation, see Peter Liberman, *Does Conquest Pay? The Exploitation of Occupied Industrial Societies* (Princeton, N.J.: Princeton University Press, 1996). On the German occupation of France during World War II, see Ian Ousby, *Occupation: The Ordeal of France, 1940–1944* (New York: St. Martin's, 1998).

3. On occupations undertaken by the United Nations, see Richard Caplan, *International Governance of War-Torn Territories: Rules and Reconstruction* (New York: Oxford University Press, 2005); Simon Chesterman, *You, the People: The United Nations, Transitional Administration, and State-Building* (New York: Oxford University Press, 2004); and James Dobbins et al., *The UN's Role in Nation-Building: From the Congo to Iraq* (Santa Monica, Calif.: RAND, 2005).

4. For a more detailed typology, including seventeen different forms of occupation, see Adam Roberts, "What Is a Military Occupation?" *British Year Book of International Law,* 55 (1984), 249–305.

5. On the Treaty of Frankfort ending the Franco-Prussian War and the postwar occupation of France, see Robert I. Giesberg, *The Treaty of Frankfort* (Philadelphia: University of Pennsylvania Press, 1966); Michael Howard, *The Franco-Prussian War: The German Invasion of France, 1870–1871* (New York: Routledge, 1961), 453; Allan Mitchell, *The German Influence in France After 1870* (Chapel Hill, N.C.: University of North Carolina Press, 1979), 27–34; and Otto Pflanze, *Bismarck and the Development of Germany,* vol. 2, *The Period of Consolidation, 1871–1880* (Princeton, N.J.: Princeton University Press, 1990), 6.

6. See Robert E. Quirk, *An Affair of Honor: Woodrow Wilson and the Occupation of Veracruz* (Lexington: University of Kentucky Press, 1962).

7. David Fromkin, *A Peace to End All Peace: The Fall of the Ottoman Empire and the Creation of the Modern Middle East* (New York: Henry Holt, 1989), 411. See also Stephen Hemsley Longrigg, *Syria and Lebanon under French Mandate* (New York: Oxford University Press, 1958).

8. On the intervention in Nicaragua, see Ivan Musicant, *The Banana Wars: A History of United States Military Intervention in Latin America from the Spanish-American War to the Invasion of Panama* (New York: Macmillan, 1990), 285–361.

9. Quoted in Sarah E. Mendelson, *Changing Course: Ideas, Politics, and the Soviet Withdrawal from Afghanistan* (Princeton, N.J.: Princeton University Press, 1988), 63–64.

10. See Andrew Bennett, *Condemned to Repetition?: The Rise, Fall, and Reprise of Soviet-Russian Military Intervention, 1973–1996* (Cambridge, Mass.: MIT Press, 1999); Diego Cordovez and Selig S. Harrison, *Out of Afghanistan: The Story of the Soviet Withdrawal* (New York: Oxford University Press, 1995); and Mendelson, *Changing Course.*

11. Quoted in A. J. P. Taylor, *The Struggle for Mastery in Europe, 1848–1918* (Oxford: Oxford University Press, 1954), 289.

12. On the Philippines see, Brian McAllister Linn, *The Philippine War, 1899–1902* (Lawrence: University Press of Kansas, 2000); Glenn Anthony May, *A Past Recovered* (Quezon City: New Day, 1987); and Stuart Creighton Miller, *"Benevolent Assimilation": The American Conquest of the Philippines, 1899–1903* (New Haven, Conn.: Yale University Press, 1982). U.S. leaders intensely debated whether or not to annex the Philippines after the Spanish-American War of 1898.

13. Theodore Roosevelt letter to William Howard Taft, August 21, 1907. Quoted in E. Berkeley Tompkins, *Anti-Imperialism in the United States: The Great Debate, 1890–1920* (Philadelphia: University of Pennsylvania Press, 1970), 275.

14. Cited in Benny Morris, *Righteous Victims: A History of the Zionist-Arab Conflict, 1881–1999* (London: John Murray, 1999), 330.

15. On this debate, see Morris, *Righteous Victims,* 329–36; Michael B. Oren, *The Six Days of War: June 1967 and the Making of the Modern Middle East* (New York: Oxford University Press, 2002), 312–17; and Mark Tessler, *A History of the Israeli-Palestinian Conflict* (Bloomington: Indiana University Press, 1994), 407–14. Finally, for an interesting discussion of the Israeli consideration of whether the West Bank should be treated as an "occupied territory" under the Fourth Geneva Convention, see Gershom Gorenberg, *The Accidental Empire: Israel and the Birth of the Settlements* (New York: Times Books, 2006), 97–102.

APPENDIX 2

1. This number is representative since the size of occupying forces often varies widely over the course of an occupation.

2. Thomas Dwight Veve, *The Duke of Wellington and the British Army of Occupation in France, 1815–1818* (Westport, Conn.: Greenwood, 1992).

3. Michele Cunningham, *Mexico and the Foreign Policy of Napoleon III* (New York: Palgrave, 2001).

4. Immanuel C. Y. Hsü, *The Ili Crisis: A Study of Sino-Russian Diplomacy, 1871–1881* (Oxford: Clarendon Press, 1965).

5. See chapter 3.

6. Ibid.

7. Robert L. Beisner, *Twelve Against Empire: The Anti-Imperialists, 1898–1900* (New York: McGraw-Hill, 1968); H. W. Brands, *Bound to Empire: The United States and the Philippines* (New York: Oxford University Press, 1992); Brian McAllister Linn, *The Philippine*

War, 1899–1902 (Lawrence: University Press of Kansas, 2000); Brian McAllister Linn, *The U.S. Army and Counterinsurgency in the Philippine War, 1899–1902* (Chapel Hill: University of North Carolina Press, 1989); Glenn Anthony May, *A Past Recovered* (Quezon City: New Day, 1987); Stuart Creighton Miller, *"Benevolent Assimilation": The American Conquest of the Philippines, 1899–1903* (New Haven, Conn.: Yale University Press, 1982).

8. Ivan Musicant, *The Banana Wars: A History of United States Military Intervention in Latin America from the Spanish-American War to the Invasion of Panama* (New York: Macmillan, 1990), 37–78.

9. See chapter 1.

10. Bruce J. Calder, *The Impact of Intervention: The Dominican Republic during the U.S. Occupation of 1916–1924* (Austin: University of Texas Press, 1984); Stephen M. Fuller and Graham A. Cosmas, *Marines in the Dominican Republic, 1916–1924* (Washington, D.C.: U.S. Marine Corps, History and Museums Division, 1974); Melvin Moses Knight, *The Americans in Santo Domingo* (New York: Arno Press, 1970); Dana G. Munro, *The United States and the Caribbean Republic, 1921–1933* (Princeton, N.J.: Princeton University Press, 1974).

11. Nur Bilge Criss, *Istanbul under Allied Occupation, 1918–1923* (Boston: Brill, 1999).

12. Ernst Fraenkel, *Military Occupation and the Rule of Law: Occupation Government in the Rhineland, 1918–1923* (New York: Oxford University Press, 1944); Keith L. Nelson, *Victors Divided: America and the Allies in Germany, 1918–1923* (Berkeley: University of California Press, 1975); *The Occupation of the Rhineland, 1918–1929* (London: Her Majesty's Stationery Office, 1987); U.S. Army, *American Military Government of Occupied Germany, 1918–1920* (Washington: U.S. Government Printing Office, 1943); David G. Williamson, *The British in Germany, 1918–1930: The Reluctant Occupiers* (New York: Berg, 1991).

13. Christopher Catherwood, *Churchill's Folly: How Winston Churchill Created Modern Iraq* (New York: Carroll and Graf, 2004); Toby Dodge, *Inventing Iraq: The Failure of Nation Building and a History Denied* (New York: Columbia University Press, 2003); Phebe Marr, *The Modern History of Iraq*, 2d ed. (Boulder, Colo.: Westview Press, 2004); David E. Omissi, *Air Power and Colonial Control: The Royal Air Force, 1919–1939* (New York: St. Martin's Press, 1990); Kristen Coates Ulrichsen, "The British Occupation of Mesopotamia, 1914–1922," *The Journal of Strategic Studies* 30, no. 2 (April 2007): 349–77.

14. Michael Joseph Cohen, *Palestine, Retreat from the Mandate: The Making of British Policy, 1936–45* (New York: Holmes and Meier, 1978); Albert Montefiore Hyamson, *Palestine under the Mandate, 1920–1948* (London: Methuen, 1950); Tom Segev, *One Palestine, Complete: Jews and Arabs under the Mandate* (New York: Metropolitan Books, 2000); J. Stoyanovsky, *The Mandate for Palestine: A Contribution to the Theory and Practice of International Mandates* (Westport, Conn.: Hyperion Press, 1976).

15. Walter A. McDougall, *France's Rhineland Diplomacy, 1914–1924: The Last Bid for a Balance of Power in Europe* (Princeton, N.J.: Princeton University Press, 1978); Frank M. Russell, *The Saar: Battleground and Pawn* (New York: Russell and Russell, 1970).

16. Elena Agarossi, *A Nation Collapses: The Italian Surrender of September 1943*, trans. Harvey Fergusson II (New York: Cambridge University Press, 2000); Henry L. Coles and Albert K. Weinberg, *Civil Affairs: Soldiers Become Governors* (Washington, D.C.: Department of the Army, Office of the Chief of Military History, 1964); David W. Ellwood, *Italy, 1943–1945* (Leicester: Leicester University Press, 1985); Muriel Grindrod, *The New Italy: Transition from War to Peace* (London: Royal Institute of International Affairs, 1947); John Lamberton Harper, *America and the Reconstruction of Italy, 1945–1948* (New York: Cambridge University Press, 1986); C. R. S. Harris, *Allied Military Administration of Italy, 1943–1945* (London: Her Majesty's Stationery Office, 1957); Norman Kogan, *A Political History of Postwar Italy* (New York: Praeger, 1966); James Edward Miller, "The Search for Stability: An Interpretation of American Policy in Italy, 1943–46," *Journal of Italian*

History 1, no. 2 (1978); Luigi Villari, *The Liberation of Italy, 1943–1947* (Appleton, Wis.: C. C. Nelson, 1959).

17. William B. Bader, *Austria between East and West, 1945–1955* (Stanford, Calif.: Stanford University Press, 1966); Audrey Kurth Cronin, *Great Power Politics and the Struggle over Austria, 1945–1955* (Ithaca: Cornell University Press, 1986); William Lloyd Stearman, *The Soviet Union and the Occupation of Austria* (Geneva: University of Geneva, 1960).

18. Bader, *Austria Between East and West, 1945–1955;* Cronin, *Great Power Politics and the Struggle over Austria, 1945–1955;* Donald R. Whitnah and Edgar L. Erickson, *The American Occupation of Austria: Planning and Early Years* (Westport, Conn.: Greenwood, 1985).

19. See chapter 1.

20. See chapter 3.

21. Arnold G. Fisch Jr., *Military Government in the Ryukyu Islands, 1945–1950* (Washington, D.C.: United States Army Center of Military History, 1988); Nicholas Evan Sarantakes, *Keystone: The American Occupation of Okinawa and U.S.–Japanese Relations* (College Station: Texas A&M University Press, 2000).

22. See chapter 2.

23. Ibid.

24. The literature on the Israeli occupation of the West Bank and Gaza Strip is particularly voluminous. See, in particular, Gershom Gorenberg, *The Accidental Empire: Israel and the Birth of Settlements, 1967–1977,* 1st ed. (New York: Times Books, 2006); Benny Morris, *Righteous Victims: A History of the Zionist-Arab Conflict, 1881–1999,* 1st ed. (New York: Knopf, 1999); Michael B. Oren, *Six Days of War: June 1967 and the Making of the Modern Middle East,* 1st Presidio Press ed. (New York: Ballantine Books, 2003); Mark A. Tessler, *A History of the Israeli-Palestinian Conflict* (Bloomington: Indiana University Press, 1994).

25. Stephen J. Morris, *Why Vietnam Invaded Cambodia: Political Culture and the Causes of War* (Stanford, Calif.: Stanford University Press, 1999); Thu-Huong Nguyen-Vo, *Khmer-Viet Relations and the Third Indochina Conflict* (Jefferson, N.C.: McFarland, 1992).

26. Gil Merom, *How Democracies Lose Small Wars: State, Society, and the Failures of France in Algeria, Israel in Lebanon, and the United States in Vietnam* (New York: Cambridge University Press, 2003), 155–228; Itamar Rabinovich, *The War for Lebanon, 1970–1985* (Ithaca, N.Y.: Cornell University Press, 1985); Zeev Schiff, Ehud Yaari, and Ina Friedman, *Israel's Lebanon War* (New York: Simon and Schuster, 1984).

27. Flynt Leverett, *Inheriting Syria: Bashar's Trial by Fire* (Washington, D.C.: Brookings Institution Press, 2005); Robert G. Rabil, *Embattled Neighbors: Syria, Israel, and Lebanon* (Boulder, Colo.: Lynne Rienner, 2003); Rabinovich, *The War for Lebanon, 1970–1985;* Patrick Seale, *Asad of Syria: The Struggle for the Middle East* (Berkeley: University of California Press, 1989).

28. Dana H. Allin, *NATO's Balkan Interventions* (London: International Institute for Strategic Studies, 2002); Sumantra Bose, *Bosnia after Dayton: Nationalist Partition and International Intervention* (New York: Oxford University Press, 2002); Elizabeth M. Cousens and Charles K. Cater, *Toward Peace in Bosnia: Implementing the Dayton Accords* (Boulder, Colo.: Lynne Rienner, 2001); Jane M. O. Sharp, "Dayton Report Card," *International Security* 22, no. 3 (winter 1997–98): 101–37.

29. See chapter 4.

30. See conclusion.

31. Ibid.

Index

Page numbers with an *f* indicate figures; those with a *t* indicate tables.

**CARDS MUST REMAIN IN THIS
POCKET AT ALL TIMES**
a charge will be made for
lost or damaged cards